PRENTICE HALL
Realidades A

Peggy Palo Boyles
Oklahoma City, OK

Myriam Met
Rockville, MD

Richard S. Sayers
Longmont, CO

Carol Eubanks Wargin
Glen Ellyn, IL

PEARSON
Prentice
Hall

Needham, Massachusetts
Upper Saddle River, New Jersey

Inset image, front cover: Café on the water front, Barcelona, Spain
Front cover (background) and back cover: Parque del Buen Retiro, Madrid, Spain

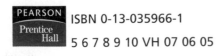

ISBN 0-13-035966-1

5 6 7 8 9 10 VH 07 06 05

Realidades Authors

Peggy Palo Boyles

During her foreign language career of over 30 years, Peggy Palo Boyles has taught elementary, secondary, and university students in both private and public schools. She currently serves as the Foreign Language/ESL Curriculum Coordinator for the Putnam City Schools in Oklahoma City, OK. She was a member of the ACTFL Performance Guidelines for K–12 Learners task force and served as a Senior Editor for the project. Ms. Boyles is currently President of the National Association of District Supervisors of Foreign Language (NADSFL). She frequently conducts foreign language workshops for state and national organizations, public school districts, and private schools throughout the country.

Myriam Met

For most of her professional life, Myriam (Mimi) Met has worked in the public schools, starting as a high school teacher in New York City. Other positions include supervisor of language programs in the Cincinnati Public Schools, K–12, and Coordinator of Foreign Languages, K–12, for Montgomery County Public Schools, MD. She is currently deputy director of the National Foreign Language Center, where she is responsible for K–12 language education policy analysis. Dr. Met has served on the Advisory Board for the National Standards in Foreign Language Learning, the task force that developed national standards in Spanish, and co-chaired the Pacesetter Spanish task force for the College Board.

Richard S. Sayers

Rich Sayers has been an educator in world languages for 25 years. He taught Spanish at Niwot High School in Longmont, CO, for 18 years, where he also served as department chair, Teacher on Special Assignment coordinating the district foreign language department, and board member of the Colorado Congress of Foreign Language Teachers. In 1991, Mr. Sayers was selected as one of the Disney Company's Foreign Language Teacher Honorees for the American Teacher Awards. He presently serves as a board member of the Southwest Conference on Language Teaching. Mr. Sayers is Senior National Consultant for Pearson Prentice Hall.

Carol Eubanks Wargin

Carol Eubanks Wargin has taught Spanish for 20 years at Glen Crest Middle School, Glen Ellyn, IL, and has also served as Foreign Languages department chair. In 1997, Ms. Wargin's presentation "From Text to Test: How to Land Where You Planned" was honored as the best presentation at the Illinois Conference on the Teaching of Foreign Languages (ICTFL) and at the Central States Conference on the Teaching of Foreign Languages (CSC). She was twice named Outstanding Young Educator by the Jaycees.

Contributing Writers

Eduardo Aparicio
Chicago, IL

Daniel J. Bender
New Trier High School
Winnetka, IL

Marie Deer
Bloomington, IN

Leslie M. Grahn
Howard County Public Schools
Ellicott City, MD

Thomasina Hannum
Albuquerque, NM

Nancy S. Hernández
World Languages Supervisor
Simsbury (CT) Public Schools

Patricia J. Kule
Fountain Valley School
of Colorado
Colorado Springs, CO

Jacqueline Hall Minet
Upper Montclair, NJ

Alex Paredes
Simi Valley, CA

Martha Singer Semmer
Breckenridge, CO

Dee Dee Drisdale Stafford
Putnam City Schools
Oklahoma City, OK

Christine S. Wells
Cheyenne Mountain
Junior High School
Colorado Springs, CO

Michael Werner
University of Chicago
Chicago, IL

National Consultants

Yvonne Cádiz
Tampa, FL

María R. Hubbard
Braintree, MA

Jan Polumbus
Tulsa, OK

Patrick T. Raven
Milwaukee, WI

Joseph Wieczorek
Baltimore, MD

norte
oeste — este
sur

OCÉAN
ATLÁNT

Tabla de materias

Mapas . . . . **x**

México x
América Central xii
El Caribe xiv
América del Sur *(Parte norte)* xvi
América del Sur *(Parte sur)* xviii
España • Guinea Ecuatorial xx
Estados Unidos xxii

Why Study Spanish? . . . . **xxiv**

Study Tips . . . . **xxv**

Para empezar

1 En la escuela 2

- Greet people at different times of the day
- Introduce yourself to others
- Respond to classroom directions
- Begin using numbers
- Tell time
- Identify parts of the body

2 En la clase 10

- Talk about things in the classroom
- Ask questions about new words and phrases
- Use the Spanish alphabet to spell words
- Talk about things related to the calendar
- Learn about the Aztec calendar

3 El tiempo 18

- Describe weather conditions
- Identify the seasons
- Compare weather in the northern and southern hemispheres

Repaso del capítulo 22

Go Online
PHSchool.com
For: Online Table of Contents
Visit: www.phschool.com
Web Code: jak-0001

Tema 1 Mis amigos y yo

Capítulo 1A
¿Qué te gusta hacer?

Objectives
- Talk about activities you like and don't like to do
- Ask others what they like to do
- Understand cultural perspectives on favorite activities

Video Highlights
- A primera vista: *¿Qué te gusta hacer?*
- GramActiva Videos: infinitives; making negative statements

A primera vista 26
- Vocabulario y gramática en contexto:
  - activities people like and don't like to do
- Videohistoria: *¿Qué te gusta hacer?*

Manos a la obra 32
- Vocabulario y gramática en uso
- Gramática:
  - infinitives
  - negatives
  - expressing agreement or disagreement
- Conexiones: *La música*
- Exploración del lenguaje: Cognates
- Pronunciación: The vowels *a, e,* and *i*
- El español en la comunidad

¡Adelante! 46
- Lectura: *¿Qué te gusta hacer?*
- La cultura en vivo: *¿Te gusta bailar?*
- Presentación oral: *A mí me gusta mucho...*
- El mundo hispano: España

Repaso del capítulo 52
- Vocabulario y gramática
- Preparación para el examen

Capítulo 1B
Y tú, ¿cómo eres?

Objectives
- Talk about personality traits
- Ask and tell what people are like
- Use adjectives to describe people
- Understand cultural perspectives on friendship

Video Highlights
- A primera vista: *Amigos por Internet*
- GramActiva Videos: adjectives; definite and indefinite articles; word order: placement of adjectives

A primera vista 56
- Vocabulario y gramática en contexto:
  - personality traits
- Videohistoria: *Amigos por Internet*

Manos a la obra 62
- Vocabulario y gramática en uso
- Gramática:
  - adjectives
  - definite and indefinite articles
  - word order: placement of adjectives
- Conexiones: *La literatura*
- Exploración del lenguaje: Cognates that begin with *es* + consonant
- Pronunciación: The vowels *o* and *u*
- El español en el mundo del trabajo

¡Adelante! 76
- Lectura: *Un self-quiz*
- Perspectivas del mundo hispano: *¿Qué es un amigo?*
- Presentación escrita: *Amigo por correspondencia*
- El mundo hispano: El Caribe

Repaso del capítulo 82
- Vocabulario y gramática
- Preparación para el examen

Tema 2
La escuela

Capítulo 2A
Tu día en la escuela

Objectives
- Talk about school schedules and subjects
- Discuss what students do during the day
- Ask and tell who is doing an action
- Compare your school with that of a student in a Spanish-speaking country

Video Highlights

- **A primera vista:** *El primer día de clases*
- **GramActiva Videos:** subject pronouns; present tense of *-ar* verbs

A primera vista 86
- Vocabulario y gramática en contexto:
  - the school day
- Videohistoria: *El primer día de clases*

Manos a la obra 92
- Vocabulario y gramática en uso
- Gramática:
  - subject pronouns
  - present tense of *-ar* verbs
- Conexiones: *Las matemáticas*
- Exploración del lenguaje: Connections between Latin, English, and Spanish
- Pronunciación: The letter *c*
- El español en la comunidad

¡Adelante! 108
- Lectura: *La Escuela Español Vivo*
- La cultura en vivo: *Aficionados al fútbol*
- Presentación oral: *Mis clases*
- El mundo hispano: México

Repaso del capítulo 114
- Vocabulario y gramática
- Preparación para el examen

Capítulo 2B
Tu sala de clases

Objectives
- Describe a classroom
- Indicate where things are located
- Talk about more than one object or person
- Understand cultural perspectives on school

Video Highlights

- **A primera vista:** *Un ratón en la clase*
- **GramActiva Videos:** the verb *estar;* the plurals of nouns and articles

A primera vista 118
- Vocabulario y gramática en contexto:
  - the classroom
  - expressions of location
- Videohistoria: *Un ratón en la clase*

Manos a la obra 124
- Vocabulario y gramática en uso
- Gramática:
  - the verb *estar*
  - the plurals of nouns and articles
- Conexiones: *Las matemáticas*
- Exploración del lenguaje: Language through gestures
- Pronunciación: The letter *g*
- El español en el mundo del trabajo

¡Adelante! 138
- Lectura: *El UNICEF y una convención para los niños*
- Perspectivas del mundo hispano: *¿Cómo es la escuela?*
- Presentación escrita: *Tu sala de clases*
- El mundo hispano: América Central

Repaso del capítulo 144
- Vocabulario y gramática
- Preparación para el examen

Capítulo 3A
¿Desayuno o almuerzo?

Objectives
- Talk about foods and beverages for breakfast and lunch
- Talk about likes and dislikes
- Express how often something is done
- Understand cultural perspectives on meals

Video Highlights

- **A primera vista:** *El desayuno*
- **GramActiva Videos:** present tense of *-er* and *-ir* verbs; *me gustan, me encantan*

A primera vista 148
- Vocabulario y gramática en contexto:
  - foods and beverages for breakfast and lunch
- Videohistoria: *El desayuno*

Manos a la obra 154
- Vocabulario y gramática en uso
- Gramática:
  - present tense of *-er* and *-ir* verbs
  - *me gustan, me encantan*
- Conexiones: *La historia*
- Exploración del lenguaje: Using a noun to modify another noun
- Pronunciación: The letters *h* and *j*
- El español en la comunidad

¡Adelante! 168
- Lectura: *Frutas y verduras de las Américas*
- La cultura en vivo: *Churros y chocolate*
- Presentación oral: *¿Y qué te gusta comer?*
- El mundo hispano: América del Sur *(Parte norte)*

Repaso del capítulo 174
- Vocabulario y gramática
- Preparación para el examen

Capítulo 3B
Para mantener la salud

Objectives
- Talk about foods and beverages for dinner
- Describe what people or things are like
- Discuss food, health, and exercise choices
- Understand cultural perspectives on diet and health

Video Highlights

- **A primera vista:** *Para mantener la salud*
- **GramActiva Videos:** the plurals of adjectives; the verb *ser*

A primera vista 178
- Vocabulario y gramática en contexto:
  - food groups and foods on the Food Guide Pyramid
  - activities to maintain good health
  - ways to describe food
- Videohistoria: *Para mantener la salud*

Manos a la obra 184
- Vocabulario y gramática en uso
- Gramática:
  - the plurals of adjectives
  - the verb *ser*
- Conexiones: *La salud*
- Exploración del lenguaje: Where did it come from?
- Pronunciación: The letters *l* and *ll*
- El español en el mundo del trabajo

¡Adelante! 198
- Lectura: *La comida de los atletas*
- Perspectivas del mundo hispano: *¿Qué haces para mantener la salud?*
- Presentación escrita: *Para mantener la salud*
- El mundo hispano: América del Sur *(Parte sur)*

Repaso del capítulo 204
- Vocabulario y gramática
- Preparación para el examen

Tema 4 — Los pasatiempos

Capítulo 4A
¿Adónde vas?

Objectives

- Talk about locations in your community
- Discuss leisure activities
- Talk about where you go and with whom
- Learn how to ask questions
- Understand cultural perspectives on leisure activities

Video Highlights

- **A primera vista:** *Un chico reservado*
- **GramActiva Videos:** the verb *ir;* asking questions

A primera vista 208

- Vocabulario y gramática en contexto:
  - places to go to when you're not in school
- Videohistoria: *Un chico reservado*

Manos a la obra 214

- Vocabulario y gramática en uso
- Gramática:
  - the verb *ir*
  - asking questions
- Conexiones: *La geografía; La historia*
- Exploración del lenguaje: Origins of the Spanish days of the week
- Pronunciación: Stress and accents
- El español en la comunidad

¡Adelante! 230

- Lectura: *Al centro comercial*
- La cultura en vivo: *Rimas infantiles*
- Presentación oral: *Un estudiante nuevo*
- El mundo hispano: Los Estados Unidos (Histórico)

Repaso del capítulo 236

- Vocabulario y gramática
- Preparación para el examen

Capítulo 4B
¿Quieres ir conmigo?

Objectives

- Talk about activities outside of school
- Extend, accept, and decline invitations
- Tell when an event happens
- Understand cultural perspectives on after-school activities

Video Highlights

- **A primera vista:** *¡A jugar!*
- **GramActiva Videos:** *ir + a +* infinitive; the verb *jugar*

A primera vista 240

- Vocabulario y gramática en contexto:
  - activities outside of school
- Videohistoria: *¡A jugar!*

Manos a la obra 246

- Vocabulario y gramática en uso
- Gramática:
  - *ir + a +* infinitive
  - the verb *jugar*
- Conexiones: *Las matemáticas*
- Exploración del lenguaje: Spanish words borrowed from English
- Pronunciación: The letter *d*
- El español en el mundo del trabajo

¡Adelante! 260

- Lectura: *Sergio y Lorena: El futuro del golf*
- Perspectivas del mundo hispano: *¿Qué haces en tu tiempo libre?*
- Presentación escrita: *Una invitación*
- El mundo hispano: Los Estados Unidos (Contemporáneo)

Repaso del capítulo 266

- Vocabulario y gramática
- Preparación para el examen

Apéndices

- Vocabulario adicional 268
- Resumen de gramática 270
- Verbos 273
- Expresiones útiles para conversar 275
- Vocabulario español-inglés . . 276
- English-Spanish Vocabulary . . . 283
- Grammar Index 290
- Acknowledgments 292

México

Ciudad de Guanajuato, México

El Zócalo, México, D.F.

México

Capital: México, D.F.

Population: 101.8 million

Area: 761,606 sq mi / 1,972,550 sq km

Ethnic Groups: mestizo, indigenous, Caucasian

Religions: Roman Catholic, Protestant

Government: federal republic

Currency: *peso mexicano*

Exports: manufactured products, oil and oil products, silver, coffee, cotton

Tijuana

Estados Unidos

Ciudad Juárez

Chihuahua

SIERRA MADRE OCCIDENTAL

Nuevo Laredo

SIERRA MADRE ORIENTAL

Monterrey

México

OCÉANO PACÍFICO

Golfo de México

Guadalajara

Querétaro

Paricutín

Ciudad de México

Iztaccíhuatl

Mérida

SIERRA MADRE DEL SUR

Popocatépetl

Veracruz

Puebla

Oaxaca

ISTMO DE TEHUANTEPEC

Belice

Acapulco

Guatemala

norte

oeste — este

sur

Frontera nacional

⊛ Capital

● Ciudad

▲ Volcán o montaña

0		300		600 millas
0	300		600 kilómetros	

Sierra Tarahumara

México **xi**

América Central

Guatemala

Capital: Guatemala

Population: 13 million

Area: 42,043 sq mi / 108,890 sq km

Ethnic Groups: indigenous, mestizo, Caucasian

Religions: Roman Catholic, Protestant, traditional Mayan beliefs

Government: constitutional democratic republic

Currency: *quetzal*

Exports: fuels, machinery and transport equipment, construction materials, grain

Honduras

Capital: Tegucigalpa

Population: 6.4 million

Area: 43,278 sq mi / 112,090 sq km

Ethnic Groups: mestizo, African, indigenous, Caucasian

Religions: Roman Catholic, Protestant

Government: democratic constitutional republic

Currency: *lempira*

Exports: coffee, bananas, shrimp, lobster, meat, zinc, wood

El Salvador

Capital: San Salvador

Population: 6.2 million

Area: 8,124 sq mi / 21,040 sq km

Ethnic Groups: mestizo, indigenous, Caucasian

Religions: Roman Catholic, Protestant

Government: republic

Currency: *colón salvadoreño*

Exports: offshore assembly parts, equipment, coffee, sugar, shrimp, textiles, chemicals, electricity

Canal de Panamá

México

Parque Nacional Tikal ▲

Belice

Lago Petén Itzá

Golfo de Honduras

Lago de Izabal

San Pedro Sula •

Guatemala

Quetzaltenango •

Copán ■

Honduras

⭐ Guatemala

Santa Rosa de Copán

Antigua •

Cerro El Pital ▲

⭐ Tegucigalpa

Volcán de Santa Ana ▲

Santa Ana •

El Salvador

CORDILLERA ISABELIA

San Salvador ⭐

Santa Rosa de Lima •

La Libertad •

Golfo de Fonseca

Lago de Managua

Nicaragua

CORDILLERA CHONTALEÑA

Managua ⭐ • Masaya

Granada •

Lago de Nicaragua

Los Chiles •

Costa Rica Limón •

OCÉANO PACÍFICO

⭐ San José

Golfo de Nicoya

Golfo Dulce

Mar Caribe

norte

oeste ✶ este

sur

Canal de Panamá

Colón •

• Panamá

Panamá

Golfo de Panamá

PARQUE NACIONAL DARIÉN ■

Go Online
PHSchool.com
For: Online Atlas
Visit: www.phschool.com
Web Code: jae-0002

Legend:
- – ∙ – ∙ – Frontera nacional
- ✶ Capital
- • Ciudad
- ▲ Volcán o montaña
- ■ Zona arqueológica

Scale:
0 ——— 200 ——— 400 millas
0 ——— 200 ——— 400 kilómetros

Nicaragua

Capital: Managua

Population: 4.9 million

Area: 49,998 sq mi / 129,494 sq km

Ethnic Groups: mestizo, Caucasian, African, indigenous, Zambo

Religions: Roman Catholic, Protestant

Government: republic

Currency: *córdoba oro*

Exports: coffee, shrimp, lobster, cotton, tobacco, meat, sugar, bananas, gold

Costa Rica

Capital: San José

Population: 3.8 million

Area: 19,730 sq mi / 51,100 sq km

Ethnic Groups: mestizo, Caucasian, African, indigenous

Religions: Roman Catholic, Protestant

Government: democratic republic

Currency: *colón de Costa Rica*

Exports: coffee, bananas, sugar, textiles, electronic components

Panamá

Capital: Panamá

Population: 2.8 million

Area: 30,193 sq mi / 78,200 sq km

Ethnic Groups: mestizo, African, Caucasian, indigenous, Asian

Religions: Roman Catholic, Protestant

Government: constitutional democracy

Currency: *balboa*

Exports: bananas, sugar, shrimp, coffee

América Central **xiii**

El Caribe

El Morro, San Juan,
Puerto Rico

El arrecife de coral, República Dominicana

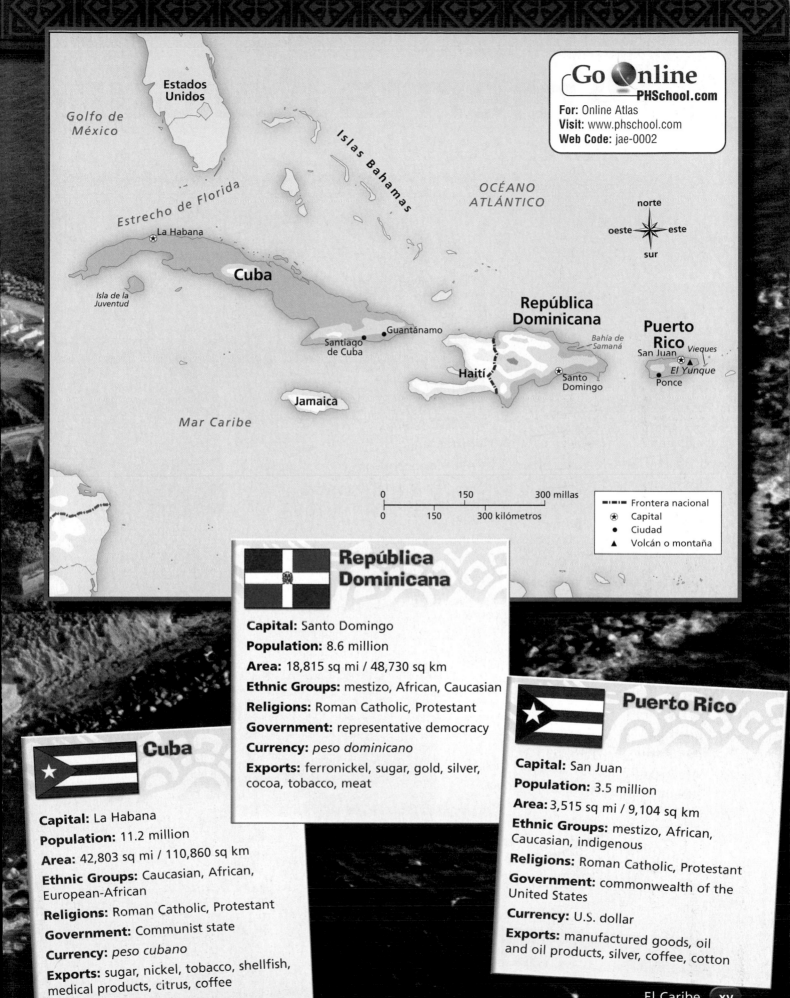

Estados
Unidos

Golfo de
México

OCÉANO
ATLÁNTICO

Islas Bahamas

Estrecho de Florida

norte

oeste — este

sur

La Habana

Cuba

Isla de la
Juventud

**República
Dominicana**

Bahía de
Samaná

**Puerto
Rico**

Vieques

San Juan

El Yunque

Guantánamo

Santiago
de Cuba

Haití

Santo
Domingo

Ponce

Jamaica

Mar Caribe

| 0 | 150 | 300 millas |
| 0 | 150 | 300 kilómetros |

–··–··– Frontera nacional
✪ Capital
● Ciudad
▲ Volcán o montaña

República Dominicana

Capital: Santo Domingo

Population: 8.6 million

Area: 18,815 sq mi / 48,730 sq km

Ethnic Groups: mestizo, African, Caucasian

Religions: Roman Catholic, Protestant

Government: representative democracy

Currency: *peso dominicano*

Exports: ferronickel, sugar, gold, silver, cocoa, tobacco, meat

Puerto Rico

Capital: San Juan

Population: 3.5 million

Area: 3,515 sq mi / 9,104 sq km

Ethnic Groups: mestizo, African, Caucasian, indigenous

Religions: Roman Catholic, Protestant

Government: commonwealth of the United States

Currency: U.S. dollar

Exports: manufactured goods, oil and oil products, silver, coffee, cotton

Cuba

Capital: La Habana

Population: 11.2 million

Area: 42,803 sq mi / 110,860 sq km

Ethnic Groups: Caucasian, African, European-African

Religions: Roman Catholic, Protestant

Government: Communist state

Currency: *peso cubano*

Exports: sugar, nickel, tobacco, shellfish, medical products, citrus, coffee

América del Sur
(Parte norte)

Colombia

Capital: Bogotá

Population: 40.3 million

Area: 439,736 sq mi / 1,138,910 sq km

Ethnic Groups: mestizo, Caucasian, African, indigenous

Religion: Roman Catholic

Government: republic

Currency: *peso colombiano*

Exports: textiles, oil and oil products, coffee, gold, emeralds, bananas, tobacco, cotton, wood, hydroelectricity

Ecuador

Capital: Quito

Population: 13.1 million

Area: 109,483 sq mi / 283,560 sq km

Ethnic Groups: mestizo, indigenous, Caucasian

Religion: Roman Catholic

Government: republic

Currency: U.S. dollar

Exports: oil, textiles, bananas, shrimp, cocoa, sugar, meat

Perú

Capital: Lima

Population: 27 million

Area: 496,226 sq mi / 1,285,220 sq km

Ethnic Groups: mestizo, indigenous, Caucasian

Religion: Roman Catholic

Government: constitutional republic

Currency: *nuevo sol*

Exports: gold, zinc, copper, fish and fish products, textiles

Las ruinas de Machu Picchu, Perú

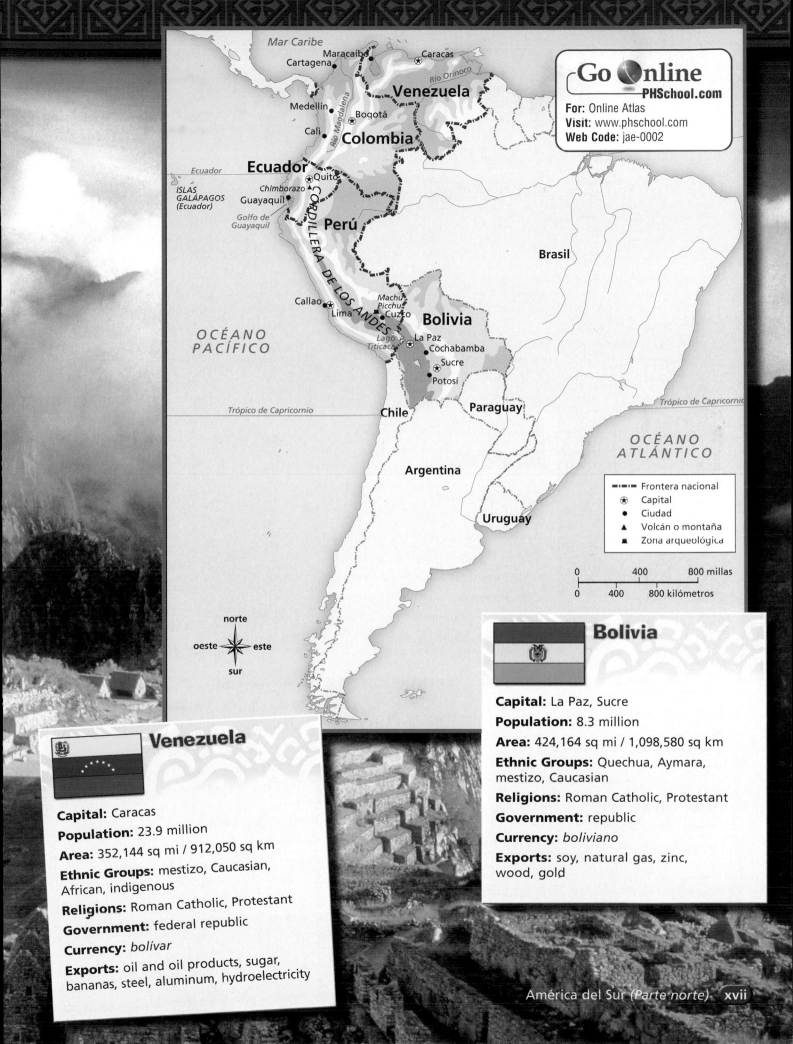

Mar Caribe

Maracaibo
Cartagena
☆ Caracas
Río Orinoco
Venezuela
Medellín
Bogotá
Cali
Colombia

Ecuador **Ecuador**
☆ Quito
Chimborazo ▲
Guayaquil ●
Golfo de Guayaquil

ISLAS GALÁPAGOS (Ecuador)

CORDILLERA DE LOS ANDES

Perú

Brasil

Callao ●
Lima ●
Machu Picchu ■
Cuzco
Bolivia
La Paz ●
Lago Titicaca ☆ Cochabamba ●
Sucre ●
Potosí ●

OCÉANO PACÍFICO

Trópico de Capricornio

Chile
Paraguay

OCÉANO ATLÁNTICO

Argentina

Trópico de Capricornio

Uruguay

norte
oeste ✦ este
sur

Legend:
- –-–-– Frontera nacional
- ☆ Capital
- ● Ciudad
- ▲ Volcán o montaña
- ■ Zona arqueológica

0   400   800 millas
0   400   800 kilómetros

Go Online
PHSchool.com
For: Online Atlas
Visit: www.phschool.com
Web Code: jae-0002

Bolivia

Capital: La Paz, Sucre

Population: 8.3 million

Area: 424,164 sq mi / 1,098,580 sq km

Ethnic Groups: Quechua, Aymara, mestizo, Caucasian

Religions: Roman Catholic, Protestant

Government: republic

Currency: *boliviano*

Exports: soy, natural gas, zinc, wood, gold

Venezuela

Capital: Caracas

Population: 23.9 million

Area: 352,144 sq mi / 912,050 sq km

Ethnic Groups: mestizo, Caucasian, African, indigenous

Religions: Roman Catholic, Protestant

Government: federal republic

Currency: *bolívar*

Exports: oil and oil products, sugar, bananas, steel, aluminum, hydroelectricity

América del Sur
(Parte sur)

Monte Fitz Roy, Patagonia, Argentina

Paraguay

Capital: Asunción

Population: 5.7 million

Area: 157,047 sq mi / 406,750 sq km

Ethnic Groups: mestizo, Caucasian

Religions: Roman Catholic, Protestant

Government: constitutional republic

Currency: *guaraní*

Exports: sugar, meat, tapioca, hydroelectricity

Chile

Capital: Santiago

Population: 15.3 million

Area: 292,260 sq mi / 756,950 sq km

Ethnic Groups: mestizo, Araucano, Caucasian

Religions: Roman Catholic, Protestant

Government: republic

Currency: *peso chileno*

Exports: copper, fish, transport equipment, fruit, paper and pulp, chemicals, hydroelectricity

Argentina

Capital: Buenos Aires

Population: 37.8 million

Area: 1,068,302 sq mi / 2,766,890 sq km

Ethnic Groups: Caucasian

Religions: Roman Catholic, Protestant, Jewish

Government: republic

Currency: *peso*

Exports: meat, edible oils, fuels and energy, cereals, feed, motor vehicles

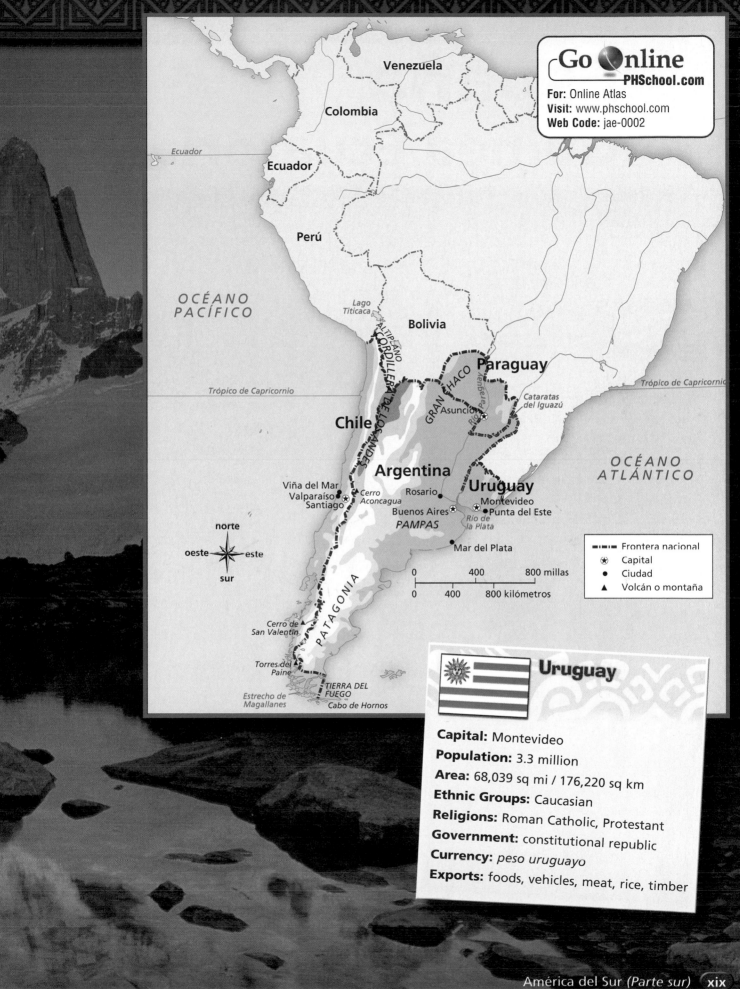

Venezuela

Colombia

Ecuador

Ecuador

Perú

OCÉANO
PACÍFICO

*Lago
Titicaca*

Bolivia

Trópico de Capricornio

Paraguay

GRAN CHACO

Asunción

*Cataratas
del Iguazú*

Trópico de Capricornio

Chile

Argentina

OCÉANO
ATLÁNTICO

Viña del Mar
Valparaíso
Santiago

*Cerro
Aconcagua*

Rosario

Uruguay

Montevideo
Punta del Este

Buenos Aires

*Río de
la Plata*

PAMPAS

Mar del Plata

norte

oeste   este

sur

0   400   800 millas

0   400   800 kilómetros

=-I=-I= Frontera nacional
✪ Capital
● Ciudad
▲ Volcán o montaña

PATAGONIA

Cerro de
San Valentín

Torres del
Paine

*TIERRA DEL
FUEGO*

*Estrecho de
Magallanes*

Cabo de Hornos

Uruguay

Capital: Montevideo

Population: 3.3 million

Area: 68,039 sq mi / 176,220 sq km

Ethnic Groups: Caucasian

Religions: Roman Catholic, Protestant

Government: constitutional republic

Currency: *peso uruguayo*

Exports: foods, vehicles, meat, rice, timber

América del Sur *(Parte sur)*   **xix**

España
Guinea Ecuatorial

España

Capital: Madrid

Population: 40 million

Area: 194,897 sq mi / 504,782 sq km

Ethnic Groups: European

Religion: Roman Catholic

Government: parliamentary monarchy

Currency: *euro*

Exports: food, machinery, motor vehicles

El Alcázar de Segovia, Segovia, España

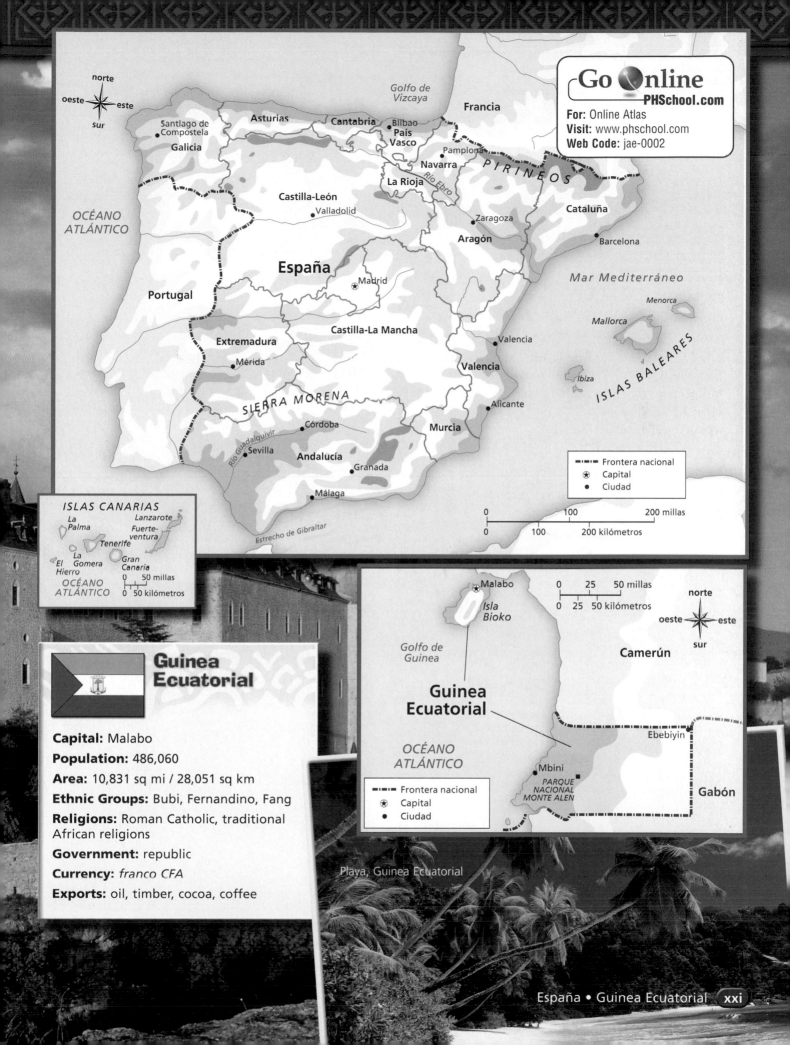

norte
oeste este
sur

Golfo de Vizcaya

Francia

OCÉANO ATLÁNTICO

Santiago de Compostela
Galicia
Asturias
Cantabria
Bilbao
País Vasco
Pamplona
Navarra
La Rioja
Río Ebro
PIRINEOS

Castilla-León
Valladolid

Zaragoza
Aragón

Cataluña

Barcelona

España
Madrid

Mar Mediterráneo

Portugal

Extremadura
Mérida

Castilla-La Mancha

Mallorca

Menorca

Valencia

ISLAS BALEARES

Ibiza

SIERRA MORENA

Valencia

Alicante

Río Guadalquivir
Córdoba
Sevilla
Andalucía
Granada

Murcia

Málaga

Estrecho de Gibraltar

Frontera nacional
⊛ Capital
• Ciudad

0   100   200 millas
0   100   200 kilómetros

ISLAS CANARIAS
La Palma
Lanzarote
Fuerte-ventura
Tenerife
El Hierro
La Gomera
Gran Canaria
OCÉANO ATLÁNTICO
0   50 millas
0   50 kilómetros

Guinea Ecuatorial

Capital: Malabo

Population: 486,060

Area: 10,831 sq mi / 28,051 sq km

Ethnic Groups: Bubi, Fernandino, Fang

Religions: Roman Catholic, traditional African religions

Government: republic

Currency: *franco CFA*

Exports: oil, timber, cocoa, coffee

Malabo
Isla Bioko
Golfo de Guinea

0   25   50 millas
0   25   50 kilómetros

norte
oeste este
sur

Camerún

Guinea Ecuatorial

OCÉANO ATLÁNTICO

Ebebiyin

Mbini
PARQUE NACIONAL MONTE ALEN

Gabón

Frontera nacional
⊛ Capital
• Ciudad

Playa, Guinea Ecuatorial

España • Guinea Ecuatorial   **xxi**

Estados Unidos

Estados Unidos

Capital: Washington, D.C.

Population: 278 million

Area: 3,717,813 sq mi / 9,629,091 sq km

Ethnic Groups: Caucasian, Hispanic, African American, Asian, Native American

Religions: Protestant, Roman Catholic, Jewish, Muslim

Government: federal republic

Currency: U.S. dollar

Exports: motor vehicles, aerospace equipment, telecommunications, electronics, consumer goods, chemicals, food, wheat, corn

Las grandes llanuras

Caras de los Estados Unidos

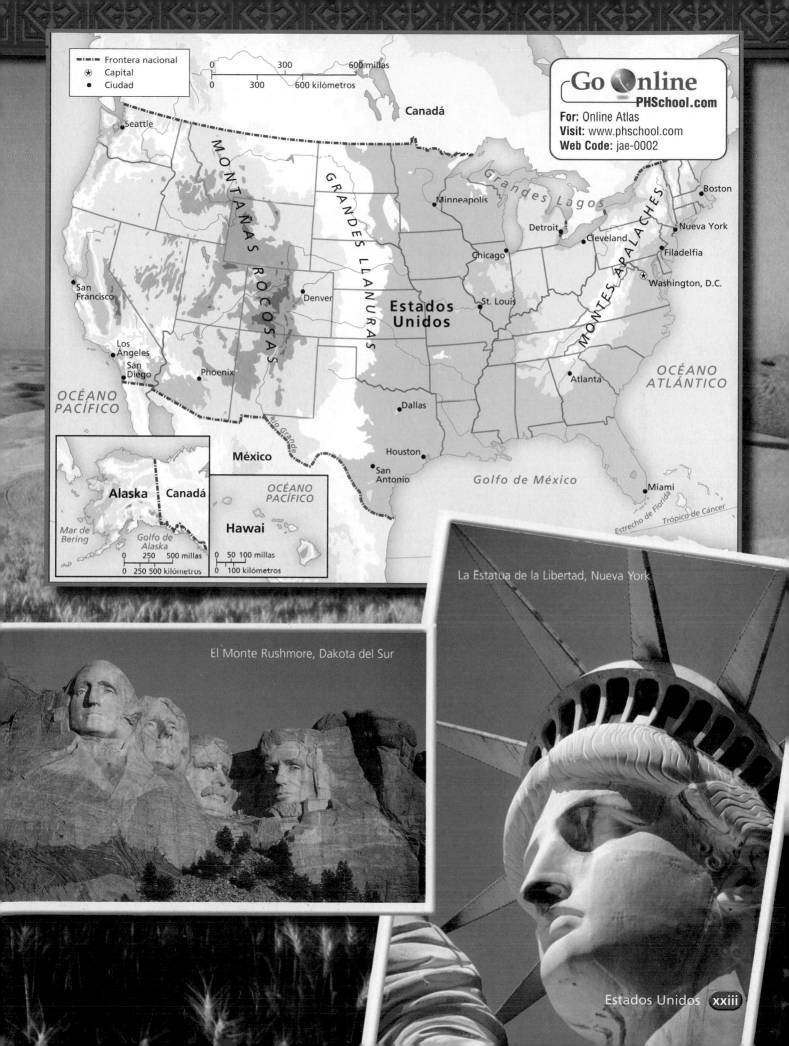

Canadá

Seattle

MONTAÑAS ROCOSAS

GRANDES LLANURAS

Grandes Lagos

Boston
Minneapolis
Detroit
Nueva York
Cleveland
Filadelfia
Chicago
Washington, D.C.
St. Louis
Denver

Estados Unidos

San Francisco

Los Ángeles
San Diego
Phoenix

MONTES APALACHES

OCÉANO ATLÁNTICO

Atlanta

OCÉANO PACÍFICO

Dallas

Houston
San Antonio

México

Golfo de México

Miami

Estrecho de Florida
Trópico de Cáncer

Río Grande

Frontera nacional
★ Capital
• Ciudad

0 300 600 millas
0 300 600 kilómetros

Mar de Bering

Alaska **Canadá**

Golfo de Alaska

OCÉANO PACÍFICO

Hawai

0 250 500 millas
0 250 500 kilómetros

0 50 100 millas
0 100 kilómetros

La Estatua de la Libertad, Nueva York

El Monte Rushmore, Dakota del Sur

Why Study Spanish?

Over 340 million people who live in Spain, 18 Latin American countries, Puerto Rico, Equatorial Guinea, the Philippines, and the United States speak Spanish. It is the second most common language in the United States and the third most commonly spoken language in the world. Studying Spanish helps you to:

Understand culture The Spanish-speaking world is rich in music, food, art, literature, history, and everyday traditions. Learning about culture helps you understand other people's perspectives, patterns of behavior, and contributions to the world at large. ▶

▲ **Expand career opportunities** Your career options expand as businesses in the twenty-first century look for employees who can communicate in Spanish.

Enjoy your Spanish experiences Climb the Incan ruins of Machu Picchu. Volunteer to build a school in Mexico. Enjoy a meal at a Mexican restaurant. Speaking Spanish enriches your experience whether at home or in another country. ▶

Improve your language skills Studying Spanish improves your first-language skills: vocabulary, grammar, reading, and writing. Research shows your test scores may improve!

Study Tips

Go Online
PHSchool.com
For: More tips for studying Spanish
Visit: www.phschool.com
Web Code: jae-0003

Take risks, relax, and be patient. The goal of studying Spanish is to communicate! So don't wait until you get it perfect. Just start talking, and you'll get better and better! You'll make some mistakes, but the longer you practice, the more improvement you'll see.

Here are some easy tips to help you learn Spanish!

Use what you already know. You already know lots of Spanish words such as *rodeo, hasta la vista, tacos, armadillo, sombrero, piñata, mesa,* and *tango.* Use your knowledge of English to help you figure out new words such as *comunicación, delicioso, limón,* and *oficina.* You'll find Spanish is easier if you use what you already know.

You don't need to understand everything. As you hear or read Spanish, you'll come across words or expressions you don't know. Try to figure out what the meaning might be. Above all, don't stop! Keep on listening or reading. You'll be surprised how much you can understand without knowing every word.

Look for Strategy and ¿Recuerdas? boxes. Throughout **Realidades,** you'll see boxes that provide strategies or remind you of something you've already learned. The information in the boxes will help you learn.

Make flashcards. One way to learn a new word is to make a flashcard. Create a picture of the word on an index card. On the back, write the word in Spanish. Then use the card to study: look at the picture and say the word or look at the picture and write the word.

Have fun! You'll find lots of activities that allow you to work with other students, play games, act out skits, explore the Internet, create projects, and use technology. Try out all of the activities and you'll have fun.

Strategy

Using graphic organizers
Drawing diagrams can help you understand how things are related.

¿ ?
madre
yo

¿Recuerdas?

Adjectives agree in gender with the masculine or feminine nouns they modify:

• **El** bistec es sabro**so**.

• **La** ensalada es sabro**sa**.

Estudiantes en México

Fondo cultural

Social relations are somewhat more formal in Spanish-speaking countries than in the United States, since new acquaintances usually greet one another with a handshake. Friends, however, greet each other with a hug or with a kiss on the cheek.

• How does this compare with the way you greet people in the United States?

Estudiantes en Cuzco, Perú

Una escuela en México

Para empezar

Objectives

1 En la escuela

- Greet people at different times of the day
- Introduce yourself to others
- Respond to classroom directions
- Begin using numbers
- Tell time
- Identify parts of the body

2 En la clase

- Talk about things in the classroom
- Ask questions about new words and phrases
- Use the Spanish alphabet to spell words
- Talk about things related to the calendar
- Learn about the Aztec calendar

3 El tiempo

- Describe weather conditions
- Identify the seasons
- Compare weather in the Northern and Southern hemispheres

1 En la escuela

¡Hola! ¿Cómo te llamas?

Objectives

- Greet people at different times of the day
- Introduce yourself to others
- Respond to classroom directions
- Begin using numbers
- Tell time
- Identify parts of the body

—**¡Buenos días, señor!**
—¡Buenos días! **¿Cómo te llamas?**
—**Me llamo** Felipe.

—**¡Buenas tardes, señora!**
—¡Buenas tardes! ¿Cómo te llamas?
—Me llamo Beatriz.
—**Mucho gusto.**
—**Encantada.**

Nota

A woman or girl says *encantada*.
A man or boy says *encantado*.

—**¡Buenas noches!** ¿Cómo te llamas?
—**¡Hola!** Me llamo Graciela. **¿Y tú?**
—Me llamo Lorenzo.
—Mucho gusto.
—**Igualmente.**

Exploración del lenguaje

Señor, señora, señorita

The words *señor, señora,* and *señorita* mean "sir," "madam," and "miss" when used alone. When they are used with people's last names they mean "Mr.," "Mrs.," and "Miss," and are abbreviated *Sr., Sra.,* and *Srta.* Note that the abbreviations are capitalized.

In Spanish you should address adults as *señor, señora,* or *señorita* or use the titles *Sr., Sra.,* and *Srta.* with their last names.

Actividad 1 · Escuchar

Buenos días

Listen as people greet each other. Then point to the clock that indicates the time of day when the greetings are probably taking place.

a.  b.  c.

Actividad 2 · Hablar

¿Cómo te llamas?

Follow the model to ask the name of the classmate on your right. After you have introduced yourself, do the same with the person on your left.

Modelo

A —¡Hola! ¿Cómo te llamas?
B —Me llamo David. ¿Y tú?
A —Me llamo Antonio. Mucho gusto.
B —Igualmente.
o: Encantado.

¿Recuerdas?

If you are a girl, you say *encantada*.

Actividad 3 · Hablar

¡Hola!

Work with a partner. Choose a clock from Actividad 1 and greet each other appropriately for the time of day. Then find out your partner's name. Follow the model. Change partners and repeat.

Modelo

A —Buenas tardes.
B —Buenas tardes. ¿Cómo te llamas?
A —Me llamo Paco. ¿Y tú?
B —Me llamo Lourdes. Mucho gusto.
A —Igualmente.

Go Online
PHSchool.com
For: List of Spanish names
Visit: www.phschool.com
Web Code: jad-0001

Los nombres

Chicas
Alicia
Ana
Beatriz
Carmen
Cristina
Dolores (Lola)
Elena
Gloria
Inés
Isabel (Isa)
Juana
Luisa
Luz María (Luzma)
Margarita
María
María Eugenia (Maru)
Marta
Teresa (Tere)

Chicos
Alejandro
Antonio (Toño)
Carlos (Chacho, Cacho)
Diego
Eduardo (Edu)
Federico (Kiko)
Francisco (Paco)
Guillermo (Guille)
Jorge
José (Pepe)
Juan
Manuel (Manolo)
Miguel
Pablo
Pedro
Ricardo
Roberto
Tomás

tres **3**
Para empezar

¡Hola! ¿Cómo estás?

—Buenos días, Adela.
¿Cómo estás?
—**Bien, gracias,** Sr. Ruiz.
¿Y usted?
—Bien, gracias.

—Buenas tardes, Sr. Ruiz.
¿Cómo está Ud.?
—**Muy** bien, gracias. ¿Y tú?
—Bien, gracias.

—Buenas noches, Miguel.
¿Qué tal?
—**Regular.** ¿Y tú, Carlos?
¿Qué pasa?
—**Nada.**

—**¡Adiós, Srta** Moreno!
¡Hasta luego!
—**¡Hasta mañana!**

—¡Hasta luego, Juan!
—**¡Nos vemos!**

● **Más práctica**
Practice Workbook P-1

¿Recuerdas?

Señor, señora, and *señorita* are abbreviated to *Sr., Sra.,* and *Srta.* before a person's last name.

Tú vs. usted

For most Spanish speakers there are two ways to say "you": *tú* and *usted*. Use *tú* when speaking to friends, family, people your own age, children, and pets. *Usted* is formal. Use it to show respect and when talking to people you don't know well, older people, and people in positions of authority. In writing, *usted* is almost always abbreviated *Ud.,* with a capital *U.*

Would you say *tú* or *Ud.* when talking to the following people?

- your brother
- your teacher
- your best friend
- your friend's mother
- your cat
- your principal
- a new acquaintance who is your age

Actividad 4   **Escuchar**

¿Hola o adiós?

Make a chart on your paper with two columns. Label one *Greeting,* the other *Leaving.* Number your paper from 1–8. As you hear each greeting or leave-taking, place a check mark in the appropriate column next to the number.

	Greeting	Leaving
1.		
2.		
3.		

Actividad 5   **Hablar**

¡Hola! ¿Qué tal?

Work with a partner. Greet each other and ask how your partner is. Say good-bye. Then change partners and repeat.

Modelo

A —*Hola, Luisa. ¿Qué tal?*
B —*Bien, Lupe. ¿Y tú?*
A —*Regular. ¡Hasta luego!*
B —*¡Adiós!*

Actividad 6   **Leer**

Mucho gusto

Read the conversation on the right, then reply *sí* or *no* to these statements.

1. The people in the dialogue knew each other already.
2. The teacher is a man.
3. We know the last names of both people.
4. The student talks to the teacher in a formal tone.
5. Neither person is feeling well today.

Profesor:	Buenos días. Me llamo Señor Guzmán. ¿Y tú?
Estudiante:	Me llamo María Rosa Hernández. Mucho gusto.
Profesor:	Igualmente. ¿Cómo estás, María Rosa?
Estudiante:	Bien, gracias. ¿Y Ud.?
Profesor:	Muy bien, gracias. Hasta luego.
Estudiante:	Adiós, señor.

● **Más práctica**
Practice Workbook P-2

¡Atención, por favor!

—¡Silencio, **por favor!** Abran el libro en la página diez.

—¡Atención! Cierren el libro.

—Repitan, por favor:
Buenos días.
—Buenos días.

—Levántense, por favor.

—Siéntense, por favor.

—Saquen una hoja de papel. Escriban los números.

—Entreguen sus hojas de papel.

Actividad 7 · Escuchar · · · · · ·

¡Siéntense!

You will hear some classroom commands. Listen carefully and act them out.

● **Más práctica** · · · · · · ·
Practice Workbook P-3

Los números

cero   uno   dos   tres   cuatro

cinco   seis   siete   ocho   nueve

10	diez		
11	once	21	veintiuno, . . .
12	doce	30	treinta
13	trece	31	treinta y uno, . . .
14	catorce	40	cuarenta
15	quince	50	cincuenta
16	dieciséis	60	sesenta
17	diecisiete	70	setenta
18	dieciocho	80	ochenta
19	diecinueve	90	noventa
20	veinte	100	cien

 Actividad 8 **Hablar**

Las combinaciones

It is the first day of school, and you are helping some Spanish-speaking exchange students learn their locker combinations. Read the combinations that you see below.

1. 09-26-17
2. 16-07-30
3. 13-20-11
4. 22-19-29
5. 04-12-27
6. 15-01-28
7. 10-06-14
8. 18-21-25

  Actividad 9 **Pensar/Hablar**

Los números

With a partner, provide the missing numbers in each sequence. Then say the number sequence aloud.

1. 1, 2, 3, . . . 10
2. 2, 4, 6, . . . 20
3. 1, 3, 5, . . . 19
4. 5, 10, 15, . . . 60
5. 3, 6, 9, . . . 39
6. 10, 20, 30, . . . 100

  Actividad 10 **Hablar/Escuchar/Escribir**

Números y más números

Tell your partner these numbers. He or she will write them using numerals, not words. Then check your partner's work.

1. the phone numbers used to dial for information and emergencies
2. the bar code number on the back of your Spanish book
3. the number of months until your next birthday
4. the number of students in your math class
5. the number of minutes it takes you to get from your home to school

Azulejos (tiles) cerámicos

Go Online
PHSchool.com
For: More practice: *los números*
Visit: www.phschool.com
Web Code: jad-0002

¿Qué hora es?

In Spanish, to ask what time it is, you say *¿Qué hora es?*
Here are some answers:

Es la una.

Son las dos.

Son las tres y cinco.

Son las cuatro y diez.

Son las cinco y cuarto.

Son las seis y media.

Son las siete menos veinte.

Son las ocho y cincuenta y dos.

Actividad 11 · Hablar

¿Qué hora es?

Work with a partner to ask and answer questions about the time. Use these clocks.

Modelo

A —*¿Qué hora es?*
B —*Son las diez.*

1.
2.
3.
4.

5.
6.

La persistencia de la memoria (1931), Salvador Dalí

Oil on canvas, 9 1/2 x 13 in. (24.1 x 33 cm). Given anonymously. © 2004 Salvador Dalí, Gala-Salvador Dalí Foundation/Artists Rights Society (ARS), New York.† A.K.G., Berlin/Super Stock.

Actividad 12 · Escuchar

La hora

Write the numbers 1–8 on a sheet of paper. Write the times you hear with numerals— 1:00, 2:15, and so on.

 Más práctica
Practice Workbook P-4

El cuerpo

la cabeza

el ojo

la nariz

la boca

el brazo

el dedo

el estómago

la mano

la pierna

el pie

66¡Ay! **Me duele** el pie.**99**

Actividad 13 · Escuchar

Señalen

You will hear some commands. Listen carefully and act out the commands. When you hear the word *señalen,* you should point to that body part.

Actividad 14 · Escuchar

Juego

Play the game *Simón dice . . .* (Simon Says). Listen and follow the leader's directions. Remember that if the leader does not say *"Simón dice,"* you should not do the action.

● **Más práctica**
Practice Workbook P-5

For: More practice: *el cuerpo*
Visit: www.phschool.com
Web Code: jad-0003

2 En la clase

Objectives

- Talk about things in the classroom
- Ask questions about new words and phrases
- Use the Spanish alphabet to spell words
- Talk about things related to the calendar

La sala de clases

el estudiante

el profesor

—¿Qué quiere decir *lápiz*?

—Quiere decir *pencil*.

la estudiante

la profesora

—¿Cómo se dice *book* en español?

—Se dice *libro*.

el cuaderno

la hoja de papel

el lápiz

el libro

el bolígrafo

la carpeta

el pupitre

Actividad 1 Escuchar

El libro, el lápiz, . . .

You will hear the names of objects in your classroom. After you hear each word, hold up the object if you have it on your desk or point to it if it is somewhere in the classroom.

También se dice . . .

In many Spanish-speaking countries or regions, you will hear different words for the same thing. Words like these are highlighted in the *También se dice . . .* sections throughout your textbook.

For example, in Spain *pencil* is **el lapicero.** In Mexico and other countries, *pen* is **la pluma.**

Actividad 2 Hablar

¿Cómo se dice...?

Discuss with a partner how you would say the following classroom objects in Spanish.

Modelo

A —¿Cómo se dice <u>book</u> en español?
B —Se dice <u>libro</u>.

1.
2.
3.
4.
5.

Now ask each other what these Spanish words mean in English.

Modelo

mano
A —¿Qué quiere decir <u>mano</u>?
B —Quiere decir <u>hand</u>.

6. estudiante
7. pie
8. cabeza
9. ojo
10. brazo

Gramática

Nouns

Nouns refer to people, animals, places, things, and ideas. In Spanish, nouns have gender. They are either masculine or feminine.

Most nouns that end in -o are masculine. Most nouns that end in -a are feminine.

Masculine	Feminine
el libro	la carpeta
el bolígrafo	la hoja de papel

The definite articles, *el* and *la,* also point out if a word is masculine or feminine. They both mean "the."

Spanish nouns that end in -e or a consonant must be learned as masculine or feminine. You should practice them with their definite articles, *el* or *la.*

Masculine	Feminine
el profesor	la noche
el lápiz	la conversación

Actividad 3 Pensar/Escribir

¿Masculino o femenino?

Look at these words and decide whether each one is masculine or feminine. Rewrite each word and add the appropriate definite article *(el* or *la).*

1. pierna
2. nariz
3. cuaderno
4. carpeta
5. pupitre
6. pie
7. profesora
8. lápiz

 Más práctica
Practice Workbook P-6

For: More practice: *en la clase*
Visit: www.phschool.com
Web Code: jad-0004

El alfabeto

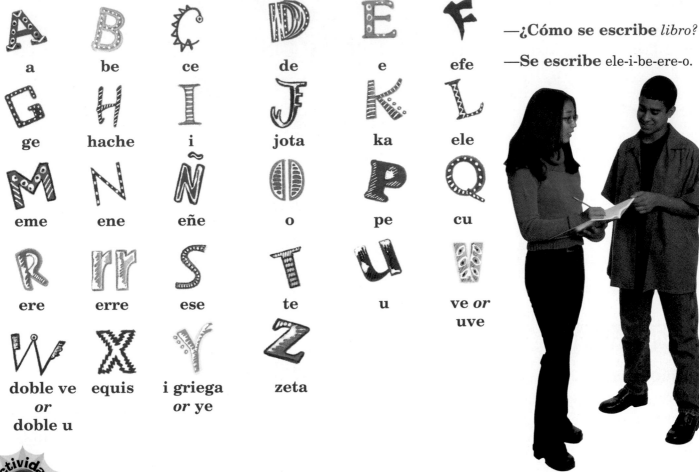

A	B	C	D	E	F
a	be	ce	de	e	efe
G	H	I	J	K	L
ge	hache	i	jota	ka	ele
M	N	Ñ	O	P	Q
eme	ene	eñe	o	pe	cu
R	rr	S	T	U	V
ere	erre	ese	te	u	ve *or* uve
W	X	Y	Z		
doble ve *or* doble u	equis	i griega *or* ye	zeta		

—¿Cómo se escribe *libro*?

—Se escribe ele-i-be-ere-o.

Escuchar/Escribir

Escucha y escribe

On a sheet of paper, write the numbers 1–8. You will hear several words you know spelled aloud. Listen carefully and write the letters as you hear them.

Hablar/Escribir

Pregunta y contesta

Work with a partner. Use the pictures to ask and answer according to the model. As Student B spells the words, Student A should write them out. When you are finished, check your spelling by looking at p. 10.

1. 2. 3.

4. 5.

> **Modelo**
>
> A —¿*Cómo se escribe lápiz?*
> B —*Se escribe ele-a acento-pe-i-zeta.*

Actividad 6

Hablar

¿Cómo te llamas?

Work with a partner. Follow the model to find out each other's names and how they are spelled. Then change partners and repeat.

Modelo

A —¿Cómo te llamas?
B —Me llamo *María*.
A —¿Cómo se escribe *María*?
B —Se escribe *eme-a-ere-i acento-a*.

Fondo cultural

The Maya were among the early civilizations in the Western Hemisphere to develop a form of writing with symbols, known as hieroglyphics *(los jeroglíficos)*. Each symbol, or glyph, represents a word or an idea.

• With what other hieroglyphic writing are you familiar?

Jeroglíficos mayas

Punctuation and accent marks

You have probably noticed that questions begin with an upside-down question mark (¿) and exclamations with an upside-down exclamation point (¡). This lets you know at the beginning of a sentence what kind of sentence you are reading.

You probably also noticed the accent marks *(el acento)* on *días* and *estás*. When you write in Spanish, you must include these accent and punctuation marks.

Try it out! Rewrite these phrases and insert the correct punctuation and accent marks.

Como estas   Que tal   Hasta luego   Y tu

Actividad 7

Escuchar/Escribir/Hablar

Juego

❶ Play this game in pairs. Each player makes a list of five Spanish words that you have learned. Don't let your partner see your words.

❷ Spell your first word aloud in Spanish. Don't forget any accent marks. Your partner will write the word as you spell it. Then your partner will spell a word for you to write. Take turns until you have spelled all the words on your lists.

❸ Check each other's papers. The winner is the player with the most words spelled correctly.

Strategy

Sustaining a conversation
If you need your partner to spell a word again, say: *Repite, por favor.*

El calendario y la fecha

AGOSTO — el mes

lunes	martes	miércoles	jueves	viernes	sábado	domingo
				1	2	3
4	5	6	7	8	9	10
11	12	13	14	15	16	17
18	19	20	21	22	23	24
25	26	27	28	29	30	31

el día

la semana

—¿Qué día es hoy?
—Hoy es lunes. Mañana es martes.
—¿Cuántos días hay en el mes de agosto?
—Hay treinta y un días.

Nota

Notice that the days of the week and the months of the year are not capitalized in Spanish, except at the beginning of sentences.

The first day of the week in a Spanish-language calendar is *lunes.*

Los meses del año

enero

febrero

marzo

abril

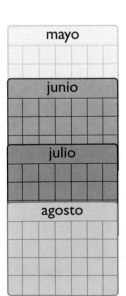

mayo

junio

julio

agosto

septiembre

octubre

noviembre

diciembre

Nota

To say the first day of the month, use *el primero*. For the other days, use the numbers *dos, tres*, and so on.

—¿Cuál es la fecha?
—Es **el** 22 **de** agosto.

—¿Cuál es la fecha?
—Es **el primero** de agosto.

Actividad 8   **Hablar**

Hoy y mañana

Ask and answer according to the model.

Modelo

lunes

A —*¿Qué día es hoy?*
B —*Hoy es lunes. Mañana es martes.*

1. martes
2. sábado
3. jueves

4. miércoles
5. viernes
6. domingo

El Cinco de Mayo es un día festivo en México.

Actividad 9   **Leer/Escribir**

Días de fiesta

Your friend never gets dates right. Correct the following sentences making the necessary changes.

1. El Día de San Patricio es el 14 de enero.
2. El Día de San Valentín es en junio.
3. Januká es en febrero.
4. La Navidad (*Christmas*) es el 25 de noviembre.

5. El Día de la Independencia de los Estados Unidos (*United States*) es el 4 de junio.
6. El Año Nuevo (*New Year's Day*) es en diciembre.
7. Hoy es el 3 de agosto.

Actividad 10

Escribir

El calendario

Answer the questions based on the calendar page at the right.

hoy

1. ¿Cuál es la fecha de hoy?
2. ¿Qué día de la semana es?
3. ¿Qué día es mañana?
4. ¿Cuál es la fecha de mañana?
5. ¿Cuántos días hay en este *(this)* mes?
6. ¿Cuántos días hay en una semana?

julio

lunes	martes	miércoles	jueves	viernes	sábado	domingo
	1	2	3	4	5	6
7	8	9	10	11	12	13
14	15	16	17	18	19	20
21	22	23	24	25	26	27
28	29	30	31			

Fondo cultural

Los sanfermines, or the "Running of the Bulls," is a popular two-week festival in Pamplona, Spain, named for the town's patron saint, San Fermín, who is commemorated on July 7 each year. The celebration includes daily bullfights, but before they begin the real fun happens! As the bulls are released from their pens and run through the streets, many people run ahead or alongside them to the bullring.

• What festivals are you familiar with in which animals play a role?

Un día de fiesta en Pamplona, España

Más práctica
Practice Workbook P-7, P-8

Go Online
PHSchool.com

For: More practice: *el calendario*
Visit: www.phschool.com
Web Code: jad-0005

Actividad 11 · Leer

El calendario azteca

The Aztecs were a nomadic tribe that finally settled in the valley of central Mexico in 1325. They established their capital, Tenochtitlán, on a swampy lake and built a mighty empire that dominated most of Mexico. The Aztec empire flourished until 1521, when it was defeated by the Spaniards, led by Hernán Cortés.

México

Conexiones
La historia

One of the most famous symbols of Mexico is the monolith, or huge stone, carved by the Aztecs in 1479. Known today as the Aztec calendar or the Sun Stone, the carving weighs almost 24 tons and is approximately 12 feet in diameter. The Aztecs dedicated it to the sun, represented by the face in the center. The calendar represents a 260-day year.

Representation of the sun, or Tonatiuh

One of the previous four world creations

This band shows the 20 days of the month.

Actividad 12 · Pensar

Los símbolos aztecas

Here are several glyphs representing days found on the Sun Stone. Match the glyph with the Spanish word. What do you think each of the glyphs represents? Why do you think the Aztecs included these symbols on their calendar?

1.

2.

3.

4.

5.

6.

a. Jaguar
b. Perro
c. Movimiento
d. Serpiente
e. Cráneo
f. Agua

3 El tiempo

Objectives

- Describe weather conditions
- Identify the seasons
- Compare weather in the northern and southern hemispheres

¿Qué tiempo hace?

Hace sol.

Hace calor.

Hace frío.

Hace viento.

Llueve.

Nieva.

Las estaciones

la primavera

el verano

el otoño

el invierno

1 Escuchar

El tiempo

You will hear descriptions of different weather conditions. Write the numbers 1–6 on a sheet of paper. Then, next to each number, write the letter of the photo for which the weather is being described.

a.  **b.**  **c.**  **d.**

2 Hablar

¿Qué tiempo hace?

Work with a partner. Ask and answer the questions based on the city and weather information for each item.

Miami / julio /

Modelo
A —*¿Qué tiempo hace en <u>Miami</u> en <u>julio</u>?*
B —*Hace sol.*

1. Denver / enero /

2. Chicago / octubre /

3. San Francisco / noviembre /

4. Washington, D.C. / junio /

5. Minneapolis / diciembre /

6. Dallas / agosto /

3 Hablar/Escribir

Las estaciones

Answer the questions based on where you live.

1. ¿Qué tiempo hace en la primavera?

2. ¿Qué tiempo hace en el otoño?

3. ¿En qué estación hace calor?

4. ¿En qué estación hace frío?

5. ¿En qué estación llueve mucho?

6. ¿En qué estación nieva?

● **Más práctica**
Practice Workbook P-9

Dos hemisferios

Read about the seasons in the Northern and Southern Hemispheres and then answer the questions.

Conexiones

La geografía

Did you know that the seasons for the Northern and Southern Hemispheres are reversed? When it's winter in the Northern Hemisphere, it's summer in the Southern Hemisphere and vice versa. So if you want to ski all year round, go from the slopes of the Rockies in Colorado in December to those of the Andes in Bariloche, Argentina in July. Or for a December getaway to a warmer climate, go to one of the coastal resorts at Viña del Mar, Chile.

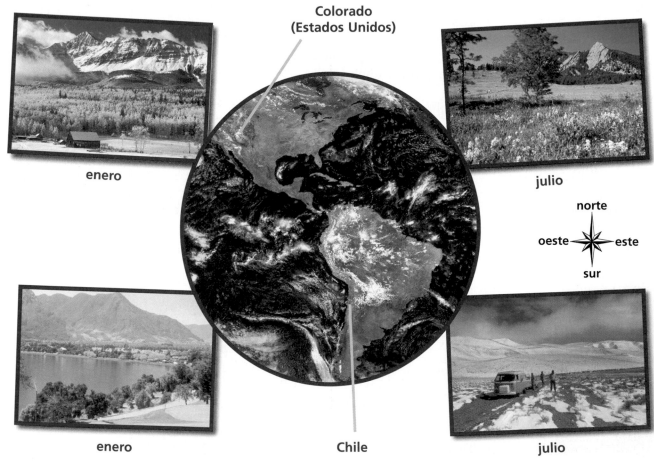

Colorado
(Estados Unidos)

enero

julio

norte

oeste — este

sur

enero

Chile

julio

1. En febrero, ¿qué tiempo hace en Chile?

2. En junio, ¿qué tiempo hace en Colorado?

3. En tu comunidad, ¿qué tiempo hace en diciembre? ¿Y en agosto?

ciudad	diciembre	julio
Chicago	36°F / 2°C	75°F / 24°C
Los Ángeles	67°F / 19°C	88°F / 31°C
Miami	76°F / 24°C	97°F / 36°C
Nueva York	41°F / 5°C	74°F / 23°C
Seattle	41°F / 5°C	66°F / 19°C
St. Louis	36°F / 2°C	81°F / 27°C
Asunción, Paraguay	85°F / 29°C	75°F / 24°C
Bogotá, Colombia	66°F / 19°C	64°F / 17°C
Buenos Aires, Argentina	78°F / 26°C	50°F / 10°C
Caracas, Venezuela	80°F / 27°C	80°F / 27°C
Ciudad de México, México	70°F / 21°C	74°F / 23°C
Guatemala, Guatemala	72°F / 22°C	74°F / 23°C
La Habana, Cuba	76°F / 24°C	82°F / 28°C
La Paz, Bolivia	58°F / 15°C	55°F / 13°C
Lima, Perú	76°F / 24°C	67°F / 19°C
Quito, Ecuador	65°F / 18°C	67°F / 19°C
San José, Costa Rica	78°F / 26°C	78°F / 26°C
San Juan, Puerto Rico	74°F / 23°C	80°F / 27°C
Santiago, Chile	82°F / 28°C	50°F / 10°C
Tegucigalpa, Honduras	70°F / 21°C	81°F / 27°C

  **Hablar** •

¿Hace calor o hace frío?

Work with a partner. Discuss the weather in six cities listed in the chart above.

Modelo

A —¿Qué tiempo hace en <u>Chicago</u> en <u>diciembre</u>?
B —<u>Hace frío.</u>

  Hablar •

La temperatura es...

Working with a partner, ask about the temperature in six different places on the chart.

Modelo

A —¿Cuál es la temperatura en <u>Quito</u> en <u>diciembre</u>?
B —<u>Sesenta y seis</u> grados.
o: <u>Dieciocho</u> grados.

 Nota

In most parts of the world, people express temperatures in Celsius. A simple way to convert from Celsius to Fahrenheit is to multiply the temperature by $\frac{9}{5}$, then add 32.

$$30°C = \underline{\ ?\ }\ F$$
$$30 \times \tfrac{9}{5} = 54 + 32$$
$$30°C = 86°F$$

Para decir más...

la temperatura temperature
grados degrees

For: More practice: *el tiempo*
Visit: www.phschool.com
Web Code: jad-0006

Repaso del capítulo

Vocabulario y gramática

En la escuela

to greet someone

Buenos días.	Good morning.
Buenas noches.	Good evening.
Buenas tardes.	Good afternoon.
¡Hola!	Hello!
¿Cómo te llamas?	What is your name?
Me llamo ...	My name is ...
Encantado, -a.	Delighted.
Igualmente.	Likewise.
Mucho gusto.	Pleased to meet you.
señor (Sr.)	sir, Mr.
señora (Sra.)	madam, Mrs.
señorita (Srta.)	miss, Miss

to ask and tell how someone is

¿Cómo está Ud.? *(formal)*	How are you?
¿Cómo estás? *(familiar)*	How are you?
¿Qué pasa?	What's happening?
¿Qué tal?	How are you?
¿Y tú? / ¿Y usted (Ud.)?	And you?
(muy) bien	(very) well
nada	nothing
regular	okay, so-so
gracias	thank you

to say good-bye

¡Adiós!	Good-bye!
Hasta luego.	See you later.
Hasta mañana.	See you tomorrow.
¡Nos vemos!	See you!

to tell time

¿Qué hora es?	What time is it?
Es la una.	It is one o'clock.
Son las ... y/ menos ...	It is ... *(time)*.
y cuarto/menos cuarto	quarter past / quarter to
y media	thirty, half-past

to count up to 100 (Turn to p. 7.)

to talk about the body (Turn to p. 9.)

En la clase

to talk about the classroom

el bolígrafo	pen
la carpeta	folder
el cuaderno	notebook
el estudiante, la estudiante	student
la hoja de papel	sheet of paper
el lápiz	pencil
el libro	book
el profesor, la profesora	teacher
el pupitre	(student) desk
la sala de clases	classroom

to say the date

el año	year
el día	day
el mes	month
la semana	week
¿Qué día es hoy?	What day is today?
¿Cuál es la fecha?	What is the date?
Es el *(number)* de *(month)*.	It is the ... of ...
Es el primero de *(month)*.	It is the first of ...
hoy	today
mañana	tomorrow

to say the days of the week and the months of the year (Turn to p. 14.)

to ask for help

¿Cómo se dice ...?	How do you say ...?
Se dice ...	You say ...
¿Cómo se escribe ...?	How is ... spelled?
Se escribe ...	It's spelled ...
¿Qué quiere decir ...?	What does ... mean?
Quiere decir ...	It means ...

other useful words

¿cuántos, -as?	how many?
en	in
hay	there is, there are
por favor	please

Más práctica
Practice Workbook Puzzle P-10
Practice Workbook Organizer P-11

Go Online
PHSchool.com
For: Test preparation
Visit: www.phschool.com
Web Code: jad-0007

El tiempo

to talk about the weather		to talk about the seasons	
¿Qué tiempo hace?	What's the weather like?	la estación, *pl.*	season
Hace calor.	It's hot.	las estaciones	
Hace frío.	It's cold.	el invierno	winter
Hace sol.	It's sunny.	el otoño	fall, autumn
Hace viento.	It's windy.	la primavera	spring
Llueve.	It's raining.	el verano	summer
Nieva.	It's snowing.		

Preparación para el examen

 1 Escuchar On the exam you will be asked to listen to and understand people as they greet each other and introduce themselves. To practice, listen to some students greet people in the school halls. Answer these questions about each greeting: What is the time of day? Was the greeting directed to an adult? How did that person respond?

To review, see pp. 2–5 and Actividades 1, 4.

 2 Escuchar You will be asked to listen to and understand someone announcing the current date and time. To practice, listen to the message and answer the questions: What is the time of day? What is the date?

To review, see pp. 7–8 and Actividad 11; pp. 14–16 and Actividad 10.

 3 Leer You will be asked to read and understand a description of the weather for a given day. To practice, read the weather forecast to the right. Answer the questions: What is the date? What are the high and low temperatures? What is the weather like?

To review, see pp. 18–21 and Actividades 2–6.

El dos de septiembre
Hoy en San Antonio hace sol.
La temperatura máxima es 75 grados y la mínima es 54.
No llueve.

 4 Leer You will be asked to read a list of school supplies and identify them. To practice, copy the school supply list below onto a sheet of paper. Please note: *un, una* mean "a" or "an." Then look to see whether you have any of the items on your desk right now. Make a check mark next to each item you have.

un cuaderno   un lápiz   una hoja de papel
un bolígrafo   una carpeta   un libro

To review, see p. 10.

Fondo cultural

Pablo Picasso (1881–1973), one of the best-known Spanish artists of the twentieth century, had a long, productive career creating art in a wide range of styles and forms. He showed remarkable artistic talent as a child and had his first exhibition when he was 13 years old. *Three Musicians* is an example of Picasso's cubist painting style.

• Study the painting and list some characteristics that show why this style is known as "cubism."

Musiciens aux masques / Three Musicians
(1921), Pablo Picasso

Oil on canvas, 6' 7" x 7' 3 3/4". Mrs. Simon Guggenheim Fund. (55.1949).
Digital Image © The Museum of Modern Art / Licensed by SCALA/ Art
Resource, NY. Museum of Modern Art, New York, N.Y., U.S.A. © 2004
Estate of Pablo Picasso/Artists Rights Society ARS, New York.

¿Qué te gusta hacer?

Chapter Objectives

- Talk about activities you like and don't like to do
- Ask others what they like to do
- Understand cultural perspectives on favorite activities

Video Highlights

A primera vista: *¿Qué te gusta hacer?*
GramActiva Videos: infinitives; making negative statements

Country Connection

As you learn to talk about what you and your friends like to do, you will make connections to these countries and places:

Texas
España
República Dominicana
México
Puerto Rico
Costa Rica
Colombia
Guinea Ecuatorial
Argentina

Go Online
PHSchool.com

For: Online Atlas
Visit: www.phschool.com
Web Code: jac-0002

Un concierto de música latina

A primera vista

Vocabulario y gramática en contexto

bailar

escuchar música

practicar deportes

nadar

correr

esquiar

—¡**Me gusta mucho** bailar!

—**A mí también. Y también** me gusta escuchar música.

—¡Hola, Beatriz! ¿**Qué te gusta hacer?** ¿**Te gusta** practicar deportes?

—¡**Sí!** Me gusta mucho practicar deportes. Me gusta correr, nadar y esquiar. ¿**Y a ti?** ¿Qué te gusta hacer?

escribir cuentos

montar en monopatín

ver la tele

usar la computadora

dibujar

cantar

montar en bicicleta

jugar videojuegos

—A mí me gusta mucho escribir cuentos y dibujar. **¡No me gusta nada** cantar!

—¡Uy! **A mí tampoco.**

—¿Qué te gusta **más,** ver la tele **o** montar en bicicleta?

—**Pues,** no me gusta **ni** ver la tele **ni** montar en bicicleta. Me gusta usar la computadora y jugar videojuegos. Y a ti, ¿qué te gusta más?

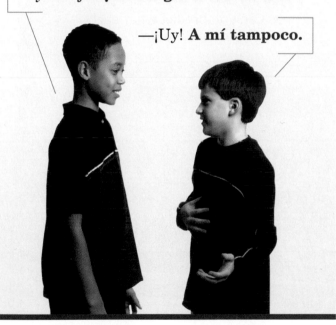

Actividad 1 Escuchar

¿Te gusta o no te gusta?

You will hear Rosa say what she likes to do and doesn't like to do. Give a "thumbs-up" sign when you hear her say what she likes to do, and a "thumbs-down" sign when she says what she doesn't like to do.

 Más práctica
Practice Workbook 1A-1, 1A-2

Actividad 2 Escuchar

Me gusta...

Listen to what some people like to do. Point to the picture of the activity each describes.

 Go Online
PHSchool.com
For: Vocabulary practice
Visit: www.phschool.com
Web Code: jad-0101

¿Qué te gusta hacer?

You're going to meet eight students from around the Spanish-speaking world and find out what they like and don't like to do. You'll be able to figure out where they live by looking at the globes on the page.

Strategy

Using visuals
Look at the pictures with each postcard to help you understand the meaning of the new words.

- Can you predict what each student likes to do?

Saludos desde Madrid

❝ Soy Ignacio.
Me gusta mucho
tocar la guitarra.❞

❝ Y yo me llamo Ana.
A mí me gusta **hablar por teléfono.❞**

Ciudad de México

66 ¡Hola! Me llamo Claudia y me gusta usar la computadora y **pasar tiempo con mis amigos. 99**

66 Yo soy Teresa. También me gusta usar la computadora, pero **me gusta más** jugar videojuegos. **99**

Recuerdos de San Antonio

66 Yo soy Esteban. A mí me gusta **patinar. 99**

66 ¡Hola, amigos! Me llamo Angélica y me gusta mucho montar en bicicleta. **99**

66 Yo me llamo Raúl. Me gusta ir a la escuela . . . más o menos . . . , pero me gusta más **leer revistas. 99**

Monteverde, Costa Rica

66 ¿Qué tal, amigos? Soy Gloria. A mí me gusta **ir a la escuela,** y también me gusta **trabajar. 99**

Leer

Actividades favoritas

The students you saw in the video are doing their favorite activities. Number your paper from 1–6 and match the picture to the activity each student likes to do.

1.
2.
3.
4.
5.
6.

a. patinar

b. montar en bicicleta

c. hablar por teléfono

d. tocar la guitarra

e. ir a la escuela

f. leer revistas

Actividad 4

Leer

¿Comprendes?

On a sheet of paper, write the numbers 1–6. Read the following statements by the characters in the *Videohistoria* and write *C (cierto)* if the statement is true, or *F (falso)* if it is false.

1. **Angélica:** No me gusta montar en bicicleta.
2. **Raúl:** Me gusta mucho leer revistas.
3. **Esteban:** Me gusta patinar.
4. **Claudia:** Me gusta pasar tiempo con mis amigos.
5. **Teresa:** No me gusta usar la computadora.
6. **Gloria:** Me gusta trabajar.

Actividad 5

Escribir/Hablar

Y tú, ¿qué dices?

Choose the activity that you prefer to do on the following days of the week and write it on a separate sheet of paper. Share your answers with a classmate.

1. Hoy es sábado. Me gusta más ___.
   a. trabajar
   b. leer revistas
   c. ver la tele

2. Hoy es lunes. Me gusta más ___.
   a. usar la computadora
   b. patinar
   c. ir a la escuela

3. Hoy es miércoles. Me gusta más ___.
   a. jugar videojuegos
   b. tocar la guitarra
   c. bailar

4. Hoy es domingo. Me gusta más ___.
   a. pasar tiempos con amigos
   b. jugar al fútbol
   c. hablar por teléfono

● **Más práctica**

Practice Workbook 1A-3, 1A-4

Go Online
PHSchool.com

For: Vocabulary practice
Visit: www.phschool.com
Web Code: jad-0102

Manos a la obra

Vocabulario y gramática en uso

Actividad 6 Escribir

Actividades populares

Use the word bank to match the vocabulary word with the appropriate picture.

dibujar	usar la computadora
correr	cantar
practicar deportes	ver la tele
bailar	montar en bicicleta
nadar	

Modelo

Me gusta <u>*practicar deportes*</u>.

1. Me gusta ___.

2. Me gusta ___.

3. Me gusta ___.

4. Me gusta ___.

5. Me gusta ___.

6. Me gusta ___.

Actividad 7 Escribir

Mi lista personal

Copy this chart on a separate sheet of paper. Using the activities from pp. 26–30, write four things that you like to do and four things that you don't like to do under the correct columns.

Modelo

Me gusta	No me gusta
correr	cantar

Actividad 8

Escribir

¿Te gusta o no te gusta?

Using the chart you made in Actividad 7, complete each of the following sentences with a different activity.

Modelo

Me gusta pasar tiempo con mis amigos.

1. Me gusta ___.
2. Me gusta mucho ___.
3. Y también me gusta ___.
4. No me gusta ___.
5. No me gusta nada ___.
6. No me gusta ni ___ ni ___.

Actividad 9

Hablar

¡A mí también!

Using the information from Actividad 7, tell your partner three activities you like to do. Your partner will agree or disagree with you. Follow the model. Then switch roles and repeat the activity.

Modelo

A —*Me gusta correr.*
B —*¡A mí también!*
o: *¡A mí no me gusta!*

Fondo cultural

Outdoor cafés are popular throughout the Spanish-speaking world. Friends go there to enjoy a snack, something to drink, or a light meal. A café is a place where young people can sit and talk with one another and watch people go by.

- Are there outdoor cafés in your area that are similar to this one in Madrid's *Plaza Mayor?* What kinds of places do you go to for a snack with your friends? Compare the places where you like to meet with the Spanish café in the photo.

En el verano, me gusta pasar tiempo con mis amigos en la Plaza Mayor.

Actividad 10 Hablar

¿Qué te gusta hacer?

Ask your partner whether he or she likes doing the activities below. Your partner will answer using one of the two responses shown. Then switch roles and answer your partner's questions.

Modelo

A —¿Te gusta <u>montar en monopatín?</u>

B —Sí, me gusta mucho.

o: No, no me gusta nada.

Estudiante A
¿Te gusta . . . ?

Estudiante B

¡Respuesta personal!

Actividad 11 · Leer/Hablar

¿Calor o frío?

With a partner, look at the following vacation brochures. Ask your partner if he or she likes to do the different activities offered at the two hotels. Then, using that information, decide which vacation destination would be best for him or her.

Hotel Las Colinas

En Las Colinas, hay actividades para toda la familia.

San Carlos de Bariloche, Argentina
Teléfono: (0924) 61 029 • Fax: (0924) 61 008

¡Bienvenidos al Club Arena!

Aquí hay sol y mucho más.

Punta Cana, República Dominicana
Teléfono: (809) 256-9872 • Fax: (809) 256-9873

Pronunciación

The vowels *a*, *e*, and *i*

The vowel sounds in Spanish are different from those in English. In Spanish, each vowel has just one sound. Spanish vowels are also quicker and shorter than those in English.

The letter *a* is similar to the sound in the English word *pop*. Listen to and say these words:

andar	cantar	trabajar
hablar	nadar	pasar

The letter *e* is similar to the sound in the English word *met*. Listen to and say these words:

tele	me	es	Elena	deportes

The letter *i* is similar to the sound in the English word *see*. As you have already seen, the letter *y* sometimes has the same sound as *i*. Listen to and say these words:

sí	escribir	patinar
lápiz	ti	mí

Try it out! Listen to and say this rhyme:

A E I El perro canta para ti.
A E I El tigre baila para mí.

Try it again, substituting *el gato* for *el perro* and *la cebra* for *el tigre*.

Gramática

Infinitives

Verbs are words that are most often used to name actions. Verbs in English have different forms depending on who is doing the action or when the action is occurring:

I **walk,** she **walks,** we walk**ed,** etc.

The most basic form of a verb is called the infinitive. In English, you can spot infinitives because they usually have the word "to" in front of them:

to swim, **to** read, **to** write

Infinitives in Spanish, though, don't have a separate word like "to" in front of them. Spanish infinitives are only one word, and they always end in *-ar, -er,* or *-ir:*

nad**ar,** le**er,** escrib**ir**

GramActiva VIDEO

Want more help with infinitives? Watch the **GramActiva** video.

hablar

12 Gramática Escribir

¿Cuál es?

On a sheet of paper, make a chart with three columns for the headings *-ar, -er,* and *-ir.* Then look at these pictures of activities. Write the infinitive for each activity under the corresponding head. Save your chart to use in Actividad 14.

Modelo		
-ar	-er	-ir
nadar		

Actividad 13 Gramática Escuchar/GramActiva

Tres papeles

Tear a sheet of paper into three equal parts. Write
-ar on one piece, *-er* on another piece, and *-ir* on
the third piece. You will hear several infinitives.
Listen carefully to the endings. Hold up the paper
with the ending that you hear.

Actividad 14 Gramática Escribir

El verbo es...

Here are some verbs in English. Look them up in the
English-Spanish glossary at the back of the book and
write down the infinitive form on the chart you made
in Actividad 12.

1. to walk   2. to see   3. to eat   4. to study
5. to talk   6. to write   7. to share   8. to play

> **Strategy**
>
> **Using a dictionary or glossary**
> When you need to look up
> a verb, always look for the
> infinitive form.

Actividad 15 Gramática Escribir

El diccionario en uso

It's easy to talk about the things you like to do once
you know the infinitive, because you just add the
infinitive to *Me gusta*. Using the glossary at the
back of the book, try writing six sentences about
what you like to do.

Modelo

I like to play soccer.
Me gusta jugar al fútbol.

Escribir/Hablar • • • • • • • • • • • • • • • • • •

Encuesta: ¿Qué te gusta hacer?

Ask four classmates to tell you two things they like to do (*¿Qué te gusta hacer?*) and two things they don't like to do (*¿Qué no te gusta hacer?*). Record their names and responses on a chart like this one.

Nombre	Me gusta	No me gusta
Beto	nadar ir a la escuela	patinar cantar

  Escribir/Hablar • • • • • • • • • • • • • • • • •

Encuesta: Los resultados

Working in a group, create a chart like the one to the right using the results of the interviews you did in Actividad 16. Use your chart to find the most popular and least popular activities among your group. Finally, share your findings with the class, using the two sentences below.

1. Las actividades más (*most*) populares:

2. Las actividades menos (*least*) populares:

Actividad	Me gusta	No me gusta
tocar la guitarra	I I I	I
cantar	I	I I I I
trabajar	I I	I I I I I

Escuchar/Escribir •

Escucha y escribe

Write the numbers 1–7 on a sheet of paper. You will hear Raúl say seven things that he likes to do. Write them down as he says them. Spelling counts!

¿Recuerdas?

Remember to include any accent marks when you spell a word.

¿Te gusta hablar por teléfono?

1. _____
2. _____
3. _____
4. _____
5. _____
6. _____
7. _____

Actividad 19   **Hablar/GramActiva**

Juego

Get together in groups and make a list of at least four things that you like to do. When everyone in the group knows how to say what they like to do in Spanish, you're ready to play.

1 The first person will start the game by saying one thing that he or she likes to do.

First Person:

Me gusta escuchar música.

2 The second person will repeat that information and add another activity.

Second Person:

Me gusta escuchar música y también esquiar.

3 The next person will repeat both activities and add a new one, and so on. See how long your group's sentence gets before someone leaves out an activity.

Next Person:

Me gusta escuchar música, esquiar y también escribir cuentos.

● **Más práctica**
Practice Workbook 1A-5

For: Practice with infinitives
Visit: www.phschool.com
Web Code: jad-0103

Cognates

Words that look alike and have similar meanings in English and Spanish are called **cognates** *(cognados)*. Here are examples from this chapter:

Spanish	English
popular	popular
usar	to use
guitarra	guitar
computadora	computer

Strategy

Recognizing cognates
Identifying cognates will help you understand what you read and will increase your vocabulary.

Try it out! Look at pp. 26–30 and make a list of seven cognates from the vocabulary on those pages.

Fondo cultural

Jaime Antonio González Colson (1901–1975) was an artist from the Dominican Republic. His works usually focused on the people and culture of his homeland.

The *merengue,* the dance shown in this painting, originated in the Dominican Republic in the nineteenth century. One of the instruments used to accompany it is the *güiro* (shown at the top right of the painting), made from a gourd and played by scraping it with a forked stick.

• What instruments set the rhythms in the music that you listen to?

Merengue (1937), Jaime Antonio González Colson
Courtesy of Museo Bellapart, Dominican Republic.

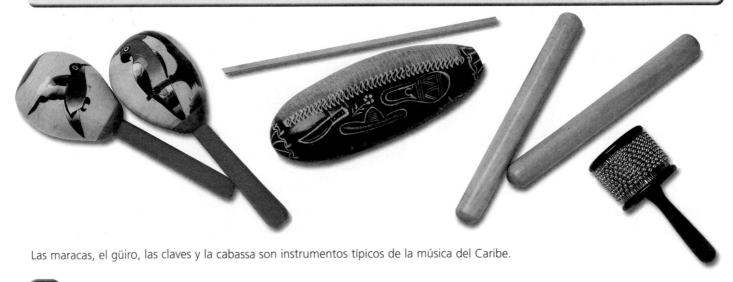

Las maracas, el güiro, las claves y la cabassa son instrumentos típicos de la música del Caribe.

El baile y la música del mundo hispano

Each country in the Spanish-speaking world has distinct musical styles and traditions. Many of the unique rhythms and dances of Spanish-speaking countries are now popular in the United States. This music features instruments such as guitars, violins, accordions, and various types of percussion such as *güiros,* sticks, cymbals, cowbells, and drums. As you read the captions, see how many words you can understand due to their similarity with English words. After you read, your teacher will play examples of each type of music. Listen for the different instruments used.

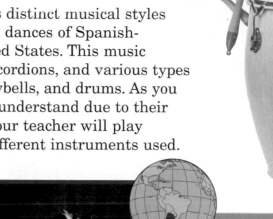

Conexiones
La música

En Argentina, el tango es muy popular. Es un baile romántico.

El flamenco es un baile típico de España. El instrumento más importante en el flamenco es la guitarra.

En Puerto Rico, la salsa es el baile preferido. El ritmo de la salsa es popular en la música de los Estados Unidos también.

En la República Dominicana, el baile tradicional es el merengue. El merengue tiene muchos ritmos africanos.

La cumbia es el baile más famoso de Colombia.

- Reread each of the captions and make a list of seven cognates.

- Make a list of instruments you heard in the different pieces of music. You might need to listen to the music again.

Gramática

Negatives

To make a sentence negative in Spanish, you usually put *no* in front of the verb or expression. In English you usually use the word "not."

No me gusta cantar.   *I do **not** like to sing.*

To answer a question negatively in Spanish you often use *no* twice. The first *no* answers the question. The second *no* says, "I do *not... (don't)*." This is similar to the way you answer a question in English.

¿Te gusta escribir cuentos?   *Do you like to write stories?*

No, no me gusta.   ***No, I don't.***

In Spanish, you might use one or more negatives after answering "*no.*"

¿Te gusta cantar?   *Do you like to sing?*

No, no me gusta **nada**.   ***No, I don't** like it **at all**.*

If you want to say that you do not like either of two choices, use *ni... ni*:

No me gusta **ni** nadar **ni** dibujar.   *I **don't** like **either** swimming **or** drawing.*

                                    *or: I like **neither** swimming **nor** drawing.*

> **¿Recuerdas?**
>
> Did you remember that *nada* has another meaning?
>
> • ¿Qué pasa? **Nada.**
>
> In this case, *nada* means "nothing."

GramActiva VIDEO

Want more help with negatives? Watch the **GramActiva** video.

ni bailar ni nadar

21 **Gramática** **Leer/Escribir**

Una persona muy negativa

Tomás is a new student in the class who is very negative. Number your paper from 1–5. Complete his conversation with Ana by writing one of these negative expressions: *no, nada, ni... ni.*

Ana: Hola, Tomás. ¿Te gusta escuchar música?

Tomás: No, **1.** me gusta.

Ana: Pues, ¿qué te gusta más, jugar videojuegos o usar la computadora?

Tomás: No me gusta **2.** jugar videojuegos **3.** usar la computadora.

Ana: ¿Te gusta practicar deportes?

Tomás: No, no me gusta **4.** practicar deportes.

Ana: Pues, Tomás, **5.** me gusta pasar tiempo con personas negativas.

Tomás: ¡A mí tampoco! *(Me neither!)*

nada

no

ni

 **Actividad 22 Gramática** • **Hablar** •

¡No, no me gusta!

Today you feel as negative as Tomás. With a
partner, respond to each question saying that
you don't like to do any of these activities.

Modelo

A —¿Te gusta ver la tele?
B —No, no me gusta ver la tele.

Estudiante A
¿Te gusta...?

Estudiante B

No, no me gusta...

También se dice...
no me gusta nada = no me
gusta para nada
(muchos países)

  Actividad 23 • **Hablar** •

¿Qué te gusta más?

Find out what your partner likes
more. Then switch roles.

Modelo

A —¿Qué te gusta más, nadar o
esquiar?
B —Pues, me gusta más nadar.
o: Pues, no me gusta ni nadar ni
esquiar.

1.

2.

3.

4.

● **Más práctica** • • • • • • • • • • • • • • •
Practice Workbook 1A-6

Go Online
PHSchool.com
For: Practice with negatives
Visit: www.phschool.com
Web Code: jad-0104

Gramática

Expressing agreement or disagreement

To agree with what a person likes, you use *a mí también*.
It's like saying "me too" in English.

Me gusta pasar tiempo con amigos.	*I like to spend time with friends.*
A mí también.	**Me too.**

If someone tells you that he or she dislikes something, you can agree by saying *a mí tampoco*. It's like saying "me neither" or "neither do I" in English.

No me gusta nada cantar.	*I don't like to sing at all.*
A mí tampoco.	**Me neither.**

también

tampoco

---

24 **Gramática** **Escribir**

Un buen amigo

You have the same likes and dislikes as Miguel, the new Spanish exchange student. Read his statements below and using either *a mí también* or *a mí tampoco*, write a sentence saying that you agree.

Modelo

Me gusta montar en monopatín.
A mí también. Me gusta mucho montar en monopatín.
No me gusta correr.
A mí tampoco. No me gusta nada correr.

1. Me gusta jugar videojuegos.
2. No me gusta ir a la escuela.
3. No me gusta escribir cuentos.
4. Me gusta pasar tiempo con mis amigos.
5. No me gusta usar la computadora.
6. Me gusta mucho patinar.
7. No me gusta tocar la guitarra.
8. No me gusta trabajar.

---

25 **Escribir/Hablar**

¿También o tampoco?

Write a list of three things that you like to do and three things that you don't like to do. Tell your partner the activities on your list. Your partner will agree or disagree based upon his or her personal preferences. Follow the model.

Modelo

A —*Me gusta mucho bailar.*
B —*A mí también.*
o: *Pues, a mí no me gusta nada bailar.*
A —*No me gusta nada cantar.*
B —*A mí tampoco.*
o: *Pues, a mí me gusta cantar.*

Actividad 26 Leer/Escribir

¿Comprendes?

Read two students' opinions on snowboarding. On a sheet of paper, answer the questions that follow.

1. Who thinks that snowboarding is "neither a fad nor a sport"? What does he or she consider it to be?

2. What does the other person consider snowboarding to be? What else does this person say about snowboarding?

3. ¿A ti te gusta el *snowboard?* En tu opinión, ¿es un deporte o una moda?

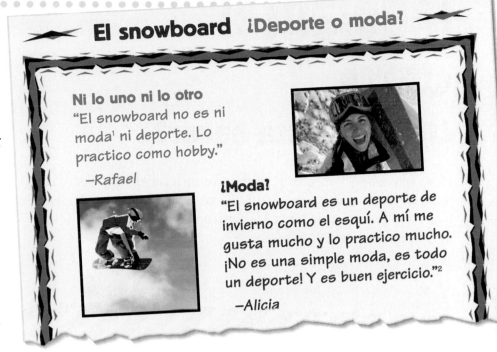

El snowboard ¡Deporte o moda!

Ni lo uno ni lo otro
"El snowboard no es ni moda[1] ni deporte. Lo practico como hobby."
—Rafael

¡Moda!
"El snowboard es un deporte de invierno como el esquí. A mí me gusta mucho y lo practico mucho. ¡No es una simple moda, es todo un deporte! Y es buen ejercicio."[2]
—Alicia

[1] fad [2] good exercise

● **Más práctica**
Practice Workbook 1A-7

Go Online
PHSchool.com
For: Practice with agreement or disagreement
Visit: www.phschool.com
Web Code: jad-0105

El español en la comunidad

People of Spanish-speaking heritage in the U.S. make up approximately 13 percent of the total population and are the fastest-growing minority group. By the year 2050, the Hispanic population is expected to be almost 25 percent of the total U.S. population. Because of this, many Spanish-language media sources—

Viajes
Tu pasaporte para el mundo
• Turismo de aventura
• Las montañas y el mar
• Exploración de los bosques

magazines, newspapers, television, radio, and Internet—are available throughout the country.

● Make a list of Spanish-language media sources in your community. Try to find local, regional, national, or even international sources. If possible, bring in examples. How much can you understand?

These sources will help you improve your Spanish, and you'll learn about Spanish-speaking cultures as well.

¡Adelante!

Objectives

- Read about favorite activities of some teenagers
- Understand cultural perspectives regarding dancing
- Give an oral presentation about your activities
- Learn facts about Spain

Lectura

¿Qué te gusta hacer?

Here are some notes that four students have written to a popular teen magazine. All four are looking for e-pals. As you read their notes, think about how their likes and interests compare to yours.

Strategy

Using cognates
Use what you already know about cognates to figure out what new words mean.

Puerto Rico
Marisol, 14 años

"¿Te gusta practicar deportes y escuchar música? ¡A mí me gusta mucho! También me gusta jugar al básquetbol. ¡Hasta luego!"

Colombia
Daniel, 13 años

"Me gusta mucho ver la tele y escuchar música clásica. También me gusta tocar el piano y pasar tiempo con amigos en un café o en una fiesta. ¿Y a ti?"

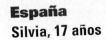

"Me gusta leer revistas, bailar y cantar. Soy fanática de la música alternativa. También me gusta hablar por teléfono con amigos. ¿Y a ti? ¿Qué te gusta hacer?"

Guinea Ecuatorial
Pablo, 15 años

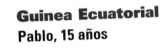

"Me gusta mucho jugar al vóleibol y al tenis. Me gusta escribir cuentos y también me gusta organizar fiestas con amigos. No me gusta ni jugar videojuegos ni ver la tele. ¡Hasta pronto!"

¿Comprendes?

1. On a sheet of paper, draw a bar graph like the one below. Indicate on the graph how many of the four young people like each of these types of activities.

ver la tele				
escuchar música				
practicar deportes				
pasar tiempo con amigos				
	1	2	3	4

2. Of the four types of activities, which are the most popular with these four students?

3. Of the four students, with whom do you have the most in common?

4. Write a personal message similar to those in the magazine. Use one of them as a model.

For: Internet link activity
Visit: www.phschool.com
Web Code: jad-0106

¿Te gusta bailar?

Thanks to the worldwide popularity of Latin music, Latin dances have captured the attention of people of all ages. As a result, people all around the United States are learning dances such as the merengue, tango, and salsa. Here is a dance you can learn. It is called the mambo, and it originated in Cuba in the 1940s.

Bailando el mambo

El mambo

Directions

Beat 1 (of the music):
Step forward with the left foot and slightly raise the right foot in a rocking motion.

Beat 2: Step back down on the right foot.

Beat 3: Place the left foot next to the right foot.

Beat 4: Hold both feet in place with the left and right feet next to each other.

Repeat the same motion, now moving backwards.

Beat 5: Step backward with the right foot and slightly raise the left foot in a rocking motion.

Beat 6: Step back down on the left foot.

Beat 7: Place the right foot next to the left foot.

Beat 8: Hold both feet in place with the left and right feet next to each other.

These steps are repeated throughout the music. If partners dance together, then the male should start with his left foot going forward and the female should start with her right foot going backward.

Think about it! How is doing the mambo with a partner different from dances you might do? What dances do you know from the United States that are danced with a partner?

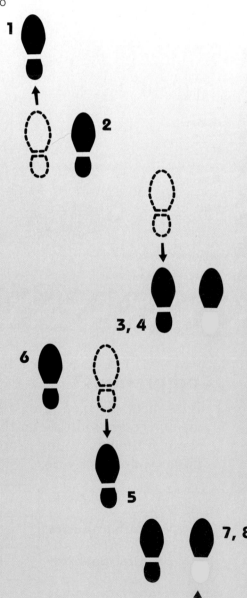

A mí me gusta mucho . . .

Task
You are a new student at school and have been asked to tell the class a little bit about your likes and dislikes.

1 Prepare Copy this diagram on a sheet of paper. Write a list of at least five activities that you can include in the three different ovals.

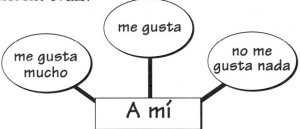

Strategy

Creating visuals
Making a diagram can help you organize a presentation.

Using your list, create a poster or other visual aid to illustrate the three categories and at least five activities. To illustrate the activities, you can make drawings, cut pictures out of magazines, or show photos of yourself doing the activity. Make sure that each activity is easy to identify. You will use this visual as part of your presentation.

2 Practice Go through your presentation with a few class members. You can use your notes the first time or two, but then practice using only the visuals.

Modelo

Me gusta mucho . . .
Me gusta . . .
No me gusta nada . . .

3 Present Talk about yourself using the visual you have created. Remember to look at the Evaluation list below so you know what you need to emphasize in your presentation. Be sure to begin the presentation with your name. During the presentation, try to:

• use complete sentences

• speak clearly

• use the visuals to keep yourself focused

4 Evaluation Your teacher may give you a rubric explaining how the presentation will be graded. You probably will be graded on:

• how much information you communicate

• how easy it is to understand you

• how clearly and neatly your visuals match what you are saying

España

The Spanish empire once included parts of Italy and the Netherlands, much of the Americas and the Caribbean, the Philippines, and colonies in Africa. Today, Spain is a country of rich regional and cultural traditions with a population of more than 40 million people.

Spain was one of the most important provinces of the ancient Roman empire. The Spanish language is very closely related to Latin, the language of that empire. Roman engineering also left its mark on the Spanish landscape, and some Roman bridges are still in use after almost 2,000 years! This photo shows the Roman aqueduct in Segovia, which was constructed entirely without mortar or clamps.

¿Sabes que . . . ?

Spain has five official languages: Spanish, Catalan, Basque, Galician, and Valencian. Originally the language of Castile in central Spain, Spanish is the primary national language and is also spoken in most of Spain's former empire in what is today North, Central, and South America.

Para pensar

Spain has been influenced by many civilizations, including those of the ancient Greeks, Romans, and Moors. What civilizations have most affected the language, culture, and customs of the United States?

Go Online
PHSchool.com

For: Online Atlas
Visit: www.phschool.com
Web Code: jae-0002

Originally a royal retreat, the Parque del Buen Retiro is now a favorite place for the traditional Sunday-afternoon *paseo* (stroll). Throngs of people come to enjoy the Retiro's lakes, gardens, and museums, or simply to spend time with friends or family. What are your favorite places to go walking with friends? Why? ▼

▲ Arabic-speaking Moors from North Africa ruled much of Spain for nearly 800 years. Córdoba in southern Spain became one of the most important cities in Islam, and its mosque, the Mezquita, was one of the largest in the world. The Alhambra in Granada (shown above) is a strongly fortified and beautiful complex of palaces and gardens. It was also the last stronghold of the Moors in Spain, falling to Spain's Catholic monarchs in 1492.

The Bilbao Guggenheim Museum opened in October 1997 and houses a collection of modern and contemporary art. The building's titanium-paneled curves and concrete blocks imitate the harbor of Bilbao, a principal seaport and former shipbuilding center in the heart of the Basque country in the north.

Repaso del capítulo

Vocabulario y gramática

Chapter Review

To prepare for the test, check to see if you...
- know the new vocabulary and grammar
- can perform the tasks on p. 53

to talk about activities

bailar	to dance
cantar	to sing
correr	to run
dibujar	to draw
escribir cuentos	to write stories
escuchar música	to listen to music
esquiar	to ski
hablar por teléfono	to talk on the phone
ir a la escuela	to go to school
jugar videojuegos	to play video games
leer revistas	to read magazines
montar en bicicleta	to ride a bicycle
montar en monopatín	to skateboard
nadar	to swim
pasar tiempo con amigos	to spend time with friends
patinar	to skate
practicar deportes	to play sports
tocar la guitarra	to play the guitar
trabajar	to work
usar la computadora	to use the computer
ver la tele	to watch television

to say what you like to do

(A mí) me gusta ___.	I like to ___.
(A mí) me gusta más ___.	I like to ___ better. (I prefer to ___.)
(A mí) me gusta mucho ___.	I like to ___ a lot.
A mí también.	Me too.

to say what you don't like to do

(A mí) no me gusta ___.	I don't like to ___.
(A mí) no me gusta nada ___.	I don't like to ___ at all.
A mí tampoco.	Me neither.

to ask others what they like to do

¿Qué te gusta hacer?	What do you like to do?
¿Qué te gusta más?	What do you like better (prefer)?
¿Te gusta ___?	Do you like to ___?
¿Y a ti?	And you?

other useful words and expressions

más	more
ni ... ni	neither...nor, not...or
o	or
pues	well...
sí	yes
también	also, too
y	and

Más práctica

Practice Workbook Puzzle 1A-8
Practice Workbook Organizer 1A-9

For *Vocabulario adicional,* see pp. 268–269.

For: Test preparation
Visit: www.phschool.com
Web Code: jad-0107

Preparación para el examen

On the exam you will be asked to...	Here are practice tasks similar to those you will find on the exam...	If you need review...
1 Escuchar Listen to and understand a description of what someone likes to do	Listen to a voice mail from a student looking for a "match-up" to the homecoming dance. a) What are two things this person likes doing? b) What is one thing this person dislikes doing?	**pp. 26–31** *A primera vista* **p. 27** Actividades 1–2 **p. 38** Actividad 18
2 Hablar Talk about yourself and what you like and don't like to do and ask the same of others	You agreed to host a student from the Dominican Republic for a week. What can you tell him or her about yourself in a taped message? Include a brief description of what you like to do. How would you ask the student to tell you something about himself or herself?	**p. 32** Actividad 7 **p. 33** Actividades 8–9 **p. 34** Actividad 10 **p. 38** Actividades 16–17 **p. 43** Actividades 22–23 **p. 49** *Presentación oral*
3 Leer Read and understand someone's description of himself or herself	Read this pen pal e-mail from a Spanish-language magazine. What does the person like to do? Does this person have anything in common with you? What is it? ¡Hola! A mí me gusta mucho usar la computadora y tocar la guitarra. No me gusta ni ir a la escuela ni leer. En el verano me gusta nadar y en el invierno me gusta esquiar. ¿Y a ti? ¿Qué te gusta hacer?	**pp. 26–31** *A primera vista* **p. 31** Actividades 3–4 **p. 35** Actividad 11 **p. 42** Actividad 21 **p. 45** Actividad 26 **pp. 46–47** *Lectura*
4 Escribir Write about yourself with a description of things you like and don't like to do	A school in the Dominican Republic wants to exchange e-mails with your school. Tell your e-pal your name and what you like to do and don't like to do.	**p. 31** Actividad 5 **p. 32** Actividades 6–7 **p. 38** Actividades 16–17 **p. 44** Actividades 24–25 **p. 47** *¿Comprendes?*, no. 3
5 Pensar Demonstrate an understanding of cultural differences regarding dancing	How would you describe the Latin dances that have become popular in the United States? With what countries do you associate each dance? With what type of music or rhythms do you associate each dance?	**p. 41** Actividad 20 **p. 40** *Fondo cultural* **p. 48** *La cultura en vivo*

Fondo cultural

■ ◆ ◆ ◇ ◆

Frida Kahlo (1907–1954) is one of the best-known Mexican painters. In spite of a childhood illness, a crippling traffic accident, and many hospital stays throughout her life, Kahlo was a successful painter and led a very active social life. She used her artwork as an outlet for her physical and emotional suffering.

• Frida Kahlo painted over fifty self-portraits. What is she saying about herself through this painting?

Autorretrato con mono (1938), Frida Kahlo

Oil on Masonite, overall: 16" x 12" (40.64 x 30.48 cm). ©Banco de México Diego Rivera & Frida Kahlo Museums Trust. Av. Cinco de Mayo No. 2, Col. Centro, Del. Cuauhtemoc 06059, México, D.F. Reproduction authorized by the *Instituto Nacional de Bellas Artes y Literatura.* Courtesy of Albright-Knox Art Gallery, Buffalo, New York. Bequest of A. Conger Goodyear, 1966.

En los Pirineos, España

Y tú, ¿cómo eres?

Chapter Objectives

- Talk about personality traits
- Ask and tell what people are like
- Use adjectives to describe people
- Understand cultural perspectives on friendship

Video Highlights

A primera vista: *Amigos por Internet*

GramActiva Videos: adjectives; definite and indefinite articles; word order: placement of adjectives

Country Connection

As you learn how to describe yourself and your friends, you will make connections to these countries and places:

Texas
Cuba
República Dominicana
México
Guatemala
Colombia
Ecuador
Perú
Bolivia
Puerto Rico
Venezuela

Go Online
PHSchool.com

For: Online Atlas
Visit: www.phschool.com
Web Code: jae-0002

A primera vista

Vocabulario y gramática en contexto

❝¿El chico? **Es mi amigo. ¿Cómo se llama?** Se llama Marcos. **¿Cómo es?** Pues . . .

el chico

. . . **él** es **deportista. Le gusta** mucho practicar deportes.

Pero a veces es **impaciente** . . .

. . . también es **un** chico **desordenado. ❞**

❝Mi amiga Sarita es **una buena** amiga. No es **muy** deportista . . .

la chica

. . . pero es una chica **artística** . . .

. . . y muy **ordenada.**

Es una chica muy **inteligente. ❞**

" Hola, me llamo Luz. ¿Yo? ¿Cómo **soy?** Pues . . .

. . . soy **estudiosa** . . .

. . . y **trabajadora** . . .

. . . y también **graciosa** . . .

. . . pero **según mi familia** ¡a veces soy **perezosa!** Y tú, ¿cómo eres? **"**

Actividad 1 Escuchar

¿Marcos o Sarita?

Look at the pictures of Marcos and Sarita, and listen to the descriptions. If a word describes Marcos, point to his picture. If a word describes Sarita, point to her picture.

Actividad 2 Escuchar

¿Cierto o falso?

You will hear some statements about Luz. Give a "thumbs-up" sign if a statement is true, or a "thumbs-down" sign if it is false.

● **Más práctica**
Practice Workbook 1B-1, 1B-2

Go Online
PHSchool.com
For: Vocabulary practice
Visit: www.phschool.com
Web Code: jad-0111

Amigos por Internet

See what happens when *Chica sociable*
sends an e-mail message to Esteban.

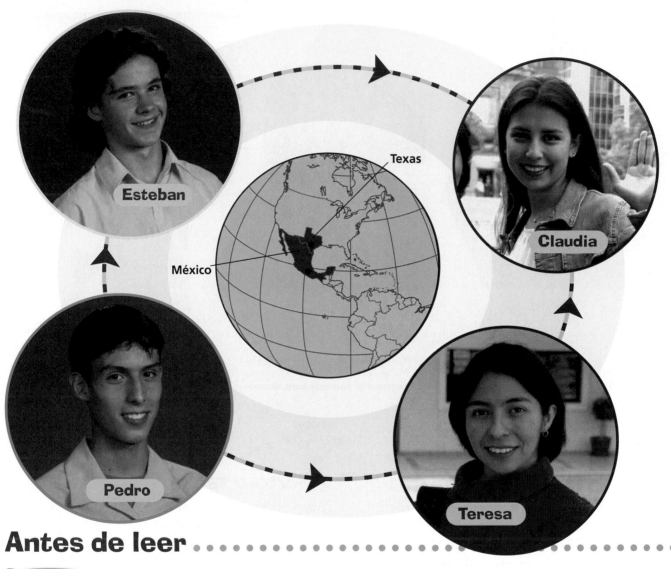

Antes de leer

Strategy **Using cognates** You will see some unfamiliar words in
this story. Many of these are cognates. Use their similarity to
English words to determine their meaning.

• What does *sociable* mean? What does *ideal* mean?

1. Look at photo 1. What are the boys doing?
2. Look at photos 3 and 4. Are the students at different locations?
   Where are they? How do you think the students in the two photos
   might be connected?

1 **Pedro:** Esteban, escucha: "Hola, ¿cómo eres? ¿Qué te gusta hacer? Me gusta mucho hablar con mis amigos. Me llamo *Chica* **sociable.** Escríbeme."

Esteban: ¡Ja! *Chica sociable.* A responder. Escribe, Pedro . . .

2 **Pedro:** "Hola. Me llamo *Chico sociable.* ¡Qué coincidencia!"

3 **Pedro:** "Me gusta pasar tiempo con mis amigos. **No soy** muy **serio.** Según mis amigos, soy gracioso."

4 **Claudia:** *¡Chica sociable!* ¡Ja!
Teresa: Yo soy *Chica sociable.*
Claudia: ¡No! ¿Tú **eres** *Chica sociable?* Mi buena amiga . . .

5 **Teresa:** "Soy muy desordenada. Me gusta hablar por teléfono. Y no me gusta ir a la escuela. Escríbeme. *Chica sociable.*"

6 **Claudia:** Un momento . . . uno más de mí. Escribe . . . "Yo soy *Chica misteriosa.* Soy amiga de *Chica sociable.* Soy muy simpática."

7 **Claudia:** "Y me gusta ir a la escuela. Soy estudiosa y trabajadora. Yo no soy tu chica ideal. *Chica misteriosa.*"

8 **Esteban:** Pues, Pedro. ¿*Chica sociable* o *Chica misteriosa?*

Pedro: *Chica misteriosa.* Me gusta la escuela y a ella le gusta la escuela también.

Esteban: Perfecto. A mí me gusta más *Chica sociable.*

Actividad 3

Escribir/Hablar · · · · · · · · · · · · · · · · · ·

¿Comprendes?

Read each of the sentences below and indicate which character is being described: *Chica sociable* or *Chica misteriosa.*

1. Me gusta hablar por teléfono.
2. Me gusta ir a la escuela.
3. Soy simpática.
4. No soy muy ordenada.
5. Soy trabajadora.

Claudia   Teresa

Actividad 4

Leer/Pensar ·

¿Qué les gusta hacer?

Number your paper 1–8. Based on the *Videohistoria,* decide which characters you think would like to do the activities below. Write the names of all of the characters you have chosen beside each number.

1. trabajar
2. estudiar
3. bailar
4. leer
5. hablar
6. ir a la escuela
7. pasar tiempo con amigos
8. usar la computadora

Esteban   Pedro

● **Más práctica** · · · · · · · · · · · · · · · · · ·
Practice Workbook 1B-3, 1B-4

PHSchool.com
For: Vocabulary practice
Visit: www.phschool.com
Web Code: jad-0112

Manos a la obra

Vocabulario y gramática en uso

Objectives
- Talk about what people are like
- Ask people to talk about themselves and others
- Describe your own personality traits

Actividad 5 · Escribir

¿Cómo es el chico o la chica?

Number your paper 1–6. Choose the correct word to describe each of the people in the pictures and write the complete sentence on your paper.

Modelo
El chico es *(impaciente / estudioso).*
El chico es impaciente.

1. La chica es *(reservada / artística).*

2. El chico es *(desordenado / atrevido).*

3. La chica es *(graciosa / perezosa).*

4. La chica es *(artística / atrevida).*

5. El chico es *(reservado / deportista).*

6. El chico es *(estudioso / desordenado).*

Actividad 6 Leer/Pensar

Nuevos amigos

Look at the profiles of the following students who are chatting online with you. Put them in pairs according to who you think would make good friends. Base your decision on personality traits and favorite activities.

1.

Catalina: Me gusta mucho correr. En general, soy deportista.

2.

Christian: Me gusta escribir cuentos. Soy estudioso.

3.

Flor: Soy reservada. No me gusta mucho hablar por teléfono.

4.

Alejandro: No me gusta nada nadar. Me gusta más jugar videojuegos.

5.

Liliana: Soy inteligente. Me gusta ir a la escuela y leer.

6.

Mayra: No soy muy sociable, pero a veces me gusta pasar tiempo con amigos.

7.

Alfonso: No soy deportista. Me gusta mucho usar la computadora.

8.

Guillermo: Me gusta practicar deportes. No soy muy artístico.

Actividad 7 Escribir

Mi amigo José

Maritza is talking about her friend José. Read the sentences, then choose the appropriate word to fill in each blank.

Modelo

No es un chico impaciente. Es muy paciente.

trabajador	deportista
paciente	estudioso
gracioso	desordenado
sociable	

1. Le gusta mucho practicar deportes. Es ___.

2. A veces no es serio. Es un chico ___.

3. Le gusta pasar tiempo con amigos. Es muy ___.

4. No es un chico ordenado. Es ___.

5. Le gusta ir a la escuela. Es ___.

6. No es perezoso. Es un chico muy ___.

Gramática

Adjectives

Words that describe people and things are called adjectives *(adjetivos).*

- In Spanish, most adjectives have both masculine and feminine forms. The masculine form usually ends in the letter *-o* and the feminine form usually ends in the letter *-a.*

- Masculine adjectives are used to describe masculine nouns.

    Marcos es ordenad**o**   *Marcos is organized*
    y simpátic**o.**   *and nice.*

- Feminine adjectives are used to describe feminine nouns.

    Marta es ordenad**a**   *Marta is organized*
    y simpátic**a.**   *and nice.*

- Adjectives that end in *-e* describe both masculine and feminine nouns.

    Anita es inteligent**e.**   *Anita is smart.*

    Pedro es inteligent**e**   *Pedro is also smart.*
    también.

Masculine	Feminine
ordenad**o**	ordenad**a**
trabajad**or**	trabajad**ora**
pacient**e**	pacient**e**
deportist**a**	deportist**a**

- Adjectives whose masculine form ends in *-dor* have a feminine form that ends in *-dora.*

    Juan es trabajad**or.**   *Juan is hardworking.*
    Luz es trabajad**ora.**   *Luz is hardworking.*

- Some adjectives that end in *-a,* such as *deportista,* describe both masculine and feminine nouns. You will need to learn which adjectives follow this pattern.

    Tomás es deportist**a.**   *Tomás is athletic.*

    Marta es deportist**a**   *Marta is also*
    también.   *athletic.*

GramActiva VIDEO

Want more help with masculine and feminine adjectives? Watch the **GramActiva** video.

talentoso

8 Gramática   Escribir

Roberto y Yolanda

Copy the Venn diagram on a sheet of paper. Which words from the list could only describe Roberto? Write them in the oval below his name. Which words could only describe Yolanda? Write them in the oval below her name. Which words could describe either Roberto or Yolanda? Write them in the overlapping area.

Modelo

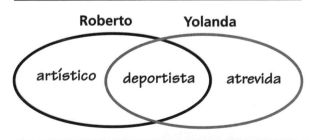

Roberto   Yolanda

artístico   deportista   atrevida

artístico	graciosa	ordenada	serio
atrevida	impaciente	paciente	sociable
deportista	simpático	perezosa	talentosa
estudiosa	inteligente	reservado	trabajador

Actividad 9
Gramática · **Hablar**

¿Cómo es Paloma?

Work with a partner to ask and answer questions about the people shown below.

Paloma

1. Elena

2. Marisol

3. Felipe

4. Juan

5. Lola

6. Gloria

Actividad 10
Gramática · **Hablar/GramActiva**

Juego

Choose an adjective to act out for a small group. The other students in the group will take turns asking you questions to guess which word you are demonstrating. The first student to guess the correct adjective, in the correct form, gets to perform the next charade.

Para decir más . . .

¡Claro que sí!   Of course!

¡Claro que no!   Of course not!

¿De veras?   Really?

Modelo

A —¿Eres ordenada?
B —¡Claro que sí! Soy ordenada.
o: ¡Claro que no! No soy ordenada.

Actividad 11 · Escribir

Yo soy . . .

Make a chart like the one on the right. Write at least three adjectives in each column to say what you are like and are not like. Include *muy* and *a veces* when they are appropriate. Save your chart to use in later activities.

Modelo

Soy	No soy
estudiosa	perezosa
muy trabajadora	impaciente
deportista	

Actividad 12 · Hablar/Escribir

¿Cómo eres?

Working with a partner, use the chart that you made in Actividad 11 to talk about your personality traits. Take notes on what your partner tells you. You will be asked to use this information in the next Actividad.

Modelo

A —¿Cómo eres?
B —Soy estudiosa y muy trabajadora. También soy deportista. ¿Y tú?
A —Soy artístico. Según mis amigos, soy talentoso. No soy perezoso.

Actividad 13 · Escribir/Hablar

Mi amigo(a)

Use the information from Actividades 11 and 12 to write a short description of yourself and your partner. Follow the model, and be prepared to report back to the class.

Modelo

Me llamo Luisa. Soy estudiosa y trabajadora. Y soy artística. Mi amiga se llama Susana. Ella es simpática. También es artística y trabajadora.

Actividad 14

Hablar •

¿Qué te gusta hacer?

Working with a partner, ask each other if you like to do the following activities and answer according to the model.

Modelo

A —¿Te gusta *correr*?

B —Sí, soy *deportista*.

o: No, no soy *deportista*.

o: Sí, pero no soy muy *deportista*.

Estudiante A

Estudiante B

trabajador, -a
sociable
artístico, -a
deportista
estudioso, -a
talentoso, -a

¡Respuesta personal!

Actividad 15

Escribir •

Una persona famosa

Who is your favorite celebrity? Copy the paragraph on a separate piece of paper, filling in the blanks with words that describe your favorite celebrity and what he or she likes to do.

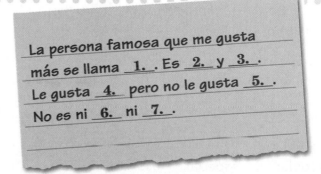

La persona famosa que me gusta más se llama __1.__ . Es __2.__ y __3.__ . Le gusta __4.__ pero no le gusta __5.__ . No es ni __6.__ ni __7.__ .

Simón Bolívar (1783–1830) liberated the territory that is now Venezuela, Colombia, Ecuador, Peru, and Bolivia. Bolívar helped these areas gain their independence from Spain. Simón Bolívar is remembered as a brave and daring leader and is known throughout South America as *El Libertador* (The Liberator).

• Name three leaders who had a similar influence on events of their time.

Simón Bolívar (siglo XIX), Anónimo
Chromolitho. Artist Unknown (pre 20th century). Private Collection / Archives Charmet / Bridgeman Art Library.

Actividad 16 Pensar/Escribir

¿Qué es un buen líder?

A good leader has to have certain qualities. Copy this chart onto your paper, and fill in the adjectives that, in your opinion, describe what a good leader is and is not.

Es...	No es...

Exploración del lenguaje

Cognates that begin with *es* + consonant

Many words in Spanish that begin with *es* + consonant are easy to understand because they have the same meaning as English words. Knowing this pattern helps you recognize the meaning of new Spanish words and learn them quickly.

Try it out! Look at these words, then cover up the *e* at the beginning. Name English words that come from the same root word.

estudiante **es**tudioso **es**cuela **es**tómago

esquiar **es**pecial **es**tricto **es**cena

Es muy deportista. Le encanta esquiar.

Actividad 17

Leer/Escribir . . . .

El poema "Soy Elena"

The following poem is called a *diamante*. Can you guess why?
After you've read the poem, answer the questions.

Conexiones

La literatura

Soy Elena
En general, soy
reservada y ordenada.
A veces, soy atrevida,
graciosa o impaciente.
No soy ni deportista
ni artística.
¡Yo soy yo!

1. Which activity would you invite Elena to do based on what she has told you about herself?

dibujar   montar en monopatín   escuchar música

2. Rewrite the poem replacing *Soy Elena* with *Soy Tomás*.

Actividad 18

Escribir . . . .

Un poema personal

Write *un poema diamante* about yourself.
Choose adjectives that best describe you. Look
back at your chart from Actividad 11 for some
ideas. Substitute your adjectives in the poem
above. Be sure to write the poem in the form of
a diamond. You might want to use calligraphy
or an appropriate font on the computer and
add pictures to illustrate your work.

 Más práctica . . . .
Practice Workbook 1B-5

Go Online
PHSchool.com
For: Practice with adjective agreement
Visit: www.phschool.com
Web Code: jad-0114

Gramática

Definite and indefinite articles

El and *la* are called definite articles and are the equivalent of "the" in English. *El* is used with masculine nouns; *la* is used with feminine nouns. You've already seen words with definite articles:

el libro   ***the*** book   **la** carpeta   ***the*** folder

Un and *una* are called indefinite articles and are the equivalent of "a" and "an" in English. *Un* is used with masculine nouns; *una* is used with feminine nouns.

un libro   ***a*** book   **una** carpeta   ***a*** folder

el	the
la	the

un	a, an
una	a, an

Strategy

Learning by repetition
When you learn a new noun, say it aloud, along with its definite article. Eventually you will find that words just "sound right" with the correct definite article and you will know whether the nouns are masculine or feminine.

GramActiva VIDEO

Want more help with definite and indefinite articles? Watch the **GramActiva** video.

Actividad 19 · Gramática · Escuchar/GramActiva

¿El o la?

Write the word *el* in large letters on a sheet of paper or an index card. Write *la* in large letters on another sheet. You will hear eight words you already know. When you hear a masculine word, hold up the paper with *el*. When you hear a feminine word, hold up the paper with the word *la* on it.

Actividad 20 · Gramática · Escribir

Buenos días, Doctor

Julian is at the doctor's office for a check-up. As he examines Julian, the doctor follows a list to be thorough. Copy the list on your paper and help the doctor by adding the appropriate definite article for each body part.

☑ 1. ___ brazo
☑ 2. ___ cabeza
☑ 3. ___ nariz
☑ 4. ___ pierna
☑ 5. ___ estómago
☑ 6. ___ mano

Actividad 21 Gramática Escribir

La escuela de Diego

Diego is talking about people at his school. Copy the sentences on your paper and complete each one with *un* or *una*.

1. La Sra. Secada es ___ profesora simpática.

2. Alicia es ___ estudiante trabajadora.

3. Juan Carlos es ___ chico perezoso.

4. Víctor es ___ chico sociable.

5. El Sr. Guzmán es ___ profesor gracioso.

6. Adriana es ___ chica muy seria.

7. La Srta. Cifuentes es ___ profesora paciente.

8. Arturo es ___ estudiante talentoso.

Actividad 22 Gramática  Hablar

¿Qué es?

Tell your partner the name of each object or body part pictured below.

> **Modelo**
> A —¿Qué es?
> B —Es un brazo.

1.

2.

3.

4.

5.

6.

7.

8.

Pronunciación

The vowels *o* and *u*

In Spanish, the pronunciation of the letter *o* is similar to the vowel sound in the English word *boat,* except that it is short. Listen then say these words, concentrating on making a short *o* sound:

bolígrafo	gracioso	cómo
teléfono	tampoco	otoño

In Spanish, the pronunciation of the letter *u* is similar to the vowel sound in the English word *zoo.* Listen to and say these words:

mucho	lunes	usted
octubre	estudioso	según

¡Ojo! Careful! Sometimes the words we mispronounce most are the ones that remind us of English words.

Try it out! Pronounce these words, concentrating on the Spanish vowel sounds:

agosto	regular	tropical	música
gusto	universidad	Uruguay	Cuba

El mundo

 Más práctica
Practice Workbook 1B-6

For: Practice with articles
Visit: www.phschool.com
Web Code: jad-0113

Word order: Placement of adjectives

In Spanish, adjectives usually come after the noun they describe. Notice how *artística* follows *chica* in this Spanish sentence:

Margarita es una **chica artística**.   *Margarita is an **artistic girl**.*

Did you notice in the English sentence that the adjective comes before the noun?

Here's a simple pattern you can follow when writing a sentence in Spanish:

¿Recuerdas?

To make a sentence negative, you place the word *no* before the verb.

- **Eduardo no es un chico serio.**
- **No me gusta jugar videojuegos.**

Subject	Verb	Indefinite Article + Noun	Adjective
Margarita	es	una chica	muy artística
Pablo	es	un estudiante	inteligente
La señora Ortiz	es	una profesora	muy buena

Actividad 23 **Gramática** **Escribir**

Frases desordenadas

Create five sentences using the words in the following bubbles. Follow the "building blocks" pattern above and be sure to add a period at the end of each sentence.

una
Patricia
chica
deportista
es

Modelo

Patricia es una chica deportista.

1. artística
es
una
Marina
chica

2. Marcos
chico
es
reservado
un

3. es
un
Tito
perezoso
chico

4. chica
Teresa
es
inteligente
una

5. Enrique
es
trabajador
un
chico

24 Gramática Escuchar/Escribir • • • •

Escucha y escribe

You will hear a description of Arturo, Marta, and Belinda. Write what you hear.

25 Leer/Escribir • • • • • • • •

¿Cómo son los estudiantes?

Each of the following students is going to tell you what they like to do. Based on their statements, write a description of them. Be sure to use the correct word order.

Modelo

José: Me gusta nadar.
José es un chico deportista.

1. **Mariana:** Me gusta estudiar.
2. **Gustavo:** Me gusta mucho pasar tiempo con amigos.
3. **Luz:** Me gusta hablar por teléfono.
4. **Jorge:** Me gusta trabajar.
5. **Silvia:** Me gusta mucho bailar y cantar.
6. **Natalia:** Me gusta mucho el arte.
7. **Julian:** Me gusta usar la computadora.

El español en el mundo del trabajo

Paciente, inteligente, trabajador, ordenado . . .

These four qualities will make you a good candidate for any job. And if you add *bilingüe* to the list, your job qualifications will be enhanced.

- Make a list of careers where your knowledge of Spanish would be an asset. Which of these careers are of interest to you?

Actividad 26 Gramática Escribir

¿Cómo es...?

You are sitting in your school cafeteria with Marcos, a new exchange student from Costa Rica. Describe the other students based on their activities.

Modelo

Emilia es una chica talentosa.

Actividad 27 Escribir/Hablar

Y tú, ¿qué dices?

1. Según tu familia, ¿cómo eres?
2. Según tu mejor *(best)* amigo(a), ¿cómo eres?
3. Según tus profesores, ¿cómo eres?

Actividad 28

Leer/Escribir •

Un mensaje electrónico

You just received an e-mail message from another student in Panama City, but when you opened it up, some of the sentences were scrambled. Unscramble her message and then answer her questions by writing your own message.

Hola,

Me llamo Andreina:

una seria soy estudiante muy Yo. chica Yo artística soy una. ¿Eres inteligente? ¿Eres paciente? Mi mejor amiga es Claudia. **Claudia deportista chica una es. muy estudiante Claudia es trabajadora una.** ¿Cómo se llama tu mejor amigo? ¿Es deportista y talentoso?

Hola Andreina,

Me llamo ____.

Soy ____.

También, yo soy ____.

Mi mejor amigo(a) se llama ____.

Es ____.

También es ____.

Y a ti, ¿qué te gusta hacer?

¡Escríbeme pronto!

Fondo cultural

Cibercafés Many households in Spanish-speaking countries have computers and are online. However, *cibercafés*, places where people can access the Internet, are very popular. Some of the *cibercafés* are regular coffeehouses that serve snacks and drinks and have a few computers for customers to use, while others are equipped with dozens of computers. When people want to surf the Internet, play computer games, or e-mail friends, they can go to a *cibercafé* and get connected for a small fee.

- How much time do you spend on the computer? Would you spend money to go to a *cibercafé* if you didn't have a computer at home or at school? Why or why not?

● **Más práctica** • • • • • • • • • • • • • • • • • •
Practice Workbook 1B-7

Go Online
PHSchool.com
For: Practice with placement of adjectives
Visit: www.phschool.com
Web Code: jad-0115

¡Adelante!

Objectives
- Read an article about personality traits
- Understand cultural perspectives on friendship
- Write a letter to a pen pal
- Learn facts about the Caribbean

Lectura

Un *self-quiz*

Is there a relationship between colors and personality? According to a self-quiz in the magazine *Amigos,* your favorite colors reveal perfectly what your personality is like.

¿Cómo eres tú?

¡Los colores revelan tu personalidad!

Strategy

Using visual clues to get meaning
You have not yet learned the Spanish words for colors, but see if you can figure out what they are from the visual clues in the article.

¿Eres una chica? ¿Te gusta el rojo? ¿Eres un chico? ¿Te gusta el rojo?	Eres muy apasionada. Eres atrevido.
¿Eres una chica? ¿Te gusta el verde? ¿Eres un chico? ¿Te gusta el verde?	Eres una chica natural. Eres muy generoso.
¿Eres una chica? ¿Te gusta el azul? ¿Eres un chico? ¿Te gusta el azul?	Eres muy talentosa. Eres un chico sociable.
¿Eres una chica? ¿Te gusta el anaranjado? ¿Eres un chico? ¿Te gusta el anaranjado?	Eres una chica artística. Eres gracioso.
¿Eres una chica? ¿Te gusta el violeta? ¿Eres un chico? ¿Te gusta el violeta?	Eres una chica muy independiente. Eres un chico romántico.
¿Eres una chica? ¿Te gusta el amarillo? ¿Eres un chico? ¿Te gusta el amarillo?	Eres una chica muy trabajadora. Eres muy serio.

¿Comprendes?

1. You probably were able to understand most of the words in the quiz. Write the English meaning for these Spanish cognates from the reading:

a. revelan   **d.** generoso

b. natural   **e.** apasionada

c. independiente   **f.** romántico

2. According to the self-quiz, what should be the favorite colors of these teenagers?

a. A Beto le gusta estar con amigos.

b. A Margarita le gusta dibujar.

c. A Lorenzo le gusta el trabajo voluntario *(volunteer work)*.

d. A Lupe le gusta estudiar. Es muy seria.

e. A Isabel le gusta estar con amigos, pero también le gusta estar sola *(alone)*.

3. Which of the colors in this reading is your favorite? Do you agree with the description? Why or why not?

Modelo

amarillo
¡Sí! Soy una chica trabajadora. Me gusta la escuela.
o: *¡No! Soy una chica perezosa. Me gusta ver la tele.*

Fondo cultural

Huipil is the word for the colorful, hand-woven blouse worn by female descendents of the Maya. The color, design, and style of weaving are unique to each *huipil* and identify the background and specific village of the weaver. Hundreds of designs and styles of weaving have been identified in the Mayan regions, principally Guatemala and parts of Mexico.

• What do you wear that might help someone identify your background?

Una niña con huipil

PHSchool.com
For: Internet link activity
Visit: www.phschool.com
Web Code: jad-0116

¿Qué es un amigo?

Marcos, a Costa Rican student on an exchange program in the United States, writes:

" When I arrived in the United States, I was amazed at all the friends my host brother and sister had. They knew a lot of people. These friends came to the house frequently, and we went out in groups. People were very open when meeting me. We'd spend some time together and get to know each other in a short amount of time. And once you got to know them, you ended up talking about everything! "

Brianna, a U.S. student on an exchange program in Colombia, writes:

" After I spent my year in Colombia, I learned that the concept of friendship is a little different than in the United States. My host brother and sisters spent a lot of time with their family. They knew people at school and from after-school activities, but they had just a few close friends and we'd do things with them. It was definitely a smaller group than I was used to. It seems that it took longer to become close friends with people too. "

Dos amigas estudiando en Cozumel, México

In Spanish, two expressions are used frequently to describe friendly relationships: *un amigo,* which means "friend," and *un conocido,* which means "acquaintance." You already know the word *amigo. Conocido* comes from the verb *conocer,* which means "to meet." Each expression implies a different type of relationship.

Check it out! In many Spanish-speaking countries you'll find lots of expressions for someone who is your friend: *hermano, cuate (México), amigote (España),* and *compinche (Uruguay, Argentina, España).* Make a list of the expressions for "a friend" that are popular in your community. How would you explain them to someone from a Spanish-speaking country?

Think about it! Compare how the United States perspective on friendship is different from that of a Spanish-speaking country. Use the terms *amigo* and *conocido* as you make the comparison.

Amigos en una fiesta en España

Amigo por correspondencia

Task
Write an e-mail in which you introduce yourself to a prospective pen pal.

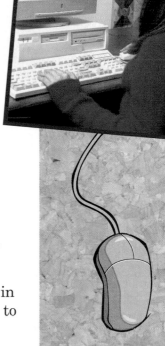

1 **Prewrite** Think about what information you want to give. Answer these questions to help you organize your e-mail message.

- ¿Cómo te llamas?
- ¿Cómo eres?
- ¿Qué te gusta hacer?
- ¿Qué no te gusta hacer?

2 **Draft** Write a first draft of your e-mail message using the answers to the questions above. Begin by introducing yourself: *¡Hola! Me llamo...* When you are finished, end with *Escríbeme pronto.* ("Write to me soon.")

Strategy

Using the writing process
To create your best work, follow each step in the writing process.

Modelo

¡Hola! Me llamo Patti. Soy atrevida y muy deportista. Me gusta mucho nadar y correr, pero me gusta más esquiar. ¡No me gusta nada jugar videojuegos! Escríbeme pronto.

3 **Revise** Review the first draft of your e-mail and share it with a partner. Your partner should check the following:

- Is it well organized?
- Does it include all the information from the Prewrite questions?
- Is the spelling accurate? Did you use the correct form of the adjectives to describe yourself?
- Did you include the opening and the closing?

Decide whether or not you want to use your partner's suggestions. Rewrite your draft.

4 **Publish** Type up the e-mail. You might want to send it to a pen pal in another class or school, send it to your teacher, or print it and give it to someone else in the class to answer.

5 **Evaluation** Your teacher may give you a rubric for grading the e-mail. You probably will be graded on:

- completion of task
- following the writing process by turning in the Prewrite and first draft
- using adjectives correctly

El Caribe

A chain of islands extending from the Bahamas in the north to Trinidad in the south, the Caribbean or West Indies is a region of extraordinary cultural and linguistic diversity. The Spanish-speaking countries are Cuba, Puerto Rico, and the Dominican Republic, which occupies the eastern portion of the island of Hispaniola.

Christopher Columbus first landed on the island of Hispaniola in 1492. He returned the following year with 1,000 colonists and founded Isabela, the first European colony in America, on the northern coast of Hispaniola.

¿Sabes que...?

Most Cubans are descendants of people who originally came to the island from Spain and Africa. Although almost all Cubans speak Spanish as their first language, some also speak Lucumi, which is closely related to West African languages. Many people in other parts of the Caribbean speak creole languages, which combine elements of African and European tongues.

Para pensar

African traditions have inspired reggae, calypso, salsa, merengue, and many other musical styles in the Caribbean. What are some of the musical styles from the United States that have been influenced by African traditions?

Go Online
PHSchool.com

For: Online Atlas
Visit: www.phschool.com
Web Code: jae-0002

The Universidad Autónoma de Santo Domingo, located in the capital of the Dominican Republic, Santo Domingo, is the oldest university in the Americas. It was founded in 1538—almost 100 years before Harvard—and continues to be one of the most important in the Caribbean.

Opened in 1963, the Arecibo Observatory in Puerto Rico has the largest single-dish radio telescope in the world. Some 200 scientists from around the world conduct research at Arecibo every year. In the early 1990s astronomers at Arecibo discovered the first planets outside our solar system.

◀ The Caribbean is famous for its diverse musical styles that fuse African and European influences. Some groups even combine salsa, rumba, cha-cha-cha, and other Caribbean musical styles with jazz, hip-hop, and rock and roll.

Repaso del capítulo

Vocabulario y gramática

Chapter Review

To prepare for the test, check to see if you...
- know the new vocabulary and grammar
- can perform the tasks on p. 83

to talk about what you and others are like

artístico, -a	artistic
atrevido, -a	daring
bueno, -a	good
deportista	athletic
desordenado, -a	messy
estudioso, -a	studious
gracioso, -a	funny
impaciente	impatient
inteligente	intelligent
ordenado, -a	neat
paciente	patient
perezoso, -a	lazy
reservado, -a	reserved, shy
serio, -a	serious
simpático, -a	nice, friendly
sociable	sociable
talentoso, -a	talented
trabajador, -ora	hardworking

to ask people about themselves or others

¿Cómo eres?	What are you like?
¿Cómo es?	What is he/she like?
¿Cómo se llama?	What's his/her name?
¿Eres...?	Are you...?

to talk about what someone likes or doesn't like

le gusta...	he/she likes...
no le gusta...	he/she doesn't like...

to describe someone

es	he/she is
soy	I am
no soy	I am not

For *Vocabulario adicional,* see pp. 268–269.

to tell whom you are talking about

el amigo	male friend
la amiga	female friend
el chico	boy
la chica	girl
él	he
ella	she
yo	I

other useful words

a veces	sometimes
muy	very
pero	but
según	according to
según mi familia	according to my family

adjectives

Masculine	Feminine
ordenado	ordenada
trabajador	trabajadora
paciente	paciente
deportista	deportista

definite articles

el	the
la	the

indefinite articles

un	a, an
una	a, an

● Más práctica

Practice Workbook Puzzle 1B-8
Practice Workbook Organizer 1B-9

Preparación para el examen

On the exam you will be asked to...	Here are practice tasks similar to those you will find on the exam...	If you need review...
1 Escuchar Listen to and understand a description of a friend	Listen as a character in a Spanish soap opera describes his ex-girlfriend. What does he think her good qualities are? What does he think her shortcomings are? Can you understand why he broke up with her?	**pp. 56–61** *A primera vista* **p. 62** Actividad 5 **p. 63** Actividades 6–7 **p. 64** Actividad 8 **p. 65** Actividad 10
2 Hablar Talk about yourself in terms of how you see yourself	While you're talking to your Spanish teacher, you realize that she doesn't know the "real you." Tell her some things about yourself that would help her understand you.	**p. 66** Actividades 11–13 **p. 69** Actividad 18 **p. 74** Actividad 27
3 Leer Read and understand a description of someone	In a popular Spanish magazine, you see an interview with the actor who plays the part of a teenager, Carlos, in a TV show you have been watching. See if you can understand what he is saying about the character he plays: ¡No me gusta nada el chico! Él es muy inteligente, pero le gusta hablar y hablar de NADA. Es ridículo. Es muy impaciente y perezoso. Él no es ni simpático ni gracioso. Yo soy un actor . . . ¡no soy como Carlos!	**pp. 56–61** *A primera vista* **p. 69** Actividad 17 **pp. 76–77** *Lectura*
4 Escribir Write a short paragraph describing yourself	The first issue of your school's online newspaper is called "Getting to Know You." Submit a brief profile of yourself. Mention what your family thinks of you and list some things you like to do. For example: Yo soy una chica deportista y muy sociable. Según mi familia, soy graciosa. Me gusta patinar y hablar por teléfono.	**p. 66** Actividades 11–13 **p. 69** Actividad 18 **p. 74** Actividad 27 **p. 75** Actividad 28 **p. 79** *Presentación escrita*
5 Pensar Demonstrate an understanding of cultural perspectives on friendship	Explain the differences between the terms *amigo* and *conocido* in Spanish-speaking cultures. How does this compare to words that we use in the United States?	**p. 78** *Perspectivas del mundo hispano*

Fondo cultural

■ ◆ ◆ ◆ ◇ ◆ ◆ ◆ ◇ ◆ ◆ ◆ ◇ ◆

Colombian artist Fernando Botero
(1932–) is among the best known and
most respected Latin American artists.
His works have been exhibited around
the world in prestigious museums,
galleries, and open-air places. Botero's
style is unique and very recognizable.
Pedrito Botero, shown in the painting,
was the artist's son. He died in a car
accident when he was four years old.

• Based upon the painting, how
  could you describe Botero's style?

Pedrito (1997), Fernando Botero
Courtesy of the Marlborough Gallery, New York.

Tu día en la escuela

Chapter Objectives

- Talk about school schedules and subjects
- Discuss what students do during the day
- Ask and tell who is doing an action
- Compare your school with that of a student in a Spanish-speaking country

Video Highlights

A primera vista: *El primer día de clases*

GramActiva Videos: subject pronouns; present tense of *-ar* verbs

Country Connection

As you learn about the school day in Spanish-speaking countries, you will make connections to these countries and places:

For: Online Atlas
Visit: www.phschool.com
Web Code: jae-0002

Jugadores de jai-alai en España

A primera vista

Vocabulario y gramática en contexto

El horario de Alicia

Objectives

Read, listen to, and understand information about
- the school day

66 Me gusta mucho mi **horario.**
**En la primera hora, tengo
la clase de** tecnología . . .
¡es mi clase **favorita!**
Es **interesante** y **práctica.**
Pero a veces es **difícil. 99**

primera hora		tecnología
segunda hora		arte
tercera hora		ciencias sociales
cuarta hora		ciencias naturales
quinta hora		el almuerzo
sexta hora		español
séptima hora		matemáticas
octava hora		inglés
novena hora		educación física

Más vocabulario
décimo, -a   tenth

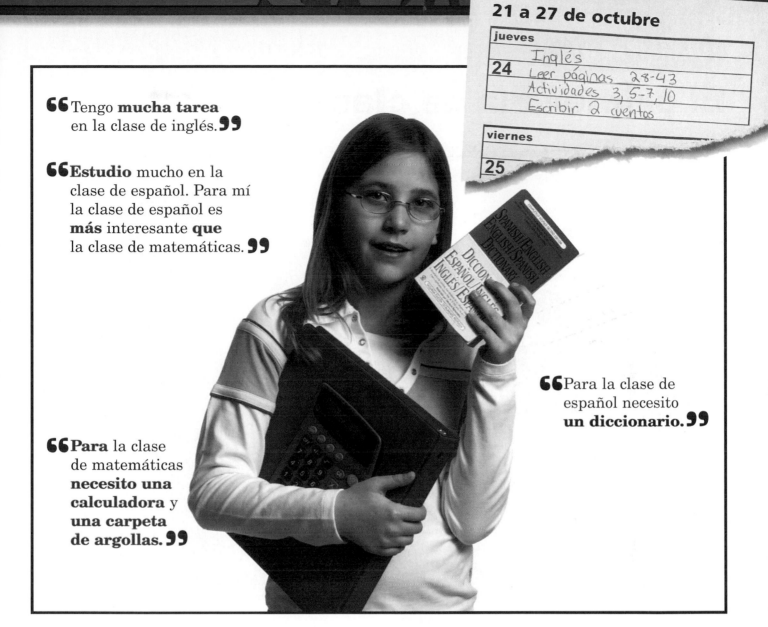

66 Tengo **mucha tarea** en la clase de inglés. **99**

66 Estudio mucho en la clase de español. Para mí la clase de español es **más** interesante **que** la clase de matemáticas. **99**

66 Para la clase de matemáticas **necesito una calculadora** y **una carpeta de argollas. 99**

66 Para la clase de español necesito **un diccionario. 99**

Actividad 1 Escuchar

¿Sí o no?

You will hear Alicia make several statements about her school day and schedule. Give a "thumbs-up" sign if what she says is true or a "thumbs-down" sign if what she says is false.

Actividad 2 Escuchar

El horario de Alicia

Listen to Alicia as she describes her class schedule. Touch the picture of each class as you hear it.

● **Más práctica**
Practice Workbook 2A-1, 2A-2

Go Online PHSchool.com
For: Vocabulary practice
Visit: www.phschool.com
Web Code: jad-0201

El primer día de clases

Es el primer día de clases en la Escuela Bilingüe de la Ciudad de México.

México

la Srta. Santoro

Matemáticas

Teresa

Claudia

el Sr. Treviño

Antes de leer

Using context clues You can often guess the meaning of new words by reading the words around them. Understanding what the rest of the sentence or paragraph is about is helpful in figuring out the meaning of individual words.

• Based on the words around it, what does *enseña* mean in panel 2?

1. What classes do you have every day? What classes do you expect the students in the *Videohistoria* to have?

2. Scan the text to find three classes that the students at the Escuela Bilingüe have. Do you have these classes?

3. Use the photos to see if you can guess what the problem is with Claudia's schedule. Then read the *Videohistoria* to find out whether your prediction was correct or not.

1 **Claudia:** Teresa, ¿qué clase **tienes** en la primera hora?

Teresa: Tengo la clase de inglés.

2 **Claudia:** ¿**Quién enseña** la clase de inglés?

Teresa: El señor Marín. Es un profesor muy **divertido.** ¿Y tú? ¿Qué clase tienes en la primera hora?

3 **Claudia:** Tengo la clase de matemáticas. Me gusta mucho. Para mí es muy **fácil.** Y, ¿qué tienes en la segunda hora?

Teresa: La clase de educación física.

4 **Teresa:** Y en la segunda hora, ¿qué clase tienes, Claudia?

Claudia: A ver... En la segunda hora, tengo la clase de matemáticas. ¡Y también tengo la clase de matemáticas en la tercera, en la cuarta, cn la quinta y cn la sexta hora!

5 **Teresa: Necesitas hablar** con el señor Treviño, en la oficina.
Claudia: Buena idea.

6 **Claudia:** Buenos días, señor Treviño. Necesito hablar con Ud. Tengo la clase de matemáticas...
Sr. Treviño: Sí, sí, Claudia, pero ahora no es posible. Mañana.

7 **Srta. Santoro:** Buenos días, estudiantes. Las matemáticas son muy interesantes y prácticas, ¿verdad?
Estudiantes: Sí, profesora.
Srta. Santoro: Y es muy importante **estudiar** y trabajar mucho...

8 **Srta. Santoro:** ¿Claudia?
Claudia: ¡Tengo seis clases de matemáticas hoy!
Srta. Santoro: ¡Seis! Es **aburrido,** ¿no?...

3 Leer/Escribir

¿Comprendes?

Read each sentence. On your paper, write *sí* if the sentence is correct or *no* if it is incorrect.

1. Es el primer día de clases.
2. A Teresa le gusta la clase de inglés.
3. Para Claudia, la clase de matemáticas es difícil.
4. Claudia tiene la clase de educación física en la segunda hora.
5. Según la Srta. Santoro, la clase de matemáticas es muy práctica.
6. Tener seis clases de matemáticas es interesante.

4 Pensar/Escribir

¿Dónde están?

Where are the students and faculty of the *Escuela Bilingüe*? Write the numbers 1–5 on your paper, and then beside each number write the name of the character who belongs in the room. Base your answers on the *Videohistoria*.

> Claudia
> Teresa
> el Sr. Marín
> la Srta. Santoro
> el Sr. Treviño

Más práctica

Practice Workbook 2A-3, 2A-4

Go Online
PHSchool.com

For: Vocabulary practice
Visit: www.phschool.com
Web Code: jad-0202

Manos a la obra
Vocabulario y gramática en uso

Objectives
- Discuss the school day
- Ask and tell about likes and dislikes
- Learn to use subject pronouns
- Learn to use verbs that end in *-ar*

Actividad 5 Leer/Escribir

Un horario

Read the list of classes offered at a school in Querétaro, Mexico, that specializes in the arts. On your paper, answer the questions about the schedule.

México

1. ¿Cuántas clases hay cada (*each*) semana?
2. ¿Cuántas horas de inglés hay?
3. ¿Cuántas clases de ciencias sociales hay?
4. ¿Cuántas clases de ciencias naturales hay?
5. Escribe los nombres de las diferentes clases de arte.

CENTRO DE EDUCACIÓN ARTÍSTICA

"IGNACIO MARIANO DE LAS CASAS"

PRIMER SEMESTRE

Español	5 h semanales
Matemáticas	5 h semanales
Historia del mundo	3 h semanales
Educación cívica y ética	3 h semanales
Biología	3 h semanales
Introducción a la física	3 h semanales
Inglés	3 h semanales
Danza	3 h semanales
Teatro	3 h semanales
Artes plásticas	3 h semanales
Música	3 h semanales

Total 37 h semanales

Actividad 6 Leer/Pensar

¿Qué les gusta?

Read the descriptions of the students below. Then, number your paper 1–6 and write the name of the class that you think each student would like.

1. A Juan le gusta mucho usar la computadora.
2. Sarita es muy deportista.
3. A Roberto le gusta leer.
4. A Miguel le gustan los números.
5. Gabriela es artística y le gusta pintar.
6. A Carolina le gusta hablar con amigos en México.

inglés
educación física
matemáticas
español
arte
tecnología

Leer/Hablar

¿Estás de acuerdo?

Yolanda has interviewed her classmates for her school newspaper, *El Diario San Miguel,* to find out what they think about their classes.

1 Number your paper 1–6. Read the article and based on your own classes, write *sí* if you agree with each statement or *no* if you disagree.

2 Now tell your partner how you would change each statement that you disagree with in order to express your own opinion.

PUEBLA, MÉXICO   22 DE SEPTIEMBRE

El Diario San Miguel

Periódico de la Escuela San Miguel   TERCERA EDICIÓN

Las clases en la Escuela San Miguel

¿Te gustan tus clases? Las opiniones de los estudiantes de la Escuela San Miguel son muy diferentes.

Alejandro Zarzalejos, octavo año

"La clase de inglés no es muy difícil. Me gusta leer y escribir." __1.__

Ángel Suzuki, séptimo año

"La clase de matemáticas es divertida. La profesora es buena." __2.__

Laura Rodríguez, séptimo año

"Mi clase favorita es la educación física. Me gusta mucho el fútbol." __3.__

Pilar Soriano, octavo año

"La tecnología es muy aburrida. No me gusta nada jugar videojuegos." __4.__

Sara Martínez, octavo año

"El arte es interesante y la profesora es muy talentosa. Me gusta mucho dibujar." __5.__

Luis Soto, séptimo año

"La clase de español es fácil. Me gusta la tarea." __6.__

Escribir •

Mi horario

Write out your class schedule. Copy the chart on a separate sheet of paper and provide the information for each of your classes.

Modelo

Hora	Clase	Profesor(a)
la primera hora	la clase de inglés	la Sra. Sánchez

¿Recuerdas?

Use *señor*, *señora*, and *señorita* when talking **to** adults. Use *el* in front of *señor* and *la* in front of *señora* or *señorita* when talking **about** adults.

Exploración del lenguaje

Connections between Latin, English, and Spanish

Many words in English and Spanish are based on Latin. Seeing the relationship between these words will help expand your English or Spanish vocabulary. Look at the list of Latin root forms for the numbers one through ten.

Try it out! For each Roman numeral listed, choose one of the root forms (if more than one is listed) and write down a Spanish and an English word you know that are based on that root.

Try it out! The Roman year used to begin with the month of March. Knowing that, can you explain why *septiembre, octubre, noviembre,* and *diciembre* use the Latin root forms for seven, eight, nine, and ten?

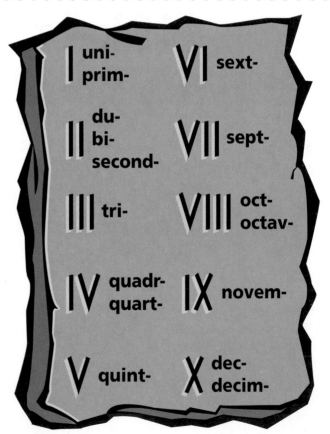

I uni- prim-
II du- bi- second-
III tri-
IV quadr- quart-
V quint-
VI sext-
VII sept-
VIII oct- octav-
IX novem-
X dec- decim-

Many Spanish words are derived from Latin because Spain was once part of the Roman Empire. Rome occupied most of Spain from about 209 B.C. to 586 A.D. During that time, massive public structures, including aqueducts and theaters, were built. Some of these, such as the aqueduct that towers over the modern city of Segovia, are still standing. The Latin name for Spain was *Hispania*.

• Can you see the similarity between *Hispania* and the country's name in Spanish, *España*?

El acueducto de Segovia

Actividad 9

 Hablar

Mucha tarea

With a partner, ask and tell if you have homework in each class.

2A+B=6

Modelo

A —¿*Tienes mucha tarea en la clase de* matemáticas?

B —*Sí, tengo mucha tarea.*

o: *No, no tengo mucha tarea.*

o: *No estudio* matemáticas.

Estudiante A

Español

El mundo

ENGLISH LITERATURE

Estudiante B

¡Respuesta personal!

Actividad 10 Escribir

Me gusta más...

On your paper, write sentences stating which of the two classes you like better and why. Use the list of adjectives to help with your responses. Save your paper for Actividad 11.

aburrida	difícil
divertida	fácil
interesante	práctica

Modelo

Me gusta más la clase de español. Es divertida.
o: *Me gusta más la clase de inglés. No es aburrida.*
o: *No me gusta ni la clase de español ni la clase de inglés.*

1.

2.

3.

4.

5.

6.

Actividad 11   **Hablar**

¿Qué te gusta más?

With a partner, ask and tell which classes from Actividad 10 you like best and why.

Modelo

A —*¿Te gusta más la clase de <u>inglés</u> o la clase de <u>español</u>?*
B —*A ver... Para mí, la clase de <u>español</u> es más divertida que la clase de <u>inglés</u>.*

Estudiantes mexicanos en una clase de inglés

Studying English While you're in Spanish class at your school, large numbers of Spanish-speaking students are studying to learn the most popular foreign language worldwide: English. Many children begin to study English in grade school and continue through high school. They often attend special language school for additional English classes. When visiting a Spanish-speaking country, you might easily find someone who is eager to practice his or her English skills with you in exchange for helping you improve your Spanish.

• Why do you think English is so popular in other countries? Are you studying Spanish for similar reasons?

El español en la comunidad

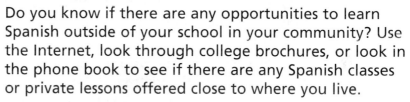

Do you know if there are any opportunities to learn Spanish outside of your school in your community? Use the Internet, look through college brochures, or look in the phone book to see if there are any Spanish classes or private lessons offered close to where you live.

• Why do you think people in your community would want to study Spanish?

Actividad 12

Escribir/Hablar

Y tú, ¿qué dices?

1. ¿Qué clase te gusta más?
2. ¿Cómo es la clase?
3. ¿En qué hora tienes la clase?
4. ¿Quién enseña la clase?
5. ¿Tienes mucha tarea en la clase?

Gramática

Subject pronouns

The subject of a sentence tells who is doing the action.
You often use people's names as the subject:

Gregorio escucha música.   **Gregory** *listens to music.*

Ana canta y baila.   **Ana** *sings and dances.*

yo tú

You also use subject pronouns *(I, you, he, she, we, they)* to tell
who is doing an action. The subject pronouns replace people's names:

Él escucha música.   **He** *listens to music.*

Ella canta y baila.   **She** *sings and dances.*

Here are all the subject pronouns in Spanish:

yo	I	**nosotros** **nosotras**	we we
tú	you *(familiar)*	**vosotros** **vosotras**	you you
usted (Ud.)	you *(formal)*	**ustedes (Uds.)**	you *(formal)*
él **ella**	he she	**ellos** **ellas**	they they

Tú, usted, ustedes, and *vosotros(as)* all mean "you."

• Use *tú* with family, friends, people your age or younger, and anyone
  you call by his or her first name.

• Use *usted* with adults you address with a title, such as *señor, señora,*
  profesor(a), etc. *Usted* is usually written as *Ud.*

• In Latin America, use *ustedes* when speaking to two or more people,
  regardless of age. *Ustedes* is usually written as *Uds.*

• In Spain, use *vosotros(as)* when speaking to two or more people you
  call *tú* individually: *tú + tú = vosotros(as).* Use *ustedes* when talking
  to two or more people you call *usted* individually.

If a group is made up of males only, or of both males and females
together, use the masculine forms: *nosotr**os**, vosotr**os**, ell**os.***

If a group is all females, use the feminine forms:
*nosotr**as**, vosotr**as**, ell**as.***

You can combine a subject pronoun and a name
to form a subject.

Alejandro y yo = **nosotros**   Pepe y tú = **ustedes**

Carlos y ella = **ellos**   Lola y ella = **ellas**

GramActiva VIDEO

Want more help
with subject
pronouns?
Watch the
GramActiva video.

yo

13 Gramática • Escuchar/GramActiva

¡Señala!

Your teacher will name several subject pronouns. Point to people in the classroom who represent the pronoun you hear. After you have practiced with your teacher, practice with a partner.

14 Gramática • Escribir

¿Es ella?

On your paper, write the subject pronouns you would use to talk about these people.

Modelo
Gloria
Ella.

1. Carlos
2. Felipe y yo
3. Pablo, Tomás y Anita
4. María y Sarita
5. el señor Treviño
6. tú y Esteban

15 Gramática • Hablar

¿Tú, Ud. o Uds.?

Tell whether you would use *tú, Ud.,* or *Uds.* with these people.

1.

2.

3.

4.

5.

6.

7.

8.

● **Más práctica**
Practice Workbook 2A-5

Go Online
PHSchool.com
For: Practice with subject pronouns
Visit: www.phschool.com
Web Code: jad-0203

Gramática

Present tense of *-ar* verbs

You already know that the infinitive forms of Spanish verbs always end in *-ar, -er,* or *-ir.*

The largest group of verbs end in *-ar. Hablar* is one of these *-ar* verbs.

In order to express who is doing an action, you have to use verbs in ways other than in the infinitive form. To do this, you have to drop the *-ar* ending and make changes.

To create the forms of most *-ar* verbs, first drop the *-ar* from the infinitive, saving the stem:

hablar → habl-

Then add the verb endings *-o, -as, -a, -amos, -áis,* or *-an* to the stem.

Here are the forms of *hablar:*

(yo)	**hablo**	(nosotros) (nosotras)	**hablamos**
(tú)	**hablas**	(vosotros) (vosotras)	**habláis**
Ud. (él) (ella)	**habla**	Uds. (ellos) (ellas)	**hablan**

¿Recuerdas?

You already know many *-ar* verbs, such as *cantar* and *bailar.*

In Spanish, the present tense form of a verb can be translated into English in two ways:

Hablo español.   *I speak Spanish.*
                  I am speaking Spanish.

The verb endings always indicate who is doing the action. Because of this, you can often use the verb without a subject:

Hablo inglés.

¿Hablas español?

Subject pronouns are often used for emphasis or clarification.

Ella habla inglés pero **él** habla español.

GramActiva VIDEO

Want more help with verbs that end in *-ar?* Watch the **GramActiva** video.

hablo

16 Gramática   Escuchar/Pensar/GramActiva

¿Una mano o dos?

You will hear eight *-ar* verbs. If the ending tells you one person is performing the action, raise one hand. If the ending tells you more than one person is doing something, raise both hands.

Strategy

Listening for information
Always listen carefully for the endings on verbs to know who is doing the action.

Actividad 17 Pensar/Escribir

El detective

Number your paper 1–10. Play the detective and figure out what everyone is doing by matching the sentences with the correct names under the magnifying glass.

1. ___ estudia mucho en la clase.
2. ___ hablan con amigos.
3. ___ pasas mucho tiempo en la clase.
4. ___ usamos la computadora.
5. ___ dibujan muy bien.
6. ___ no montas en monopatín.
7. ___ hablamos español.
8. ___ escuchas música.
9. ___ baila con Carolina.
10. ___ patinan en el parque.

Tú
María y Graciela
Federico y yo
Carlos

Actividad 18 Gramática Escribir/Hablar

¿Qué estudian?

Number your paper 1–6. Look at the pictures and tell what these people are studying.

Modelo
Tomás
Tomás estudia música.

1. Laura

2A+B=6

2. Josefina, Elena y yo

3. tú

ENGLISH LITERATURE

4. Catalina y José

Español

5. Joaquín y tú

6. yo

El mundo

 **Gramática** ♻ **Escribir** •

En la escuela

On your paper, use verbs from the box to complete the sentences about what different activities take place during school.

1. Lupe y Guillermo ___ mucho en la clase de arte.

2. Tú ___ la computadora en la clase de tecnología.

3. Yo ___ una calculadora y una carpeta para la clase de matemáticas.

4. Tomás y yo ___ deportes en la clase de educación física.

5. ¿Quién ___ la clase de ciencias naturales?

6. Marta ___ mucho en la clase de español.

Modelo

Yo estudio mucho en la clase de español.

necesitar	hablar	practicar	enseñar
dibujar	usar	patinar	bailar

 Gramática **Escuchar/Hablar/GramActiva** • • • • • • • • • • • •

Juego

1 Work with a partner and tear a sheet of paper into eight pieces of equal size. Write a different subject pronoun on each piece (*yo, tú, él, ella, Ud., nosotros, ellas, Uds.*). Place the subject pronouns face down in a pile.

2 Your teacher will say an infinitive. One partner will select the top piece of paper from the pile, read the subject pronoun, and say the correct verb form. A correct answer earns one point. Place the "used" subject pronouns in a separate pile. Take turns selecting from the pile and answering.

3 When your teacher calls time, shuffle the pieces of paper with subject pronouns and place them in a new pile face down. When the next verb is read aloud, continue play. The partner with the most correct answers is the winner.

En una escuela en México

● **Más práctica** • • • • • • • • • • • • • • • • • • •
Practice Workbook 2A-6, 2A-7

PHSchool.com
For: Practice with *-ar* verbs
Visit: www.phschool.com
Web Code: jad-0204

Actividad 21

Escuchar/Escribir • • • • •

Escucha y escribe

Listen to a student describe this photo of himself and other students during their *recreo*. Write what you hear.

El recreo

Fondo cultural

El recreo In Spanish-speaking countries, students usually have *el recreo* (recess or break) in the school patio. Students take time to relax and spend time with friends, eat a snack, or participate in activities such as a quick game of basketball, soccer, or volleyball.

• How is this similar to your school? How is it different?

Actividad 22

Gramática **Leer/Escribir** •

Durante el recreo

During recess, Lola and the others at the Escuela Rubén Darío are always busy doing something. Based on their personality traits, match the students to the activity they would most likely be doing. After you have matched the person with the activity, write complete sentences on your paper describing what everyone does during *el recreo*.

1. yo *(deportista)*

2. Isabel y Carmen *(artísticas)*

3. Geraldo y yo *(estudiosos)*

4. tú *(sociable)*

5. el Sr. Campo *(trabajador)*

a. enseñar una clase de español

b. usar una calculadora para la tarea

c. dibujar en la cafetería

d. practicar deportes

e. hablar con amigos

Actividades y más actividades

1 Work with a partner. Look at the model for Step One below. Copy the Venn diagram on a sheet of paper. Label the oval on the left *Yo*. Label the oval on the right with the name of your partner. Label the overlapping area *Nosotros* or *Nosotras*.

2 From the word box, choose five activities you do a lot. Write your activities in the oval labeled *Yo*. Be sure to use the appropriate verb in the *Yo* form. Look at the model for Step Two below.

hablar por teléfono	dibujar
estudiar	cantar
hablar español	nadar
montar en bicicleta	bailar
pasar tiempo con amigos	trabajar
practicar deportes	escuchar música
usar la computadora	

Modelo

Step One

Yo   Nosotros(as)   Amigo(a)

Modelo

Step Two

Yo   Nosotros(as)   Amigo(a)

dibujo
trabajo

③ Interview your partner. Ask questions to find out the five activities your partner wrote in the diagram. When you find an activity that your partner does, write it in the oval labeled with his or her name. Be sure to use the appropriate verb form. Look at the model for Step Three below.

④ Compare the two sides of your diagram. Write the activities that you and your partner both do in the center. Be sure to use the appropriate verb form. Look at the model for Step Four below. Then, use the completed diagram to write at least five complete sentences telling what you and/or your partner usually do.

Modelo

Step Three

Yo   Nosotros(as)   Amigo(a)

dibujo
trabajo

trabaja

Modelo

Step Four

Yo   Nosotros(as)   Amigo(a)

dibujo
trabajo

trabajamos

trabaja

Actividad 24 · Escribir

Los fines de semana

You are writing a letter to your friend Pablo who lives in Chile. Use the words that you have already learned to tell him what you and the people you know do on weekends (*los fines de semana*). Be sure to add words like *a veces* and *mucho*.

29 de Septiembre

Hola Pablo: _____

_____

¿Cómo estás? Aquí los fines de semana son muy divertidos y muy ocupados. El viernes yo __1.__ . El sábado mi amigo(a) y yo __2.__ . El domingo mis amigos __3.__ . El sábado el/la profesor(a) de español __4.__ . El viernes mi familia __5.__ .

¿Y tú? ¿Cómo pasas los fines de semana?

¡Escríbeme pronto!

Actividad 25 · Leer/Pensar

Los números maya

Long before the Spaniards set foot in the Americas, many different civilizations already existed here. One of these, the Maya, lived in southern Mexico and Central America, where their descendants still make their home. One of the accomplishments of the ancient Maya was the development of a system of mathematics.

Conexiones
Las matemáticas

The Maya used three symbols to write numbers: a dot •, a bar ——— , and a drawing of a shell. The dot equals 1, the bar equals 5, and the shell equals 0. Mayan numbers were written from bottom to top, not from left to right. Look at the Mayan numbers below.

| 0 | 1 | 2 | 3 | 4 |
| 5 | 6 | 7 | 8 | 9 |

What would these Mayan numbers be in our numbering system?

1.

2.

3.

Now write these numbers in the Mayan system.

4. 13   5. 16   6. 19

Are you familiar with any other numbering systems that remind you of the Mayan system?

The letter c

In Spanish the pronunciation of the letter *c* depends on the letter that follows it.

When the letter *c* comes before *a, o, u,* or another consonant, it is pronounced like the *c* in *cat.* Listen to and say these words:

computadora	**c**antar	es**c**uela
tampo**c**o	**c**ómo	to**c**ar
correr	practi**c**ar	**C**arlos

When the letter *c* comes before *e* or *i*, most Spanish speakers pronounce it like the *s* in *Sally.* Listen to and say these words:

ve**c**es	so**c**iable	gra**c**ioso	gra**c**ias
ha**c**er	on**c**e	do**c**e	tre**c**e

Try it out! Listen to this rhyme. Listen particularly for the sound of the letter *c.* Then repeat the rhyme.

Cero más cuatro,
o cuatro más cero,
siempre¹ son cuatro.
¿No es verdadero²?

¹always ²true

$$0 + 4 \quad 4 + 0 \quad = 4$$

Say the rhyme again, first replacing *cuatro* with *doce,* then replacing *cuatro* with *trece.* Then say the rhyme quickly several times.

Actividad 26

Escribir/Hablar

Y tú, ¿qué dices?

1. En tu escuela, ¿quién enseña la clase de arte? ¿Quién enseña la clase de educación física?

2. En tu escuela, ¿quién canta muy bien *(well)*? ¿Quién dibuja muy bien?

3. ¿Escuchan tus amigos(as) mucha música? ¿Bailan bien tú y tus amigos(as)?

4. ¿Qué estudias en la primera hora?

5. ¿Qué clase tienes en la tercera hora?

Una estudiante en la clase de matemáticas

¡Adelante!

Objectives

- Read a brochure about a school in Costa Rica
- Learn soccer fan chants
- Talk about some of your classes
- Learn facts about Mexico

Lectura

¡Estudiar español es divertido!

Consider what an immersion experience in Spanish would be like for you as you read this brochure from a Spanish language school in Costa Rica.

Strategy

Using photos
Look at the photos to help you understand the contents of a brochure or advertisement.

Costa Rica

La Escuela Español Vivo

¡Una experiencia fabulosa en Costa Rica!
¡Estudia español con nosotros en la Escuela Español Vivo!

Es verano, el mes de junio. Eres estudiante en Santa Ana, un pueblo en las montañas de Costa Rica.

¿Y cómo es una clase? Hay cinco estudiantes en tu clase. Uds. escuchan, hablan y practican el español todo el día. También usan la computadora.

En la escuela hay estudiantes de muchos países: Estados Unidos, Inglaterra, Francia, Brasil, Canadá, Japón, India, Sudáfrica y otros. ¡Todos estudian español!

Los sábados y los domingos hay actividades muy interesantes: visitar un volcán o un parque nacional, nadar en el océano Pacífico ... ¡y más!

sábados/domingos
- visitar un volcán
- visitar un parque nacional
- nadar en el océano Pacífico

El horario de clases en la escuela es:

hora	lunes a viernes
08:00–10:30	Clases de español
10:30–11:00	Recreo
11:00–13:00	Clases de español
13:00–14:00	Almuerzo
14:00–15:30	Conversaciones
15:30–16:30	Clase de música y baile

¿Por qué la Escuela Español Vivo?

- **La naturaleza de Costa Rica en el pueblo de Santa Ana**
- **Amigos de muchos países**
- **Mucha práctica y conversación en español**
- **Clases de música y baile**
- **Excursiones los sábados y domingos**

¿Comprendes?

1. When does the program take place?
2. Describe what a class is like.
3. What activities are offered on the weekends?
4. How many hours are spent on learning and using Spanish each week?
5. Would you like to study Spanish in Costa Rica? Why or why not?

Go Online
PHSchool.com
For: Internet link activity
Visit: www.phschool.com
Web Code: jad-0205

Fondo cultural

La hora in Spanish-speaking countries is usually shown using the 24-hour clock on official schedules and timetables. Times in the morning are shown as 00:00 (midnight) through 11:59 (11:59 A.M.), 1:00 P.M. is shown as 13:00, 2:00 P.M. is 14:00, and so on.

- Look at the times in the *horario* from the brochure. What times are the conversation class and the music and dance classes?

En una estación de trenes de Madrid

Aficionados al fútbol

El fútbol (soccer) is the favorite sport in most Spanish-speaking countries. In fact, it is the most popular sport in the entire world. It has grown in popularity in the United States over the past years. As with other sports you are familiar with, *fútbol* has loyal fans, cheers, team songs, and sometimes cheerleaders. If you attended a game in Venezuela at the Escuela Secundaria Bolívar you might hear the following chant:

Chiquitibúm a la bim bom bam
A la bío
A la bao
A la bim bom bam
¡Bolívar! ¡Bolívar!
¡Ra, ra, ra!

Jugando al fútbol en la Ciudad Universitaria, Madrid, España

Except for the school name, the words of this chant do not have any meaning.

Here's another cheer:

¡Se ve! ¡Se siente!	**You see it, you feel it!**
¡Bolívar está presente!	**Bolívar is here!**
¡Que sí, que no!	**Oh, yes, oh, no!**
¡Bolívar ya ganó!	**Bolívar has already won!**
¡A la bío, a la bao!	**¡A la bío! ¡A la bao!**
¡El otro está cansao!	**The other team is tired!**

Try it out! In groups of five, select one of the chants and use it for a model to create a chant for one of your school teams. Present it to the class.

Think about it! How are these cheers and fan enthusiasm similar to or different from the cheers at your school?

Aficionados al fútbol

Presentación oral

Mis clases

Task
Imagine that a student from Costa Rica has just arrived at your school. Tell the student about some of your classes.

1 Prepare Make a chart similar to the one below and fill in information for three of your classes. You will use this chart to think through what you may want to say about these classes.

Strategy

Using graphic organizers
Simple charts can help you organize your thoughts for a presentation.

Hora	Clase	Comentarios	Profesor(a)
primera	la clase de español	me gusta hablar español	la Sra. Salinas
cuarta	la clase de arte	difícil	el Sr. Highsmith
octava	la clase de ciencias naturales	divertida	la Srta. Huerta

2 Practice Go through your presentation several times. You can use your notes in practice, but your teacher may not want you to use them when you present. Try to:

- mention the information on your classes and your teachers
- use complete sentences
- speak clearly

Modelo

En la primera hora tengo la clase de español. Me gusta hablar español. La Sra. Salinas es la profesora.

3 Present Describe the three classes you selected.

4 Evaluation Your teacher may give you a rubric for how the presentation will be graded. You probably will be graded on:

- how complete your preparation is
- how much information you communicate
- how easy it is to understand you

México

With a population of more than 100 million people, Mexico is the most populous Spanish-speaking country. It has been shaped by ancient indigenous civilizations, European colonialism, and immigration, as well as by its proximity to the United States.

The Mayan city of Tulum, situated on a cliff overlooking the Caribbean, was a major port from about 1200 until the Spaniards arrived in the early 1500s. The Mayan civilization dates from 750 B.C., and includes ancient cities throughout southern Mexico, including the Yucatan Peninsula, and parts of Central America. Today many people in these areas speak one of approximately 30 languages and dialects that developed from ancient Maya.

¿Sabes que...?

The butterfly reserve at El Rosario, Michoacán, lies in the mountains not far from Mexico City. From November through February every year, millions of monarch butterflies migrate to this area from the north, covering the branches of the area's tall pine trees.

Para pensar

These two pages show a brief overview of Mexico. If you were asked to create a similar overview of the United States, what would you highlight? Select five photographs and write a brief caption for each one. Share your results with a small group or the whole class.

Estados Unidos
México
Golfo de México
OCÉANO PACÍFICO
Belice
Guatemala
El Salvador

Go Online
PHSchool.com

For: Online Atlas
Visit: www.phschool.com
Web Code: jae-0002

Mexico's most famous dance company, el Ballet Folklórico de México, is a world-class troupe of more than 75 dancers and musicians. For more than five decades, this company has been touring the globe and performing traditional Mexican dances, such as the *jarabe tapatío*, (better known in the United States as the Mexican hat dance), *la culebra*, and the *chilingo lingo*. ▶

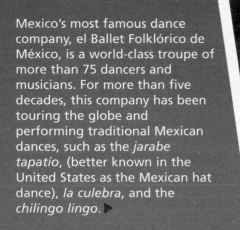

Mexico's capital is one of the largest cities in the world. It is also one of the oldest, dating back to 1500 B.C. It was here that the Aztecs built their capital, Tenochtitlán, in the 1300s. When the Spaniards arrived in 1519, Tenochtitlán had a population of more than 100,000—making it larger than most European cities of that time.

▲ Many families in Mexico spend Sundays together. A popular spot for families in Mexico City is Xochimilco, where they can relax on colorful boats while enjoying a meal and music. The canals of Xochimilco are remnants of *chinampas*, the "floating gardens" that helped feed Tenochtitlán and other ancient cities in the valley of Mexico.

Repaso del capítulo

Vocabulario y gramática

Chapter Review

To prepare for the test, check to see if you...
- know the new vocabulary and grammar
- can perform the tasks on p. 115

to talk about your school day

el almuerzo	lunch
la clase	class
la clase de...	...class
arte	art
español	Spanish
ciencias naturales	science
ciencias sociales	social studies
educación física	physical education
inglés	English
matemáticas	mathematics
tecnología	technology / computers
el horario	schedule
en la...hora	in the...hour (class period)
la tarea	homework

to describe school activities

enseñar	to teach
estudiar	to study
hablar	to talk

to talk about the order of things

*primero, -a	first
segundo, -a	second
*tercero, -a	third
cuarto, -a	fourth
quinto, -a	fifth
sexto, -a	sixth
séptimo, -a	seventh
octavo, -a	eighth
noveno, -a	ninth
décimo, -a	tenth

*Changes to *primer, tercer* before a masculine singular noun.

to talk about things you need for school

la calculadora	calculator
la carpeta de argollas	three-ring binder
el diccionario	dictionary
necesitas	you need
necesito	I need

For *Vocabulario adicional,* see pp. 268–269.

to describe your classes

aburrido, -a	boring
difícil	difficult
divertido, -a	amusing, fun
fácil	easy
favorito, -a	favorite
interesante	interesting
más... que	more...than
práctico, -a	practical

other useful words

a ver...	let's see...
mucho	a lot
para	for
¿Quién?	Who?
(yo) tengo	I have
(tu) tienes	you have

subject pronouns

yo	I	nosotros	we
		nosotras	we
tú	you (fam.)	vosotros	you
		vosotras	you
usted (Ud.)	you (form.)	ustedes (Uds.)	you (form.)
él	he	ellos	they
ella	she	ellas	they

hablar *to talk*

hablo	hablamos
hablas	habláis
habla	hablan

Más práctica

Practice Workbook Puzzle 2A-8
Practice Workbook Organizer 2A-9

Preparación para el examen

On the exam you will be asked to...	Here are practice tasks similar to those you will find on the exam...	If you need review...
1 Escuchar Listen and understand as people talk about their new schedules and what they think of their classes	Listen to two students who have just attended some of the classes on their new schedules. a) Which class does each one like? Why? b) Which class does each one dislike? Why?	**pp. 86–91** *A primera vista* **p. 87** Actividades 1–2 **p. 93** Actividad 7 **p. 96** Actividades 10–11
2 Hablar Talk about activities you and your friends have in common	To get to know you, your homeroom advisor asks you to talk or write about what you and your friends have in common, such as school subjects that you all study, and music or activities that you all like. For example, *cantamos*. You might also tell how you and your friends are different. For example, *Yo toco la guitarra y ellos practican deportes.*	**p. 96** Actividad 11 **p. 103** Actividad 21 **pp. 104–105** Actividad 23 **p. 111** *Presentación oral*
3 Leer Read and understand someone's e-mail description of his classes	Read this e-mail that your friend received from his e-pal. What does the e-pal study in school? What does he think of his classes? Do you agree or disagree? Why? *¿Cómo son mis clases? A ver... Yo tengo ocho clases. Estudio ciencias naturales, inglés, español, educación física, geografía, matemáticas, tecnología y ciencias sociales. ¡Me gusta más la clase de inglés! Necesito hablar inglés aquí en Ecuador, pero es MUY difícil. Mi clase de geografía es muy aburrida y mi clase de educación física es muy divertida. Y, ¿cómo son tus clases?*	**pp. 86–91** *A primera vista* **p. 92** Actividad 5 **p. 108–109** *Lectura*
4 Escribir Write your schedule including hour, class, and teacher's name, and give opinions about the classes	Write a note to a counselor listing reasons why you want to drop two of the classes on your schedule. What might be some reasons for wanting to change classes? You might say that your first hour class is boring and that your second hour class is difficult for you.	**p. 94** Actividad 8 **p. 95** Actividad 9 **p. 96** Actividad 10 **p. 111** *Presentación oral*
5 Pensar Demonstrate an understanding of cultural practices concerning sports	Think about the sports at your school that attract the most fans. Are these the same sports that are most popular in Spanish-speaking countries? How do spectators show their enthusiasm?	**p. 110** *La cultura en vivo*

Fondo cultural

Sor Juana Inés de la Cruz
(1648–1695), born near Mexico City, was one of the greatest intellectuals of her time. She wrote poetry, essays, music, and plays. Sor Juana also defended a woman's right to an education at a time when few women had access to it. She entered a convent at the age of 19 and over the years built a library of several thousand books. Sor Juana's living quarters in the convent became a meeting place for other writers and intellectuals, who were drawn to her because of her intelligence and knowledge.

- How are various aspects of Sor Juana's life represented in this painting? If you were to pose for a portrait, what objects would represent you and your interests?

Sor Juana Inés de la Cruz, arte mexicano del siglo XVII
Institut Amatller d'Art Hispanic-Arxiu Mas

Tu sala de clases

Chapter Objectives

- Describe a classroom
- Indicate where things are located
- Talk about more than one object or person
- Understand cultural perspectives on school

Video Highlights

A primera vista: *Un ratón en la clase*

GramActiva Videos: the verb *estar;* the plurals of nouns and articles

Country Connection

As you learn how to describe your classroom, you will make connections to these countries and places:

España
México
Puerto Rico
Guatemala
Panamá
Honduras
El Salvador
Nicaragua
Costa Rica
Colombia
Perú
Chile
Argentina

For: Online Atlas
Visit: www.phschool.com
Web Code: jae-0002

Estudiantes en una sala de clases en Cuzco, Perú

A primera vista

Vocabulario y gramática en contexto

Objectives

Read, listen to, and understand information about
- the classroom
- where objects are located

la bandera

la sala de clases

el reloj

el cartel

las ventanas

la computadora

la puerta

el sacapuntas

la mesa

el escritorio

la papelera

la silla

❝¡Hola! Me llamo Enrique. **Aquí está mi** sala de clases. Son las nueve y **los** estudiantes **están en** la clase de español. **Hay** muchos estudiantes en mi clase. **¿Cuántos** estudiantes hay en **tu** clase?**❞**

la pantalla

el disquete

el teclado

la mesa

el raton

diccionario

—Elena, ¿es tu disquete?

—No, es el disquete **de** David.

El cuaderno está **debajo de** la calculadora.

La calculadora está **encima del** cuaderno.

Los bolígrafos están **al lado del** diccionario.

La bandera está **detrás de** la computadora.

La silla está **delante de** la mesa.

 Escuchar • • • • • • • • • • • • • • • •

¿Qué hay en la sala de clases?

Look at Enrique's classroom. You will be asked if certain things are there. If you see the item mentioned, raise your hand and give a "thumbs-up" sign. If you don't see it, give a "thumbs-down" sign.

 Escuchar • • • • • • • • • • • • • • • •

En la sala de clases

Look at the picture of Enrique's classroom again. Listen to a description of various items in the room. As soon as you recognize an item, touch it.

● **Más práctica** • • • • • • • • • • • • • •
Practice Workbook 2B-1, 2B-2

Go Online
PHSchool.com
For: Vocabulary practice
Visit: www.phschool.com
Web Code: jad-0211

Un ratón en la clase

¿Qué pasa en la clase de ciencias sociales? Lee la historia.

México

Manolo

Teresa

Carlos

Claudia

Antes de leer

Strategy

Predicting outcomes Look at the pictures before you read to help you predict what will happen.

- What is causing the disturbance in Teresa's class?

1. Find at least five cognates in the *Videohistoria*. How do these cognates help you understand the story?

2. Look at the photos in the *Videohistoria* and try to predict if Manolo will get away with his prank.

1 Claudia: ¿Qué es esto?

Teresa: Es mi hámster. Es para la clase de ciencias naturales.

Claudia: ¿Cómo se llama?

Teresa: Paquito.

2 Manolo: ¡Carlos! No tengo mi tarea.

Carlos: ¿Qué?

Manolo: Tengo una idea...

3 Carlos: ¡Un ratón! Profesora, ¡hay un ratón debajo del escritorio!

Profesora: ¿Un ratón en la clase de ciencias sociales? **¿Dónde** está? ¿Dónde?

4 Estudiante: Ahora está debajo de la silla.

Manolo: Y ahora está al lado de la puerta. **Es un** ratón muy impaciente.

Teresa: ¡No es un ratón! Es mi hámster, y se llama Paquito.

5 **Claudia:** ¡Está **allí,** delante de la mesa!

Teresa: ¡Ay, mi Paquito!

Manolo: Pues, ahora está detrás de la computadora, encima de los disquetes.

Teresa: ¡Manolo! Es el ratón de la computadora. No es mi Paquito.

6 *El director de la escuela, el Sr. Treviño, entra en la clase.*

Carlos: ¡Ay! ¡Aquí está! Está en mi **mochila.**

Sr. Treviño: ¡Silencio, por favor!

7 **Sr. Treviño:** Teresa, hablamos en mi oficina.

Teresa: Sí, señor.

8 **Profesora:** Y ahora, Manolo, ¿tu tarea?

Manolo: Pues, profesora . . .

Actividad 3   Leer

¿Comprendes?

Match each of the sentences with the *Videohistoria* character whom it describes.

el Sr. Treviño

Paquito

Claudia

Teresa

Manolo

1. No tiene la tarea.

2. Está debajo de la silla.

3. Tiene un hámster.

4. Es amiga de Teresa.

5. Es muy serio.

Actividad 4   Leer/Escribir

Un hámster en la escuela

It's not a typical day at Claudia's school. Find out what is going on by putting the sentences below in the correct order. Rewrite the story on a separate sheet of paper.

a. El Sr. Treviño entra en la clase.

b. El hámster está debajo de la silla.

c. El Sr. Treviño y Teresa hablan en la oficina.

d. La profesora quiere *(wants)* la tarea de Manolo.

e. Teresa habla con *(with)* Claudia del ratón para la clase de ciencias naturales.

f. El hámster está en la mochila de Carlos.

● **Más práctica**
Practice Workbook 2B-3, 2B-4

For: Vocabulary practice
Visit: www.phschool.com
Web Code: jad-0212

Manos a la obra

Vocabulario y gramática en uso

Objectives

- Communicate about a classroom
- Ask and tell how someone feels
- Talk about where someone or something is located
- Learn to use the verb *estar* and the plurals of nouns and articles

Actividad 5 · Leer

¿Es lógico o no?

Juan Carlos is telling you about what he has in his backpack. Decide if what he is saying is logical or not. Number your paper from 1–6 and write *sí* if it is logical or *no* if it is not.

1. Un teclado está en mi mochila.
2. Hay un disquete en mi mochila.
3. Hay una mesa en mi mochila.
4. Un bolígrafo está en mi mochila.
5. Mi tarea está en mi mochila.
6. Hay una papelera en mi mochila.

Actividad 6 · Escribir

¿Qué hay?

Write the names of the things you see.

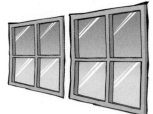

Modelo

Hay una bandera.

1.

2.

3.

4.

5.

6.

7.

8.

7 **Leer/Escribir** •

¿Dónde está?

Write the numbers from 1–9 on a sheet of paper. Complete the sentences
to tell where the following items are located in Beto's bedroom. Choose
from the words below and add the correct definite article.

| al lado de |
| debajo de |
| delante de |
| detrás de |
| encima de |

Modelo

El escritorio está debajo de la ventana.
La computadora está encima del escritorio.

1. El reloj está ____ mesa.

2. La papelera está ____ escritorio.

3. La silla está ____ escritorio.

4. El teclado está ____ disquete.

5. La computadora está ____ mesa.

6. El ratón está ____ teclado.

7. El cartel está ____ ventana.

8. La mochila está ____ silla.

 Nota

When the preposition *de* is
followed by the masculine
definite article *el*, the
contraction *del* must be
used.

• La papelera está al lado
del escritorio.

Actividad 8 Escribir

¿Estás preparado(a) para la clase?

You want to make sure that you are prepared for class. Copy the checklist below onto your own paper. Place a check mark next to the items that you have and tell where they are.

el libro	✔	encima del escritorio
un cuaderno		
un disquete		
la tarea		
un lápiz		
un bolígrafo		
un sacapuntas		
una mochila		
un diccionario		

Actividad 9   Hablar/Escribir

Juego

1 Work with a partner. Your partner will face away from you and have a blank piece of paper and a pen or a pencil.

2 Choose four classroom items and arrange them on your desk, putting objects on top of others, next to each other, and so forth.

3 Your partner will ask you questions about what is on your desk and how the items are positioned. Based on your answers, he or she will try to draw the arrangement on your desk.

4 When your teacher calls time, see how closely the picture matches the actual arrangement. Then switch roles.

Modelo

A —¿Tienes un disquete?
B —No, no tengo un disquete.
A —¿Tienes una calculadora?
B —Sí, tengo una calculadora.
A —¿Dónde está?
B —Está encima de la carpeta.

Para decir más...

a la izquierda de   to the left of
a la derecha de   to the right of

Language through gestures

In Spanish, just as in English, nonverbal body language in the form of gestures, or *gestos*, is very important to communication.

You saw the expression *¡Ojo!* in the video *Un ratón en la clase*. The word literally means "eye," but it is used to mean "be careful" or "pay attention." It is usually accompanied by a gesture, and often people use the *¡Ojo!* gesture without saying the word.

¡Ojo!

Unas estudiantes en uniforme

Fondo cultural

School uniforms Many schools in Spanish-speaking countries require their students to wear uniforms. Often students wear a full uniform, like the ones you see in the photo. Sometimes the uniform consists of something more like a smock that is worn over a student's regular clothes and helps protect them from becoming dirty or torn during the school day.

• How are these uniforms similar to or different from those worn by high school students in the United States?

Actividad 10

Escribir/Hablar

Y tú, ¿qué dices?

Describe your classroom.

1. ¿Dónde está la puerta?
2. ¿Hay un reloj en tu clase? ¿Dónde está?
3. ¿Cuántos escritorios y sillas hay?
4. ¿Hay una bandera en tu clase? ¿Dónde está?
5. ¿Qué más (*What else*) hay en tu clase?

Gramática

The verb estar

The -ar verbs you have used until now are called **regular verbs** because they follow a regular pattern. Verbs that do not follow a regular pattern are called **irregular verbs.**

Estar is irregular because the *yo* form doesn't follow a regular pattern and because the forms *estás, está,* and *están* require accent marks.

Use *estar* to tell how someone feels or where someone or something is located.

(yo)	estoy	(nosotros) (nosotras)	estamos
(tú)	estás	(vosotros) (vosotras)	estáis
Ud. (él) (ella)	está	Uds. (ellos) (ellas)	están

¿Recuerdas?

You have used the verb *estar* to ask how someone is.

• ¿Cómo **estás?**

• ¿Cómo **está** Ud.?

GramActiva VIDEO

Want more practice with the verb *estar?* Watch the **GramActiva** video.

están debajo de . . .

Actividad 11 Gramática **Leer**

¿Están en clase hoy?

Your teacher asks you to take attendance. Find out who is present and who isn't by matching the people in the first column with the completion of the sentence in the second column.

1. Tú
2. Martina y Clarisa
3. Carmen y yo
4. Guillermo
5. Yo

a. está en clase hoy.
b. estoy en clase hoy.
c. no estás en clase hoy.
d. estamos en clase hoy.
e. no están en clase hoy.

Actividad 12 Gramática **Escribir**

¡Hola! ¿Cómo estás?

Write the correct forms of *estar* on a separate sheet of paper.

Marcos: ¡Buenos días! ¿Cómo __1.__ Uds.?

Paula y Roberta: ¡Hola, Marcos! Nosotras __2.__ bien, gracias. ¿Y tú?

Marcos: __3.__ muy bien. ¿Dónde __4.__ Pedro y Juana?

Roberta: Pedro __5.__ en la sala de clases. Juana __6.__ en la oficina.

Actividad 13 Gramática  Hablar •

¿En qué clase están?

Following the model, take turns with a partner to give the correct forms of *estar*.

 ella

Modelo

Ella está en la clase de tecnología.

1. yo

2. los profesores

3.  la profesora

4. nosotros

5. ella

6.  tú

Actividad 14 Gramática Hablar •

¿Están los amigos allí?

The following people are supposed to study together in the library, but nobody is there. Explain that they are not there and tell where they are by using the correct form of *estar* and any of the places listed below.

Modelo

Paco no está allí. Está en la clase de educación física.

1. Yo
2. María
3. Tú

4. Natalia y Roberto
5. Uds.
6. Timoteo

estar

en la clase de inglés
en la oficina del director
en la clase de matemáticas
en la sala de clases
en la clase de español
en la clase de arte

Actividad 15 Hablar/Escribir •

En mi clase

Look around your classroom. Tell where the following people and things are located in relationship to the word in parentheses. Use the verb *estar*, and follow the model.

Modelo

yo (mi silla)
Yo estoy en mi silla.

1. la papelera (el escritorio)
2. el teclado (la computadora)
3. los estudiantes (la sala de clases)

4. yo (mi escritorio)
5. mi mochila (la silla)
6. los estudiantes (el/la profesor(a))

¿Cierto o falso?

Write the numbers 1–6 on a sheet of paper. Listen to the statements about Javier's Spanish club photo and write *cierto* or *falso* based on the information provided as you view the photograph from *your* perspective.

 Gramática Hablar

¿Y dónde están todos?

Work with a partner. Using the club picture above, find out where the various students are located from *Javier's* perspective.

Modelo
A —¿Y dónde está <u>Lucita</u>?
B —Lucita está <u>encima de la mesa</u>.

1. Julián y Mateo   **3.** Sara   **5.** el Sr. Salas   **7.** Benito

2. Rosa   **4.** yo   **6.** Lucita y José   **8.** Sara y yo

  Escribir/Hablar

Juego

Work with a partner. Write down the name of someone in the classroom. Your partner can only ask *sí* or *no* questions to find out the name. When your partner has guessed the mystery student's identity, switch roles.

Modelo
A —¿Está al lado de Tomás?
B —No.
A —¿Está detrás de mí?
B —Sí.
A —¿Es Patricia?
B —Sí.

Para decir más...
a la izquierda   detrás de mí
to the left   behind me
a la derecha   detrás de ti
to the right   behind you

Los precios de las mochilas en el mundo hispano

Conexiones

Las matemáticas

Most countries have their own currencies. In Mexico, people pay in *pesos,* in Peru they use *nuevos soles,* and so on. The value of each currency can go up or down daily in relation to other countries' currencies. For example, a dollar might be worth 10 Mexican *pesos* one day and 9.5 *pesos* the following day. Read the prices for *una mochila* in six different countries.

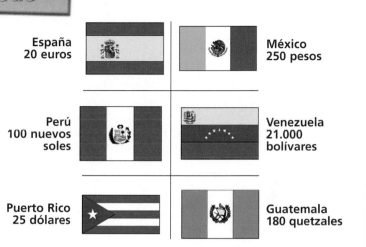

España
20 euros

México
250 pesos

Perú
100 nuevos soles

Venezuela
21.000 bolívares

Puerto Rico
25 dólares

Guatemala
180 quetzales

1. How much does a typical *mochila* cost in your community?

2. Convert the prices for *una mochila* into dollars. You can find a currency converter on the Internet.

3. How do these prices compare to those in your community? Why might the same item have different values in different countries?

De vacaciones

The following people are spending their vacations in various Spanish-speaking countries. Based on the currency they are using, say where they are. Use the information in Actividad 19 to help you.

Modelo

Clara usa quetzales.
Clara está en Guatemala.

1. Yo uso euros.

2. Ellos usan pesos.

3. Tú usas nuevos soles.

4. Ustedes usan quetzales.

5. Federico usa bolívares.

● **Más práctica**
Practice Workbook 2B-5

Go Online
PHSchool.com
For: Practice with *estar*
Visit: www.phschool.com
Web Code: jad-0214

Gramática

The plurals of nouns and articles

In Spanish, to make nouns plural you usually add -s to words ending in a vowel and -es to words ending in a consonant.

silla → silla**s**   teclado → teclado**s**   cartel → cartel**es**

Singular nouns that end in *z* change the *z* to *c* in the plural.

el lápiz → los lápi**ces**

The plural definite articles are *los* and *las*. Like *el* and *la*, they both mean "the."

las sillas   *the chairs*

The plural indefinite articles are *unos* and *unas*. They both mean "some" or "a few."

unos carteles   *some posters*

Singular	Plural
el reloj	**los** reloj**es**
la ventana	**las** ventana**s**
un disquete	**unos** disquete**s**
una mesa	**unas** mesa**s**

¿Recuerdas?

You have used the definite and indefinite articles in the singular form.

el, la *the*

un, una *a (an)*

GramActiva VIDEO

Want more help with the plurals of nouns and articles? Watch the **GramActiva** video.

los, las
unos, unas

21 Gramática   **Leer/Hablar**

¡A estudiar!

Marta and Berta are getting ready for school. Read the dialogue with a partner, completing the sentences with the correct definite articles.

Marta: ¿Dónde están __1.__ lápices?

Berta: Aquí están, en __2.__ mochila.

Marta: ¿Y tienes __3.__ bolígrafos y __4.__ libros?

Berta: No. Están allí, encima de __5.__ mesa, y debajo de __6.__ ventanas.

Marta: Ah, sí. ¿Y __7.__ cuadernos y __8.__ carpetas? ¿Dónde están?

Berta: Están encima de __9.__ mesa, y detrás de __10.__ computadoras.

22 Gramática   **Escuchar/Hablar**

Las palabras plurales

You will hear eight words. Say the plural form of the words as you hear them.

Modelo

You will hear: *el libro*
You will say: *los libros*

 **Gramática** ♻ **Escribir** •

Más plurales

On a sheet of paper, write the plural forms of the articles and nouns below.

1. el cuaderno   **3.** la bandera   **5.** la papelera   **7.** el profesor

2. una clase   **4.** una mochila   **6.** un escritorio   **8.** un pupitre

24 **Hablar** •

Una mesa desordenada

Sometimes your classmates are disorganized and they leave their things
all over the table. With a partner, look at the drawing and take turns
asking and telling where different things are located.

Modelo

A —¿Dónde _están las carpetas?_
B —_Las carpetas están debajo de los disquetes._

Estudiantes mexicanas

In some countries such as Mexico, Colombia, Costa Rica, and Chile, students attending public schools generally do not have lockers in which to store their things before each class. Most students carry the books and school supplies they need for the day in book bags. In some countries, such as Mexico, students will wear their gym clothes instead of their required school uniforms on the days they have physical education.

• If you didn't have a locker at school, what books and schools supplies would you bring every day and which ones would you leave at home?

 **Gramática** **Escribir** • • • • • • • • • • • • • • • •

El armario de Ramón

You are looking at Ramón's messy locker. Write five sentences about what you see. Be sure to use the indefinite articles.

Modelo

Hay unos disquetes.

26 Gramática **Escribir**

Necesito mucho

You need some of the things that the following people have. Look at the photos and write eight sentences following the model.

Flor

Modelo

Necesito los cuadernos de Flor.

Nota

In Spanish, you can express possession by using *de* and the name of the owner of the item.

• el escritorio **de** la profesora
the teacher's desk

1.

Ricardo

2.

el profesor

3.

Carmen

4.

el director

5.

Milagros

6.

Rosa

7.

Enrique

8.

Juan

27 **Hablar**

Es el cuaderno de...

Work in a group of four. Each of you should choose a classroom object you have brought to class. Show your group what you have chosen. Your teacher will collect all the items, then place them in view in different parts of the classroom. Ask your group where your object is.

Modelo

A —*¿Dónde está mi calculadora?*
B —*Tu calculadora está debajo de la silla de Margarita.*

Actividad 28 Escribir

Una clase de inglés

Look at this picture of an English class in Chile and write five sentences about what you see.

Modelo

Los disquetes de Claudia están encima del escritorio.

Actividad 29 Escribir/Hablar

En el dibujo hay...

Write at least three questions about the picture in Actividad 28, and then ask your partner those questions. Use some of the phrases in the box below.

¿Qué es esto?	¿Quién está . . . ?
¿Cuántos(as) . . . hay?	¿Hay . . . ?
¿Dónde está(n) . . . ?	¿Qué hay . . . ?

Modelo

A —¿*Cuántos estudiantes hay en la clase?*
B —*Hay cuatro estudiantes.*
A —¿*Dónde está la profesora?*
B —*Está al lado de la bandera.*

El español en el mundo del trabajo

School districts in the United States have many positions in which employees need to speak Spanish. For example, school counselors work with new students and parents from Spanish-speaking countries. Counselors help them set up schedules, talk about school policies, and answer questions. Both the parents and the new students feel much more comfortable when the counselor can communicate with them in Spanish.

- Does your district need employees who speak Spanish? In what other jobs within a school system would speaking Spanish be helpful?

Actividad 30 · Escribir

Y tú, ¿qué dices?

Look around your classroom and write at least five sentences describing objects and people that you see. Be sure to tell where they are located.

● **Más práctica**

Practice Workbook 2B-6, 2B-7

For: Practice with plurals
Visit: www.phschool.com
Web Code: jad-0213

Pronunciación

The letter g

In Spanish, the letter *g* sounds like *g* in *go* when it is followed by *a*, *o*, or *u*, although it often has a slightly softer sound than in English. Listen to and say the following words:

Gustavo	domingo	tengo
agosto	pregunta	luego
amigo	argollas	gato

In Spanish, the letter *g* sounds like the letter *h* in *hot* when it is followed by *e* or *i*. Listen to and say the following words. Some of these words you have not yet heard or seen. Can you guess the meanings of these cognates?

inteligente	generoso	general
gimnasio	tecnología	biología

Try it out! See if you can guess how to pronounce the following Spanish first names. Say each name in Spanish, keeping in mind the pronunciation rules for the *g* sound.

Gabriela	Ángela	Gerardo
Gilberto	Gustavo	Rodrigo
Olga	Rogelio	Gregorio

¡Adelante!

Lectura

Lee este artículo sobre el UNICEF.

Objectives

- Read about an important program of the United Nations
- Learn about cultural differences in schools
- Write a note describing your classroom
- Learn facts about Central America

Strategy

Predicting outcomes
Think about what you would consider to be basic rights for children around the world. Jot down four of them on a piece of paper. As you read the article, see if your ideas are included.

El UNICEF y una convención para los niños[1]

Esta convención dice que[5] los niños de todas[6] las naciones necesitan:

- dignidad
- una casa
- protección
- una buena dieta
- la práctica de deportes
- atención especial para los niños con problemas físicos
- amor y la comprensión de la familia
- expresar sus opiniones
- una comunidad sin[7] violencia
- ir a la escuela para ser inteligentes y sociables

[5]says that   [6]all   [7]without

¿Sabes que es un privilegio estar en una escuela, tener una mochila con libros, unos lápices, una calculadora, unas hojas de papel y un profesor bueno? En ciertas[2] naciones, ir a la escuela es difícil o no es posible.

El UNICEF es la organización internacional de las Naciones Unidas que trabaja para los niños. UNICEF es una sigla[3] inglesa que significa "Fondo Internacional de Emergencia de las Naciones Unidas para los Niños." Tiene siete oficinas regionales en diversas naciones y un Centro de Investigaciones en Italia.

El 20 de noviembre de 1989, la Organización de las Naciones Unidas escribió[4] "una convención para los niños" en inglés, árabe, chino, ruso y francés.

[1]children   [2]certain   [3]acronym   [4]wrote

¿Comprendes?

1. It is easy for students of every nation to attend school and own a backpack. True or false?

2. How many offices in different nations does UNICEF have?

3. What do the letters UNICEF stand for?

4. Where is the *Centro de Investigaciones?*

5. The convention is for children of all nations. True or false?

6. According to the convention, what are four things that children need?

For: Internet link activity
Visit: www.phschool.com
Web Code: jad-0215

¿Cómo es la escuela?

Did you know that students in many Spanish-speaking countries spend more time in school than you do? The graph to the right shows the length of the school year in various countries.

Here are some other facts you may not know:

- In many schools, when a teacher enters the classroom, the students stand.
- The teacher may call the students by their last name.
- The students, on the other hand, are more likely to address their teacher simply as *maestro(a), profesor(a),* or just *profe,* without a last name.
- Class time is generally spent with the teacher lecturing rather than with class discussion.
- Many public and private schools require uniforms.

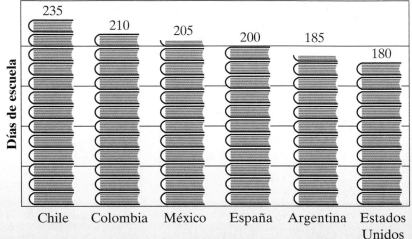

Días de escuela

| 235 | 210 | 205 | 200 | 185 | 180 |

Chile   Colombia   México   España   Argentina   Estados Unidos

País

Check it out! How are other schools in your area similar to or different from yours? How are they similar to or different from those in Spanish-speaking countries? Make a list of schools in your area and describe these similarities and differences. Are some schools more formal? Do students take classes that are different from the ones you take?

Think about it! Based on the information above, what might you assume are the attitudes toward school in Spanish-speaking cultures? How are these the same or different from attitudes in your community? List five suggestions that might help an exchange student from Mexico City adjust to your school's system.

Tu sala de clases

Task
Your pen pal from Mexico is coming to visit your school next semester and would like to know what to expect. Write her a note describing your Spanish classroom.

1 **Prewrite** Draw a simple sketch of your classroom, showing the classroom items you intend to describe in your note. Label the items.

2 **Draft** Write the first draft of your note. Your sketch will help you remember which items you want to describe and where they are located. Use the model to help you organize your writing.

Strategy

Creating visuals
Creating a sketch or a drawing can help you remember the things you want to write about in a description.

Modelo

En mi sala de clases hay cuatro ventanas. Mi pupitre está delante del escritorio de la profesora. La bandera está al lado de la puerta. Las computadoras están encima de la mesa.

3 **Revise** Read through your paragraph and check for correct spelling as well as for the criteria under Evaluation.

Share your work with a partner. Your partner should check the following:

• Is your paragraph easy to understand?

• Is there other information you could add?

• Are there are any errors?

Rewrite your paragraph making any necessary changes.

4 **Publish** Make a final copy of your note. You may exhibit it in the classroom or add it to your portfolio.

5 **Evaluation** Your teacher may give you a rubric for how the paragraph will be graded. You probably will be graded on:

• use of vocabulary

• correct use of the verb *estar*

• amount of information provided

América Central

Central America is made up of seven countries: Belize, Guatemala, El Salvador, Honduras, Nicaragua, Costa Rica, and Panama. Spanish is the official language in all of these countries except Belize, which was colonized by the British.

Costa Rica has set aside large tracts of land for conservation, helping to preserve fragile ecosystems. The oldest park in Costa Rica, Santa Rosa, protects endangered sea turtle nesting sites and the last dry tropical forest in Central America.

¿Sabes que...?

Carlos I of Spain first proposed a canal across the Isthmus of Panama in 1524. In the 1880s, French efforts to build a canal across the isthmus were hindered in large part by diseases. When Panama won its independence from Colombia in 1903, a treaty was signed with the United States granting rights to the Canal Zone. The United States completed the canal in 1914, and it was turned over to Panama in 1999.

Para pensar

In the early nineteenth century some people imagined that the United States would extend south to Panama. How do you think the United States would be different today if their predictions had come true? How do you think Mexico and Central America would be different?

México
Belice
Guatemala   Honduras
El Salvador   Nicaragua
Mar Caribe
Costa Rica
Panamá
OCÉANO PACÍFICO

Go Online
PHSchool.com

For: Online Atlas
Visit: www.phschool.com
Web Code: jae-0002

Founded by the Spanish in 1524, the Nicaraguan city of Granada became an important trading center. The town enjoys easy access to the Caribbean, yet is located less than 100 miles from the Pacific. In the nineteenth and twentieth centuries Nicaragua was proposed as an alternate site for a canal linking the Atlantic and Pacific oceans.

Much of Guatemala's large indigenous population is of Mayan descent. These women are wearing the traditional hand-woven *huipil*, which is a very "communicative" part of their clothing. The *huipil* identifies the wearer's village, her marital status, her religious beliefs, wealth, and personality. A well-woven *huipil* may last between 20 to 30 years.

From the 1500s to the end of the 1700s, the coasts of Spanish America were plagued by pirates. Panamanian ports were perfect targets, since the silver and gold mined in Peru were loaded on Panama's Pacific coast and carried overland to the Atlantic, where they were put on ships bound for Spain. Fuerte San Lorenzo, on Panama's Atlantic coast, was part of a network of forts that were meant to protect ships and their precious cargo.

Repaso del capítulo

Vocabulario y gramática

Chapter Review

To prepare for the test, check to see if you . . .

- know the new vocabulary and grammar
- can perform the tasks on p. 145

to talk about classroom items

la bandera	flag
el cartel	poster
la computadora	computer
el disquete	diskette
la mochila	bookbag, backpack
la pantalla	(computer) screen
la papelera	wastepaper basket
el ratón	(computer) mouse
el reloj	clock
el sacapuntas	pencil sharpener
el teclado	(computer) keyboard

to talk about classroom furniture

el escritorio	desk
la mesa	table
la silla	chair

to talk about parts of a classroom

la puerta	door
la sala de clases	classroom
la ventana	window

to indicate location

al lado de la / del	next to, beside
allí	there
aquí	here
debajo de la/del	underneath
delante de la/del	in front of
detrás de la/del	behind
¿Dónde?	Where?
en	in, on
encima de la/del	on top of

to indicate possession

de	of
mi	my
tu	your

For *Vocabulario adicional,* see pp. 268–269.

to identify (description, quantity)

¿Cuántos, -as?	How many?
Es un(a) . . .	It's a (an) . . .
Hay	There is, There are
¿Qué es esto?	What is this?

to identify gender and quantity of nouns

los, las	the
unos, unas	some

estar *to be*

estoy	estamos
estás	estáis
está	están

● Más práctica

Practice Workbook Puzzle 2B-8
Practice Workbook Organizer 2B-9

Preparación para el examen

On the exam you will be asked to...	Here are practice tasks similar to those you will find on the exam...	If you need review...
1 Escuchar Listen to and identify classrooms and locations	Listen as a student frantically asks some of his friends where he left his homework. Can you identify all the classrooms and places they suggest that he look?	**pp. 118–123** *A primera vista* **p. 124** Actividades 5–6 **p. 135** Actividad 27
2 Hablar Talk about where someone is located by describing where that person is in relation to objects in the classroom	You are trying to find out the name of someone in your class. You ask the person next to you, but he doesn't understand whom you are talking about. Give at least three statements that would help him identify the person. You might include where he or she is in relation to the teacher's desk, the window, someone else's desk, and so on.	**pp. 118–123** *A primera vista* **p. 125** Actividad 7 **p. 126** Actividad 9 **p. 130** Actividades 16–17 **p. 133** Actividad 24 **p. 135** Actividad 27 **p. 136** Actividad 29
3 Leer Read and understand a letter that contains questions and concerns about school issues	The school counselor has asked you to help out read a note written by a new Spanish-speaking student at school. After reading it, tell the counselor what questions the student has about her classes? *Necesito una clase para la primera hora. ¿Cómo es la clase de tecnología, fácil o difícil? ¿Qué necesito para la clase? ¿Cuántos alumnos hay en las clases? ¿Hay mucha tarea?*	**pp. 118–122** *A primera vista* **p. 128** Actividad 11 **pp. 138–139** *Lectura*
4 Escribir Write an e-mail to a friend about one of her classes	You have just moved to a new town and are sending an e-mail to a friend from your old school. You have lots of questions for your friend about her classes. Write at least three questions about one of her classes: whether she likes it, how many students are in it, where her desk is in the room, what else is in the room, etc.	**pp. 118–123** *A primera vista* **p. 124** Actividad 6 **p. 125** Actividad 7 **p. 136** Actividad 28 **p. 137** Actividad 30
5 Pensar Demonstrate an understanding of cultural differences in schools	Think about how students and teachers interact within a typical classroom in a Spanish-speaking country. What are at least four things that you might find different from most schools in the United States?	**p. 127** *Fondo cultural* **p. 134** *Fondo cultural* **p. 140** *Perspectivas del mundo hispano*

Fondo cultural

Bartolomé Murillo (1617–1682) was the first Spanish painter to become famous throughout Europe. Several of his early paintings featured children from his native Sevilla. Murillo used color, light, and a natural portrayal of his subjects to create memorable masterpieces.

• Study the painting and come up with three adjectives that describe it. Would you say the impression Murillo gives of the boys is positive or negative? Why?

Niños comiendo fruta (ca. 1650), Bartolomé Murillo
© ARS, NY. Copyright Scala/Art Resource, NY. Alte Pinakothek, Munich, Germany.

¿Desayuno o almuerzo?

Chapter Objectives

- Talk about foods and beverages for breakfast and lunch
- Talk about likes and dislikes
- Express how often something is done
- Understand cultural perspectives on meals

Video Highlights

A primera vista: *El desayuno*

GramActiva Videos: present tense of *-er* and *-ir* verbs; *me gustan, me encantan*

Country Connection

As you learn about foods and meals, you will make connections to these countries and places:

España
Venezuela
Costa Rica
Colombia
Ecuador
Perú
Bolivia
Chile

Go Online
PHSchool.com

For: Online Atlas
Visit: www.phschool.com
Web Code: jae-0002

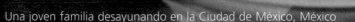
Una joven familia desayunando en la Ciudad de México, México

A primera vista

Vocabulario y gramática en contexto

El Supermercado de la Plaza

¡Abierto las 24 horas!

¡Ofertas de hoy!

¡Toda la comida que necesitas!

- las salchichas $2.29
- el tocino $2.45
- el jamón $2.35
- el cereal $3.59 — SALVADO CON PASAS
- el queso $3.25
- el yogur de fresa $.79
- los huevos $1.29
- los plátanos $.69
- el jugo de manzana $1.80
- el jugo de naranja $2.50
- la limonada $1.39
- la leche $1.75
- el té $2.40
- el pan $1.89
- las galletas $2.29
- el agua* $1.09

*Note that *agua* is a feminine noun. However, you use the masculine article *el* to make it easier to say.

❝ El desayuno es mi **comida** favorita. **En el desayuno,** yo **como** cereal **con** leche, tocino y **pan tostado. Todos los días bebo** jugo de naranja. **Nunca** bebo té **sin** leche. Y tú, ¿qué **comes** en el desayuno? **❞**

66 **Me encanta** el Restaurante de la Plaza. La comida es muy buena. **En el almuerzo,** como una ensalada de frutas o un sándwich de jamón y queso. **Siempre** bebo agua. Es importante **beber** mucha agua, ¿verdad? **99**

El Restaurante de la Plaza

¡Para un almuerzo rápido!

$3.25
la ensalada de frutas

$3.50
el sándwich de jamón y queso

$1.75
la pizza

$3.75
la hamburguesa

$1.00
el café

$1.50
el perrito caliente

$1.00
los refrescos

$1.25
las papas fritas

$1.35
los jugos

$1.80
la sopa de verduras

$1.00
el té helado

Actividad 1   Escuchar

¿Beber o comer?

Listen to the names of ten foods or beverages. If an item is a food, pantomime eating. If it's a beverage, pantomime drinking.

Actividad 2   Escuchar

¿El desayuno o el almuerzo?

Listen as different people tell what they are eating. Hold up one hand if the meal is *el desayuno* and hold up both hands if it is *el almuerzo.*

● **Más práctica**
Practice Workbook 3A-1, 3A-2

Go Online
PHSchool.com
For: Vocabulary practice
Visit: www.phschool.com
Web Code: jad-0301

El desayuno

Tomás es de los Estados Unidos. Está en Costa Rica para estudiar.
¿Qué come el primer día? Lee la historia.

Costa Rica

Papá

Mamá

Tomás

Raúl

Gloria

Antes de leer

Strategy

Using prior experience You can use experiences
that you have already had to help you understand what
you read. Think about eating breakfast. Do you like a
big breakfast? A small one? No breakfast at all?

• What do you think Tomás and Raúl have for breakfast?

1. Look at photo 2. Can you figure out from the picture what *¡Qué asco!*
means?

2. Look at the photos and describe the problem Tomás is having at
breakfast.

1 **Mamá:** A ver ... tocino, salchichas, huevos ...

Papá: ¡Uy! Es mucha comida. No **comprendo.** Tú nunca comes el desayuno.

Mamá: No es mi desayuno. Es para Tomás, **por supuesto.** Los americanos comen mucho en el desayuno.

2 **Raúl:** No comes mucho en el desayuno, ¿verdad?

Tomás: ¡No! ¡Qué asco!

3 **Tomás:** No me gusta nada el desayuno. A veces bebo jugo de naranja y como pan tostado.

Raúl: Yo tampoco como mucho.

4 **Mamá:** Buenos días, Tomás. Aquí tienes tu desayuno. Huevos, tocino, salchichas, pan tostado, cereal con leche ...

Tomás: Gracias. Es un desayuno muy bueno. **Me encantan** los huevos y el tocino.

5 **Tomás: Comparto** los huevos, el tocino y las salchichas.

Raúl: ¿Compartes tu desayuno? Muchas gracias, Tomás.

6 **Raúl:** ¿Y qué **bebes?**

Tomás: Jugo de naranja, por favor.

Mamá: Te gusta la leche, ¿no?

Tomás: Más o menos.

7 **Raúl:** Papá, ¿unos huevos?

Papá: No, gracias. ¡La comida es para Uds.!

8 **Mamá:** ¿**Cuál** es tu almuerzo favorito, Tomás?

Tomás: Me gustan las hamburguesas, la pizza, **la ensalada...**

Mamá: Bueno... ¡pizza, hamburguesas y ensalada en el almuerzo!

Escribir •

La lista

Copy Raúl's mother's shopping list on a separate sheet of paper. Then scan the *Videohistoria* and place a check mark next to the items that she uses to make breakfast for Raúl and Tomás.

Lista para el supermercado	
yogur	tocino
queso	jugo de naranja
salchichas	huevos
jamón	pan
galletas	cereal
plátanos	leche

Leer/Hablar •

Los gustos de Tomás

Read the following sentences and tell how Tomás would react, according to the *Videohistoria*. If he would like what is mentioned, say *"¡Me encanta!"* If he wouldn't like it, say *"¡Qué asco!"*

1. En el desayuno hay pan tostado.
2. En el desayuno hay jugo de naranja.
3. En el almuerzo hay pizza.
4. Hoy hay un desayuno muy grande.
5. Hoy hay ensalada en el almuerzo.

Actividad 5 **Leer** • • • • • • • • • • • • • • • • • •

¿Comprendes?

Read the following sentences. Write the numbers 1–6 on your paper and write *C (cierto)* if a sentence is true, or *F (falso)* if it is false.

1. Tomás está en Costa Rica.
2. La mamá de Raúl siempre come mucho en el desayuno.
3. A Tomás le gusta comer mucho en el desayuno.
4. Hoy Tomás no come mucho en el desayuno.
5. Tomás comparte el desayuno con Raúl.
6. A Tomás le gustan las hamburguesas y la pizza.

● Más práctica • • • • • • • • • • • • •
Practice Workbook 3A-3, 3A-4

Go Online
PHSchool.com
For: Vocabulary practice
Visit: www.phschool.com
Web Code: jad-0302

Manos a la obra

Vocabulario y gramática en uso

Objectives

- Talk about foods and beverages for breakfast and lunch
- Ask and tell what people eat and drink for breakfast and lunch
- Express likes and dislikes
- Learn to use the present tense of *-er* and *-ir* verbs and *me gustan* / *me encantan*

Actividad 6   Pensar/Escribir

Las diferencias

The two kitchens below look identical, but there are several differences. Make a list of as many differences between *la cocina de Ana* and *la cocina de Lola* as you can find.

Modelo

No hay papas fritas en la cocina de Lola.

la cocina de Ana

la cocina de Lola

Pensar/Escribir •

El desayuno y el almuerzo

Think about what people usually eat for breakfast and lunch. Copy the Venn diagram on a sheet of paper. Which foods pictured in Actividad 6 would usually be eaten for breakfast or lunch? Write the Spanish words in the appropriate oval for *el desayuno* or *el almuerzo*. Which items could be eaten for either breakfast or lunch? Write them in the overlapping area.

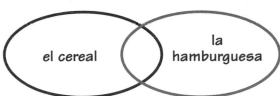

Modelo

el desayuno   los dos   el almuerzo

el cereal   la hamburguesa

 ♻ **Escuchar/Escribir** •

¿Dónde están?

You will hear eight descriptions of the drawing of *la cocina de Ana* in Actividad 6. Write the numbers 1–8 on your paper and write the correct food or beverage.

Escribir •

¿Qué bebes?

1 On a sheet of paper, make three columns with these headings: *Todos los días, A veces, Nunca.* Under each heading, write the names of the beverages pictured below based on how often you drink them.

1.    2.    3.    4.

5.    6.    7.

2 Write complete sentences telling how often you drink these beverages.

Modelo

Bebo limonada todos los días.

Actividad 10 **Hablar**

¿Qué comes?

Working with a partner, discuss the things that you eat and don't eat.

Estudiante A

1. 2. 3.
4. 5. 6. 7.

Estudiante B

Sí, todos los días...
Sí, a veces...
Sí, siempre...
No, nunca...
No, ¡qué asco!

Exploración del lenguaje

Using a noun to modify another noun

In English, we often use one noun to describe another noun: *vegetable soup, strawberry yogurt.* Notice that the noun that is being described comes second.

In Spanish, however, the noun that is being described comes first and is followed by *de* + the describing noun: *sopa* **de** *verduras, yogur* **de** *fresa.* Notice that you don't use a definite article in front of the second noun.

The form of the noun following *de* does not change even when the first noun becomes plural.

el sándwich de **jamón**
los sándwiches de **jamón**

Try it out! Name five or more examples of foods or beverages from this chapter that follow this pattern.

• Now that you know the pattern, say what the food or beverage would be in Spanish using the words paired with the pictures below.

el tomate   la lechuga

la piña   el pollo

Actividad 11

Hablar

¿Qué preparas?

You are preparing a meal for your friend. Use *de* and any of the words in the box below to come up with something special. (Some of your combinations may be a bit strange!) Tell your partner what you are making and he or she will respond with *¡Qué asco!* or *¡Me encanta(n)!*

Modelo

un sándwich
A —*Preparo un sándwich de manzanas y huevos.*
B —*¡Qué asco!*
o: *¡Me encanta!*

1. un sándwich
2. una sopa
3. un jugo
4. una ensalada
5. un yogur

verduras	salchichas	plátanos	frutas
fresas	jamón	tocino	perritos calientes
manzanas	queso	huevos	

También se dice...

la naranja = la china *(el Caribe)*

el sándwich = el bocadillo *(España);* la torta *(México)*

el plátano = la banana, el guineo *(el Caribe)*

las papas = las patatas *(España)*

el jugo = el zumo *(España)*

beber = tomar *(México)*

Actividad 12

Hablar

Mis comidas favoritas

With a partner, talk about the foods you like and don't like.

Modelo

A —*Te gustan los plátanos, ¿verdad?*
B —*Sí, ¡por supuesto! Me encantan.*

Estudiante A

Estudiante B

Sí, ¡por supuesto! Me encantan.
Sí, más o menos.
No, no me gustan.
No, ¡qué asco!

¡Respuesta personal!

Escribir/Hablar •

Juego

1 Copy this blank Bingo card on a separate piece of paper. You will need to make it big enough to write a vocabulary word and a person's name in each square.

2 After you have made your Bingo card, write the name of a food or drink from the *Repaso del capítulo* on p. 174 in any order that you want. Be sure to leave enough space at the bottom of each square to write a person's name.

3 Now that you have made your game card, you are ready to interview your classmates. Ask a classmate if he or she drinks a beverage or eats a food item that you have on your card. If the answer is *no,* you will need to ask someone else the same question. If the answer is *sí,* write the classmate's name at the bottom of that square. You can only have a classmate's name on your card once, so after you have found a classmate who says "*sí,*" look for a different person for each of the remaining items on your card. The first person to say "*¡Bingo!*" after completing a horizontal or vertical row wins.

Bingo de comer y beber

Modelo

A —*Marco, ¿bebes limonada?*
B —*No, ¡qué asco!*
A —*Sarita, ¿bebes limonada?*
C —*Sí. Me encanta.*
You write: *Sarita*

Actividad 14 Leer/Pensar

El intercambio entre dos mundos

Think about how your meals would be different without chicken, pork, beef, milk, cheese, sugar, grapes, and food made from the grains wheat and barley. Europeans brought all these foods to the Americas.

Both sides of the Atlantic Ocean benefited from a product exchange. Starting in the fifteenth century, Columbus took back to Europe a wide range of foods from the Americas that Europeans had never seen before. These foods included corn, beans, squash, tomatoes, limes, avocados, chiles, peanuts, cashews, turkey, pineapples, yams, potatoes, vanilla, and chocolate. Today these foods are found in dishes in many countries.

• What is your favorite meal? Do the ingredients originally come from the Americas, Europe, or elsewhere?

Actividad 15 Leer/Escribir

Enchiladas de pollo

Read the list of ingredients for a traditional Mexican dish of *enchiladas*. Based upon the information you just read and saw in the map, write which ingredients had their origins in the Americas and which came from Europe.

**Enchiladas
de pollo[1] con salsa de tomate**

Ingredientes

12 tortillas de maíz[2]

1 taza[3] de pollo

1 taza de queso fresco[4]

6 tomates grandes[5]

2 cebollas[6] no muy grandes

crema

aceite[7] de maíz

[1]chicken [2]corn [3]cup [4]fresh [5]large

[6]onions [7]oil

Present tense of *-er* and *-ir* verbs

To create the present-tense forms of *-er* and *-ir* verbs, drop the endings from the infinitives, then add the verb endings *-o, -es, -e, -emos / -imos, -éis / -ís,* or *-en* to the stem.

Here are the present-tense forms of *-er* and *-ir* verbs using *comer* and *compartir:*

(yo)	**como**	(nosotros) (nosotras)	**comemos**
(tú)	**comes**	(vosotros) (vosotras)	**coméis**
Ud. (él) (ella)	**come**	Uds. (ellos) (ellas)	**comen**

(yo)	**comparto**	(nosotros) (nosotras)	**compartimos**
(tú)	**compartes**	(vosotros) (vosotras)	**compartís**
Ud. (él) (ella)	**comparte**	Uds. (ellos) (ellas)	**comparten**

- Regular *-er* verbs that you know are *beber, comer, comprender, correr,* and *leer.*
- Regular *-ir* verbs that you know are *compartir* and *escribir.*
- You also know the verb *ver.* It is regular except in the *yo* form, which is *veo.*

¿Recuerdas?

The pattern of present-tense *-ar* verbs is:

toco	tocamos
tocas	tocáis
toca	tocan

GramActiva VIDEO

Want more practice with *-er* and *-ir* verbs? Watch the **GramActiva** video.

16 Gramática Escribir

¿Quiénes comparten el almuerzo?

On a separate sheet of paper, write complete sentences saying what each person is sharing and with whom.

Modelo

Elena / una manzana / Raúl
Elena comparte una manzana con Raúl.

1. Tomás / una pizza / María
2. tú / unos sándwiches / Ramón
3. nosotros / unas papas fritas / los estudiantes
4. Uds. / unas galletas / el profesor
5. ellas / unos perritos calientes / nosotros
6. tú y yo / unos plátanos / Luis y Roberta
7. yo / ¿–? / mi amigo

Una familia almorzando

17 **Gramática** • **Leer/Escribir** •

Una tarjeta postal

Read the following postcard from your friend Carolina in Venezuela.
Number your paper from 1–8 and write the correct form of the
appropriate verb in parentheses.

¡Hola!

Elena y yo estamos en Caracas. Nosotras __1.__
(comprender / correr) todos los días y __2.__
(comer / ver) muy bien.

Los estudiantes aquí __3.__ (comer / leer)
mucha pizza y __4.__ (ver / beber) mucho café.
Ellos __5.__ (leer / beber) muchos libros y
__6.__ (escribir / ver) mucho también para
las clases. Las clases son difíciles pero
me encantan.

En la clase de español nosotros __7.__
(correr / leer) revistas y cuentos en español.
Elena __8.__ (comprender / beber) muy bien
pero para mí es un poco difícil.

Tengo que estudiar. Hasta luego.

Tu amiga,
Carolina

¡Bienvenidos a Venezuela!

18 **Gramática** • **Escribir** •

El desayuno con la familia Acevedo

You have been invited to Sunday breakfast at the Acevedo house.
Write five sentences to describe what everyone is doing. Be sure to
use a different subject and a different verb for each sentence.

Modelo

Nosotros vemos la tele.

| el Sr. Acevedo
yo
Francisco y Marta
la Sra. Acevedo
nosotros | ver la tele
leer una revista
correr a la puerta
compartir un desayuno muy bueno
beber jugo de manzana
comer yogur de fresas

¡Respuesta personal! |

Actividad 19 Gramática — Hablar

¿Qué beben y qué comen?

Work with a partner. Use the verbs *comer* and *beber* to ask questions. Then answer them, following the models.

Juan / desayuno

Modelo

A —¿Qué come Juan en el desayuno?
B —Juan come pan tostado.

Miguel y Carlos / almuerzo

Modelo

A —¿Qué beben Miguel y Carlos en el almuerzo?
B —Miguel y Carlos beben limonada.

> **Para decir más...**
>
> la crema de cacahuates   peanut butter
> el pan dulce   breakfast pastry
> el panqueque   pancake
> el pollo   chicken

1. Raúl y Gloria / desayuno

2. tú / almuerzo

3. Graciela y Carlos / desayuno

4. Carolina / almuerzo

5. tu familia y tú / desayuno

6. tú / almuerzo

¡Respuesta personal!

Actividad 20 — Hablar/Escribir

Los sábados y la comida

Talk about what you and your classmates eat and drink for breakfast and lunch on Saturdays. Make a chart like the one below on a sheet of paper and complete each box with information about yourself. Then survey two classmates to find out what their habits are. Record the information in the chart.

Modelo

Los sábados, ¿qué comes en el desayuno? ¿Qué bebes?
¿Qué comes en el almuerzo? ¿Qué bebes?

	¿Qué comes?	¿Qué bebes?
el desayuno	yo: huevos, pan tostado, tocino Sandra: cereal, plátanos	
el almuerzo		

Actividad 21

Escribir/Hablar •

Los hábitos de la clase

Use your completed chart from Actividad 20 to write summary statements based on your survey. Be prepared to read your sentences to the class.

Sandra y yo comemos huevos y cereal en el desayuno.
Gregorio no bebe jugo de naranja en el desayuno y le gusta mucho la leche.
Sofía come cereal y bebe leche en el desayuno.

Actividad 22

 Escribir/Hablar • • • • • • • • • • • • • • • •

Y tú, ¿qué dices?

1. ¿Qué comen tú y tus amigos en el almuerzo?
2. ¿Compartes la comida con tus amigos? ¿Qué compartes?
3. ¿Qué bebes en el desayuno?
4. ¿Qué libros lees en tu clase de inglés?
5. ¿Quién corre rápido *(fast)* en tu clase de educación física?
6. ¿Ves la tele en tu clase de ciencias sociales? ¿Qué ves?

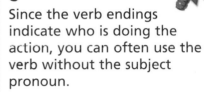

¿Recuerdas?

Since the verb endings indicate who is doing the action, you can often use the verb without the subject pronoun.

- **escribo** *I write*
- **escribimos** *we write*

¿Qué comen en el desayuno?

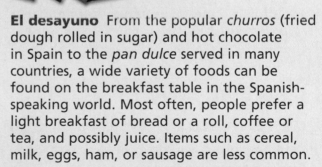

El desayuno From the popular *churros* (fried dough rolled in sugar) and hot chocolate in Spain to the *pan dulce* served in many countries, a wide variety of foods can be found on the breakfast table in the Spanish-speaking world. Most often, people prefer a light breakfast of bread or a roll, coffee or tea, and possibly juice. Items such as cereal, milk, eggs, ham, or sausage are less common.

- In Spain you can ask for a *desayuno americano.* What do you think you would be served?

● **Más práctica** •
Practice Workbook 3A-5

Go Online
PHSchool.com
For: Practice with *-er* and *-ir* verbs
Visit: www.phschool.com
Web Code: jad-0303

Gramática

Me gustan, me encantan

Use *me gusta* and *me encanta* to talk about a singular noun.

> Me gusta **el té** pero me encant**a el té helado.**

Use *me gustan* and *me encantan* to talk about plural nouns.

> Me encant**an las fresas** pero no me gust**an** mucho **los plátanos.**

When you use *me gusta(n)* and *me encanta(n)* to talk about a noun, include *el, la, los,* or *las.*

> Me encanta **el** jugo de naranja pero no me gusta **la** leche.

> ¿Qué te gustan más, **las** hamburguesas o **los** perritos calientes?

GramActiva VIDEO

Want more help with *me gusta(n)/ me encanta(n)?* Watch the **GramActiva** video.

Actividad 23 **Gramática** Escuchar/GramActiva

¿Gusta o gustan?

1 Tear a sheet of paper in thirds. On the first piece, write *No.* On the second piece write *me gusta.* On the third piece, write *n.*

2 You will hear eight food items. Indicate when you like or don't like the items by holding up one, two, or all three pieces of paper. Remember to use *me gustan* when the item you hear is plural.

Actividad 24 **Gramática** Escribir

¿Qué te gusta?

Indicate how much you do or do not like the following foods.

Modelo

Me gustan las manzanas.
o: *No me gustan nada las manzanas.*
o: *Me encantan las manzanas.*

1.

2.

3.

4.

5.

6.

Actividad 25

Leer/Escribir •

Un *quiz* personal

A popular magazine has provided this survey to see how much you and a friend have in common. Read the survey. Then, for each item on the quiz, write a sentence describing which choice you like the most. Write your sentences on a sheet of paper.

Modelo

Me gusta más la comida italiana.

¿Qué te gusta más?

¿Tu amigo(a) y tú son muy similares o muy diferentes?

Completa este quiz y compara tus respuestas con las de un(a) amigo(a).

1. **la comida mexicana o la comida italiana**
2. **el desayuno o el almuerzo**
3. **el cereal con fruta o el cereal sin fruta**
4. **las revistas o los libros**
5. **la música rock o la música rap**
6. **los amigos graciosos o los amigos serios**
7. **las hamburguesas con queso o las hamburguesas sin queso**

Respuestas similares:

7–6	**¡Uds. son gemelos!**[1]
5–4	**Tienen mucho en común, ¿verdad?**
3–2	**¡Un poco similar y un poco diferente!**
1–0	**¿Los opuestos[2] se atraen?[3] ¡Por supuesto!**

[1]twins   [2]opposites   [3]attract

Actividad 26

  Hablar •

¿Amigos similares o diferentes?

Working in pairs, take turns asking your partner about the survey items in Actividad 25. Keep track of your similarities and differences. See how the magazine rates you.

Modelo

A —*¿Qué te gusta más, la comida mexicana o la comida italiana?*
B —*Me gusta más la comida italiana.*
o: *No me gusta ni la comida mexicana ni la comida italiana.*
A —*A mí me gusta la comida mexicana.*
o: *A mí también.*
o: *A mí tampoco.*

Necesito mucho del supermercado

You and your friend are going food shopping in San Antonio, Texas. Look at the following advertisement and decide with your partner what items you should put on your shopping list. When you decide that you need an item, write it on your list.

Modelo

A —¿*Necesitamos huevos?*
B —*Sí, me encantan los huevos.*
o: *No, ¡qué asco! No me gustan los huevos.*

El Supermercado Mendoza

$3.50	$1.75	$2.39	$0.99	$2.00

las galletas Chocolífico	el tocino Rancho Tejano	el cereal Salvado con pasas	los plátanos centroaméricanos	las papas de Idaho
$2.05	$1.19	$2.35	$1.09	$0.89

la leche Vacarica 1/2 galón	los huevos	las fresas frescas	los refrescos Mendoza	las manzanas de Washington

El español en la comunidad

Foods from different Spanish-speaking countries have become very popular in the United States. Visit a local grocery store and make a list of different foods that come from Spanish-speaking countries.

- Which of these foods have you tried? How do they compare to foods that you normally eat?

The letters *h* and *j*

In Spanish, the letter *h* is never pronounced. Listen to and say these words:

| hora | hablar | hasta | hola |
| hoy | hace | hacer | hotel |

The letter *j* is pronounced like the letter *h* in *hat* but with more of a breathy sound. It is made far back in the mouth—almost in the throat. Listen to and say these words:

| trabajar | dibujar | jugar | videojuegos |
| hoja | jueves | junio | julio |

Try it out! Find and say five or more examples of foods or beverages from this chapter that have *h* or *j* in their spelling.

Try it out! Say this *trabalenguas* (tongue twister) three times, as fast as you can:

Debajo del puente de Guadalajara había un conejo debajo del agua.

Leer/Escribir

¿Qué comida hay en el Ciberc@fé @rrob@?

Menú del Ciberc@fé @rrob@

Desayunos

No. 1 Huevos: *(jamón, tocino, chorizo¹)* $18.00
Con cóctel de fruta $20.00

No. 2 Sincronizadas: *(tortilla de harina,²*
queso amarillo, jamón) $22.00
Con cóctel de fruta $24.00

No. 3 Cuernitos: *(jamón, queso, tomate*
y lechuga) $20.00
Con cóctel de fruta $22.00

No. 4 Chilaquiles: *verdes o rojos*
(con pollo o huevos) $14.00
Con cóctel de fruta $16.00

No. 5 Omelet: *(con pollo, jamón, tomate,*
cebolla, champiñones³ o queso) $18.00

No. 6 Crepas *(champiñones, jamón, pollo)* $12.50

Refrescos $5.00   Café $4.00   Jugos $7.50   Té o té helado $4.00

Tel: 212 03 95   **16 de septiembre #65, Col. Centro**

¹spicy sausage   ²flour   ³mushrooms

Strategy

Skimming
Look quickly through the menu. What meal is featured? Find three dishes you recognize and two that are new to you.

1 Read the menu and answer the questions on a separate sheet of paper.

1. Comes el desayuno No. 1 con té. ¿Cuál es el precio (price) del desayuno?

2. No te gustan nada los huevos. ¿Qué comes del menú?

3. Te encanta la fruta. ¿Qué bebes?

2 Use the cyber café menu as a model menu to create a lunch menu using the vocabulary in this chapter.

Más práctica
Practice Workbook 3A-6, 3A-7

Go Online
PHSchool.com
For: Practice with *me gusta(n)/me encanta(n)*
Visit: www.phschool.com
Web Code: jad-0304

¡Adelante!

Objectives

- Read about fruits that are native to the Americas
- Learn about a snack in Spanish-speaking countries, *churros y chocolate*
- Maintain a conversation about what you like, including your food preferences
- Learn facts about the northern part of South America

Frutas y verduras de las Américas

Hay muchas frutas y verduras que son originalmente de las Américas que hoy se comen en todos los países. Las verduras más populares son la papa, el maíz, los frijoles y muchas variedades de chiles. También hay una gran variedad de frutas como la papaya, la piña y el aguacate. Estas frutas y verduras son muy nutritivas, se pueden preparar fácilmente y son muy sabrosas. La papaya y la piña son frutas que se comen en el desayuno o de postre. ¿Cuáles de estas frutas comes?

Strategy

Making guesses
When you find an unknown word, try to guess the meaning. Is it a cognate? What might it mean within the context of the reading and other words around it? Keep reading and the meaning may become clear.

la papaya

Es una fruta con mucha agua. Es perfecta para el verano. Tiene más vitamina C que la naranja.

el aguacate

La pulpa del aguacate es una fuente de energía, proteínas, vitaminas y minerales. Tiene vitaminas A y B.

el mango

Aunque[1] el mango es originalmente de Asia, se cultiva en las regiones tropicales de muchos países de las Américas. Tiene calcio y vitaminas A y C como la naranja.

[1]Although

Licuado de plátano

El licuado es una bebida muy popular en los países tropicales. ¡Es delicioso y muy nutritivo!

Ingredientes:
1 plátano
2 vasos de leche
1 cucharadita de azúcar
hielo

Preparación:
1. Cortar el plátano.
2. Colocar los ingredientes en la licuadora.
3. Licuar por unos 5 ó 10 segundos.

¿Comprendes?

1. ¿Qué vitaminas tienen las frutas en la página anterior?

2. De las frutas y verduras en el artículo, ¿cuáles (which ones) te gustan? ¿Cuáles no te gustan?

3. ¿Qué otras frutas te gustan? ¿Comes estas frutas en el desayuno o en el almuerzo?

4. ¿Qué fruta no es originalmente de las Américas?

Fondo cultural ■ ■ ◆ ◆ ◻ ◆

Frutas y verduras During winter, the United States imports a wide range of fruits from Chile such as cherries, peaches, and grapes. When you purchase grapes from a supermarket in January, look to see if they have a label that says *Producto de Chile* or *Importado de Chile*.

• What are some other fruits and vegetables in your local market that are products of other countries?

Chile

Go Online PHSchool.com

For: Internet link activity
Visit: www.phschool.com
Web Code: jad-0305

Churros y chocolate

In many Spanish-speaking countries, a popular snack is the combination of *churros y chocolate*. *Churros* are long, slender doughnut-like pastries fried in hot oil. Small restaurants called *churrerías* specialize in *churros* and cups of delicious hot chocolate. You can also find *churros* being sold in stands on the street.

Try it out! Here's the recipe to try. *Churros* are high in fat and calories, so you won't want to sample too many of them!

Churros

1 cup water	$\frac{1}{2}$ cup unsalted butter *(= 1 stick)*
$\frac{1}{4}$ teaspoon salt	1 cup all-purpose flour
4 large eggs	oil for deep-frying
1 cup sugar	

Chocolate y churros

Un molinillo

In a heavy saucepan, bring water, butter, and salt to a full boil. Remove from heat. Add the flour all at once, stirring briskly. Stir until the mixture pulls away from the side of the pan and forms a ball. Put the mixture in a bowl. With an electric mixer on medium speed, add one egg at a time. After adding the last egg, beat the mixture for one more minute.

With adult supervision, heat 2–3 inches of oil to 375° F in a deep, heavy pan. Fit a pastry bag or cookie press with a $\frac{1}{2}$-inch star tip. Pipe out 6 inch-long tubes of dough into the oil. **Be extremely cautious adding dough to the oil, because the oil may spatter and burn you!** Fry, turning a few times, for 3–5 minutes or until golden brown. Place the sugar on a plate. Drain the *churros* well on paper towels and then roll them in the sugar.

Chocolate caliente

To make hot chocolate in Mexico, cacao beans are ground to a powder. Cinnamon, powdered almonds, and sugar are then added, and hot milk is poured in. The mixture is whipped with a wooden whisk called *un molinillo* or *un batidor*. You can find Mexican-style chocolate for making *chocolate caliente* in many supermarkets.

Think about it! What kinds of food and drink do you and your friends like? Is chocolate among the popular choices? Can you think of combinations of food and drink that are popular with many people in the United States? Are these combinations popular elsewhere?

Presentación oral

¿Y qué te gusta comer?

Task

An exchange student from the United States is going to Uruguay. You and a partner will role-play a telephone conversation in which you each take one of the roles and gather information about the other person.

1 Prepare You will role-play this conversation with a partner. Be sure to prepare for both roles. Here's how to prepare:

Host Student: Make a list of at least four questions that you might ask the exchange student. Find out what he or she likes to study, his or her favorite activities, and what he or she likes to eat and drink for breakfast and lunch.

Strategy

Making lists
Making lists of questions can help you in conversations where you need to find out specific information.

Exchange Student: Jot down some possible answers to questions that the host student might ask and be prepared to provide information about yourself.

2 Practice Work in groups of four in which there are two exchange students and two host students. Work together to practice different questions and different responses. Here's how you might start your phone conversation:

Host Student:	¡Hola, Pablo! Soy Rosa.
Exchange Student:	Hola, Rosa. ¿Cómo estás?
Host Student:	Bien, gracias. Pues Pablo, ¿te gusta...?

Continue the conversation using your notes. You can use your notes in practice, but not during the role-playing.

3 Present You will be paired with another student, and your teacher will tell you which role to play. The host student begins the conversation. Listen to your partner's questions and responses and keep the conversation going.

4 Evaluation Your teacher may give you a rubric for how the presentation will be graded. You probably will be graded on:

• completion of task

• how well you were understood

• your ability to keep the conversation going

América del Sur

Parte norte

Venezuela, Colombia, Ecuador, Peru, and Bolivia form a region of contrasts, with mountains and lowlands, rain forests and deserts, immense wealth and extreme poverty, remote villages and modern cities. A rugged geography, ancient indigenous civilizations, and abundant natural resources have made this one of the most culturally diverse regions in the world.

Constructed more than 500 years ago, the terraced fields in the highlands of Bolivia were a sophisticated system for conserving soil and water, and some remain in use today. In the 1980s archaeologists reconstructing ancient agricultural systems on the shore of Lake Titicaca (at 12,500 feet the highest navigable body of water in the world) found that these ancient systems worked better in this difficult environment than many modern agricultural techniques.

¿Sabes que . . . ?

The term *America* first appeared on a German map in 1507. The Americas are named for the Italian navigator Amerigo Vespucci, who produced the first European charts of mainland South America in 1497.

Para pensar

The countries of northern South America are lands of varied geography. Think about the North American continent. It is also a land of geographical contrasts. In what ways are both regions rich in natural resources, environmentally protected areas, and ancient civilizations?

For: Online Atlas
Visit: www.phschool.com
Web Code: jae-0002

"Rediscovered" in 1911, the mountaintop city of Machu Picchu in Peru was part of the Incan empire, which in the sixteenth century extended from present-day Ecuador to Chile. Machu Picchu's buildings were made of huge, precisely carved stone blocks that were hauled into place without wheels or heavy draft animals. ▶

◀ Venezuela is one of the most important sources of oil consumed in the United States. Other important Latin American oil producers include Mexico, Colombia, Ecuador, and Peru, with new deposits being found every year. Latin America and Canada account for approximately 48 percent of oil imports to the United States. In contrast, the Middle East accounts for approximately 30 percent.

The Galapagos Islands, also called *las islas encantadas* (the enchanted islands), lie 600 miles off the coast of Ecuador. It is believed that the Incas may have traveled to the islands in large ocean-going rafts. In 1835, the naturalist Charles Darwin spent weeks here studying the islands' unique animal life. *Galápagos* are giant tortoises that are native to these islands, which are now a national park and wildlife sanctuary.

Repaso del capítulo

Vocabulario y gramática

Chapter Review

To prepare for the test, check to see if you...
- know the new vocabulary and grammar
- can perform the tasks on p. 175

to talk about breakfast

en el desayuno	for breakfast
el cereal	cereal
el desayuno	breakfast
los huevos	eggs
el pan	bread
el pan tostado	toast
el plátano	banana
la salchicha	sausage
el tocino	bacon
el yogur	yogurt

to talk about lunch

en el almuerzo	for lunch
la ensalada	salad
la ensalada de frutas	fruit salad
las fresas	strawberries
la galleta	cookie
la hamburguesa	hamburger
el jamón	ham
la manzana	apple
las papas fritas	French fries
el perrito caliente	hot dog
la pizza	pizza
el queso	cheese
el sándwich de jamón y queso	ham and cheese sandwich
la sopa de verduras	vegetable soup

to talk about beverages

el agua *f.*	water
el café	coffee
el jugo de manzana	apple juice
el jugo de naranja	orange juice

Más práctica

Practice Workbook Puzzle 3A-8
Practice Workbook Organizer 3A-9

For *Vocabulario adicional,* see pp. 268–269.

la leche	milk
la limonada	lemonade
el refresco	soft drink
el té	tea
el té helado	iced tea

to talk about eating and drinking

beber	to drink
comer	to eat
la comida	food, meal
compartir	to share

to indicate how often

nunca	never
siempre	always
todos los días	every day

to say that you like / love something

Me / te encanta(n) ___.	I / you love ___.
Me / te gusta(n) ___.	I / you like ___.

other useful words

comprender	to understand
con	with
¿Cuál?	Which? What?
más o menos	more or less
por supuesto	of course
¡Qué asco!	How awful!
sin	without
¿Verdad?	Really?, Right?

present tense of *-er* verbs

como	comemos
comes	coméis
come	comen

present tense of *-ir* verbs

comparto	compartimos
compartes	compartís
comparte	comparten

Preparación para el examen

On the exam you will be asked to...	Here are practice tasks similar to those you will find on the exam...	If you need review...
1 Escuchar Listen and understand as people describe what they eat and drink for lunch	Listen as three students describe what they typically eat and drink for lunch. Which is most like the kind of lunch you eat? Did they mention anything you could not buy in your school cafeteria?	**pp. 148–153** *A primera vista* **p. 149** Actividades 1–2 **p. 155** Actividad 8
2 Hablar Tell someone what you typically eat for breakfast and ask the same of others	Your Spanish club is meeting for breakfast before school next week. Find out what other people in your class typically eat for breakfast. After you tell at least two people what you eat for breakfast, ask what they like to eat. Does everyone eat the same kind of breakfast or do you all like to eat different things?	**p. 156** Actividad 10 **p. 157** Actividad 12 **p. 162** Actividades 19–20 **p. 163** Actividad 21 **p. 171** *Presentación oral*
3 Leer Read and understand words that are typically found on menus	You are trying to help a child order from the lunch menu below, but he is very difficult to please. He doesn't like any white food. And he refuses to eat anything that grows on trees. Which items from the menu do you think he would refuse to eat or drink? **ALMUERZO** hamburguesa plátanos pizza manzana ensalada leche	**pp. 148–153** *A primera vista* **p. 159** Actividad 15 **p. 167** Actividad 28 **pp. 168–169** *Lectura*
4 Escribir Write a list of foods that you like and others that you dislike	Your Spanish club is sponsoring a "Super Spanish Saturday." Your teacher wants to know what foods the class likes and dislikes so that the club can buy what most people like. Write the headings *Me gusta(n)* and *No me gusta(n)* in two columns. List at least four items that you like to eat and drink for breakfast and four items for lunch. Then list what you don't like to eat and drink for these same meals.	**p. 155** Actividades 7, 9 **p. 160** Actividad 16 **p. 163** Actividad 21 **p. 164** Actividad 24
5 Pensar Demonstrate an understanding of cultural differences regarding snacks	Think about food combinations in the United States. What combination in Spanish-speaking countries is similar to coffee and doughnuts? Where are you able to buy it?	**p. 170** *La cultura en vivo*

Fondo cultural

Diego Rivera This detail of a mural entitled *La Gran Tenochtitlán* by Mexican artist Diego Rivera (1886–1957) is located in the Palacio Nacional in Mexico City. It shows *el tianguis,* the bustling marketplace at Tenochtitlán, capital of the Aztec Empire. In the foreground there are many kinds of merchandise being traded, including corn and different varieties of beans. This mural is one of many by Rivera that focus on pre-Columbian life and civilizations.

• What impression do you think Rivera is giving about life in a pre-Columbian civilization?

Detalle de *La Gran Tenochtitlán* (1945), Diego Rivera

Detail of mural. Patio Corridor, National Palace, Mexico City, D.F., Mexico. Photo by Robert Frerck, Odyssey Productions, Inc. © Banco de México Diego Rivera & Frida Kahlo Museums Trust. Av. Cinco de Mayo No. 2, Col. Centro Del. Cuautehmoc 06059, México, D.F. Reproduction authorized by the *Instituto Nacional de Bellas Artes y Literatura.*

Para mantener la salud

Chapter Objectives

- Talk about foods and beverages for dinner
- Describe what people or things are like
- Discuss food, health, and exercise choices
- Understand cultural perspectives on diet and health

Video Highlights

A primera vista: *Para mantener la salud*

GramActiva Videos: the plurals of adjectives; the verb *ser*

Country Connection

As you learn about foods and health, you will make connections to these countries and places:

España

México

Guatemala

Costa Rica

Ecuador

Paraguay

Uruguay

Chile

Argentina

Go Online
PHSchool.com

For: Online Atlas
Visit: www.phschool.com
Web Code: jae-0002

Un mercado en Puebla, México

A primera vista

Vocabulario y gramática en contexto

Objectives

Read, listen to, and understand information about
- food groups and foods on the Food Guide Pyramid
- activities to maintain good health
- ways to describe food

La pirámide nutritiva es la forma más práctica de indicar la comida que **debes** comer **cada día. Para mantener la salud,** es importante comer de **todos** los grupos.

el pollo

el bistec

el pescado

la mantequilla

las grasas

la carne   la leche

la cebolla

los guisantes

las papas

las verduras   las frutas

las uvas

los espaguetis

el pan y los cereales

el arroz

66 ¡Me encantan las verduras! Como **muchas** ensaladas con lechuga y tomates. 99

66 También me gustan las zanahorias y las judías verdes. 99

las zanahorias

la lechuga

los tomates

las judías verdes

66 ¡Mi amiga Claudia no come comida buena **para la salud!** Come muchos pasteles y helado. **Son horribles.** 99

el helado

los pasteles

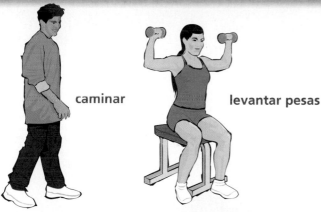

caminar levantar pesas

—¿Qué **haces** para mantener la salud?

—Pues, cada día **hago ejercicio.** Camino, monto en bicicleta y practico deportes.

—¡Uf! **Tengo hambre. ¿Por qué** no comemos **algo** en el restaurante "A tu salud"? Los sándwiches son muy **sabrosos.**

—¡Por supuesto!

Actividad 1 Escuchar

Debes comer...

Your teacher is giving a lecture on foods that you should eat from the Food Guide Pyramid. Touch each item as it is mentioned. You won't understand everything in the sentences, so listen carefully for the names of the foods.

● **Más práctica**
Practice Workbook 3B-1, 3B-2

Actividad 2 Escuchar

Para mantener la salud

Listen to students talk about things they do. Give a "thumbs-up" sign if they are describing things that are healthy and a "thumbs-down" sign if the things are unhealthy.

Go Online
PHSchool.com
For: Vocabulary practice
Visit: www.phschool.com
Web Code: jad-0311

Para mantener la salud

¿Qué hacen Raúl, Tomás y Gloria para mantener la salud?
Lee la historia.

Costa Rica

Raúl

Gloria

Tomás

Antes de leer

Strategy

Using visuals to make predictions Use the pictures
to try to predict what will happen before you read the
story. As you read, predicting what will happen next will
help you understand the story better.

- How did your predictions compare with what you read?

1. Look at photo 1. Does Tomás think that coffee is good for your health?
2. Look at photo 5. What does Tomás do for exercise?
3. Look at photo 6. How is Tomás feeling?

1 **Tomás:** Tengo sed...

Raúl: ¿Qué **prefieres?** ¿Te gusta el café? El café de Costa Rica es muy bueno.

Tomás: ¡Pero el café es **malo** para la salud! **Prefiero** una **bebida** como... un jugo de fruta.

2 **Raúl:** ¡Ah! **Estoy de acuerdo,** un refresco.

Tomás: Raúl, ¿por qué hablas de *refrescos?* A mí me gustan los jugos de fruta.

Gloria: Porque, Tomás, ¡un *refresco* en Costa Rica *es* un jugo de fruta!

3 **Raúl:** Dos refrescos de mango con leche.

Gloria: Y un refresco de mango con agua, por favor.

4 **Tomás:** ¡Es *muuuy* sabroso!

Gloria y Raúl: Sí, sí... ¡y todos los refrescos aquí son buenos para la salud!

Gloria: Tomás, ¿qué haces para mantener la salud?

5 **Tomás:** ¡Me gusta hacer algo cada día! Hago ejercicio, levanto pesas o camino todos los días.

6 **Tomás:** Tengo hambre.
Raúl: ¿Por qué no comemos en la soda?*

*La soda is the word for a casual restaurant in Costa Rica.

7 **Tomás:** La comida aquí es muy buena. Ahora no tengo hambre. ¿Y tú?
Raúl: ¡Creo que no!
Gloria: Pues, **creo que** debemos ir a casa.

8 **Mamá:** ¡A comer **la cena**!
Los jóvenes: ¡Uf!

3 Leer/Escribir

¿Quién dice...?

Number your paper 1–6. Based on what you read in the *Videohistoria*, write the name(s) of the character(s) who would make each of these statements.

1. Prefiero el café de Costa Rica.

2. Creo que es bueno hacer ejercicio.

3. Prefiero jugo de fruta.

4. Creo que los refrescos en Costa Rica son sabrosos.

5. Creo que el café es malo para la salud.

6. No debemos comer la cena.

Raúl

Gloria

Tomás

4 Leer/Escribir

¿Estás de acuerdo?

Read each statement, and write *Cierto* if the statement is true, or *Falso* if it is not. Base your answers on what you read in the *Videohistoria*.

1. Raúl tiene sed.

2. Según Tomás, el café es bueno para la salud.

3. Un refresco en Costa Rica es un jugo de fruta.

4. Gloria bebe un refresco de mango con leche.

5. Tomás nada todos los días.

6. A Tomás no le gusta nada la comida de la soda.

7. Según Gloria, los jóvenes deben ir a casa.

8. La mamá de Raúl y Gloria no prepara *(doesn't prepare)* la cena.

● **Más práctica**

Practice Workbook 3B-3, 3B-4

Go Online
PHSchool.com

For: Vocabulary practice
Visit: www.phschool.com
Web Code: jad-0312

Manos a la obra

Vocabulario y gramática en uso

Objectives

- Talk about dinner foods
- Express food preferences
- Describe people and foods
- Talk about healthy and unhealthy lifestyles
- Learn to use the plurals of adjectives and the verb *ser*

Actividad 5 Leer/Escribir

¡Claro que no!

For each group of words, choose the word or expression that doesn't belong and write it on your paper. Then write one more word or expression that would fit with the group.

Modelo

la cebolla   la lechuga   las uvas
las uvas… las zanahorias

1.	el pollo	el pescado	el arroz
2.	las zanahorias	los pasteles	las judías verdes
3.	caminar	correr	ver la televisión
4.	comer mucho	levantar pesas	hacer ejercicio
5.	los tomates	el pan	los espaguetis
6.	el bistec	las papas	el pollo
7.	la mantequilla	el helado	el pescado

Actividad 6 Escribir/Leer

Juego

① Working in a group, make one large food pyramid identical to the one you see on the right.

② Cut or tear a sheet of paper into ten small pieces, and write the word for one food or drink item on each piece of paper. Exchange the pieces of paper with another group.

③ When your teacher tells you to start, correctly place each of the vocabulary words in the appropriate spot on the food pyramid you have created. The first group to fill in a correct pyramid wins!

las grasas

la carne   la leche

las verduras   las frutas

el pan y los cereales

Fondo cultural

El mate is the national beverage of Argentina, Paraguay, and Uruguay. This herbal tea is shared among family and friends. It is served hot in a hollow gourd, also called *un mate,* with a straw called *una bombilla.*

• What national beverage does the United States have that compares to *mate?*

Actividad 7 **Escribir** •

La fiesta

You and a friend are preparing a surprise meal for your parent's birthday, using what's already in your kitchen. Look in the refrigerator at right, and make a list of eight items that you would use to prepare the meal. Be creative!

Actividad 8 **Hablar** •

¿Qué comemos en la fiesta?

Compare your list from Actividad 7 with your partner's list. Tell your partner what you think you need for the party. Your partner will agree or disagree.

Modelo
A —*Creo que necesitamos queso.*
B —*Estoy de acuerdo. ¡Me encanta!*
o: *No estoy de acuerdo. ¡Qué asco!*

Actividad 9

Escribir

Menú del día

You're in charge of the menu! Decide what you would serve your family for each meal. Copy the chart below on a sheet of paper, and fill in items that you would serve. Be sure to include at least five logical items for each one.

el desayuno	el almuerzo	la cena

Una cena grande con toda la familia

Actividad 10

Pensar/Hablar

¿Sí o no?

With a partner, talk about the things that you should eat and drink in order to be healthy.

Modelo

A —*¿Debo beber leche cada día para mantener la salud?*

B —*Creo que sí.*

o: *Creo que no.*

Estudiante A

Estudiante B

Creo que . . .

Hablar

¿Qué prefieres?

Ask your partner which of two foods he or she prefers. Your partner will answer and ask you which one you prefer.

Modelo

A —¿Qué prefieres, _carne_ o _pescado_?

B —Prefiero _carne_. Y tú, ¿qué prefieres?

o: _No como ni carne ni pescado. Y tú, ¿qué prefieres?_

A —Prefiero _pescado_.

Estudiante A

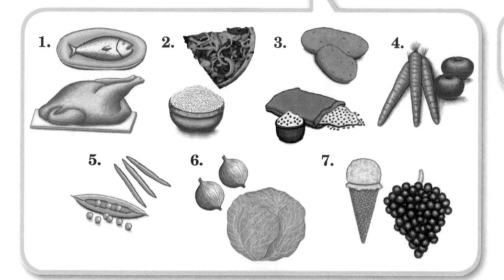

1.
2.
3.
4.
5.
6.
7.

Estudiante B

¡Respuesta personal!

En los supermercados de Texas hay muchas frutas y verduras de México.

Hablar •

¿Hay algo para comer?

Working with a partner, talk about what you should
eat and drink at the following times.

Para decir más...

de la mañana	in the morning
de la tarde	in the afternoon
de la noche	in the evening

 **Modelo**

A —*Son las ocho de la mañana y tengo hambre y sed.
¿Qué debo comer y beber?*
B —*Debes comer cereal y debes beber té.*

Estudiante A

1. 2. 3.

4. 5. 6.

Estudiante B

¡Respuesta personal!

 Leer/Escribir • • • • • • • • • • •

Los buenos consejos

Give advice about what's good or bad
for your health. Copy and complete
each sentence.

1. Para mantener la salud, debes ___
   todos los días.

2. Necesitas beber ___ cada día.

3. Debes comer ___ en la cena.

4. ___ es malo para la salud.

5. El jugo de zanahoria es ___.

6. Debes comer ___ todos los días.

7. Nunca debes comer ___.

 Hablar • • • • • • • • • • • • • • •

Compartir consejos

Compare the advice you gave in Actividad 13
with the advice your partner gave. If you
disagree with your partner's advice, suggest
something else.

Modelo

A —*Para mantener la salud, debes practicar
deportes todos los días.*
B —*Estoy de acuerdo.*
o: *No estoy de acuerdo. Debes correr todos
los días.*

También se dice...

los guisantes = los chícharos *(México);*
las arvejas *(Argentina)*

las papas = las patatas *(España)*

el tomate = el jitomate *(México)*

Leer/Escribir/Hablar •

Un "quiz" para la salud

1 Take the following quiz on healthy activities. Write your answers in complete sentences on a sheet of paper.

¿Qué haces para mantener la salud?

Contesta las preguntas según las actividades que haces cada día. Cada "sí" = 1 punto.

❑ **1.** ¿Haces ejercicio?

❑ **2.** ¿Practicas deportes?

❑ **3.** ¿Comes verduras?

❑ **4.** ¿Comes frutas?

❑ **5.** ¿Caminas o corres?

❑ **6.** ¿Comes un buen desayuno?

❑ **7.** ¿Comes comida que es buena para la salud?

❑ **8.** ¿Bebes cinco vasos* de agua?

❑ **9.** ¿Pasas tiempo con amigos?

❑**10.** ¿No ves más de tres horas de televisión?

> **9–10 puntos** ¡Felicidades! ¡Haces mucho para mantener la salud!
>
> **6–8 puntos** Bueno, pero debes hacer más para mantener la salud.
>
> **0–5 puntos** ¡Ay, ay, ay! Necesitas hacer algo para mantener la salud.

---

*glasses

2 Get together with a partner and ask each other all of the questions on the quiz. Keep track of your partner's *sí* and *no* answers and see how he or she scored.

3 Write five recommendations suggesting what your partner should do every day to have a healthier lifestyle.

Modelo
Debes <u>hacer ejercicio</u> todos los días.

Gramática

The plurals of adjectives

Just as adjectives agree with a noun depending on whether it's masculine or feminine, they also agree according to whether the noun is singular or plural. To make adjectives plural, just add an -s after the vowel at the end of the adjective. If the adjective ends in a consonant, add -es.

La hamburguesa es sabrosa. Las hamburguesas son sabrosas.

El pastel es muy popular. Los pasteles son muy populares.

When an adjective describes a group including both masculine and feminine nouns, use the masculine plural form.

La lechuga, las zanahorias y los tomates son buenos para la salud.

Don't forget that in the singular form, *mucho(a)* means "much," but in the plural form, *muchos(as)* means "many."

No como mucha carne, pero como muchas verduras.

> **¿Recuerdas?**
> Adjectives agree in gender with the masculine or feminine nouns they modify:
> - El bistec es sabroso.
> - La ensalada es sabrosa.

GramActiva VIDEO

Want more help with the the plurals of adjectives? Watch the **GramActiva** video.

hamburguesas sabrosas

16 Gramática   Pensar/Leer/GramActiva

¿Sabroso o sabrosa?

Your teacher will give you a GramActiva worksheet. Tear or cut apart the different adjective stems and endings that are printed on the sheet. Then your teacher will show you pictures of several foods. Show how you feel about each food item by holding up the appropriate adjective stem and the appropriate ending.

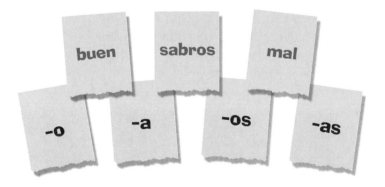

17 Gramática Escribir

Exageramos un poco

Exaggerate a little by rewriting the following sentences in plural form.

Modelo
La hamburguesa es sabrosa.
Todas las hamburguesas son sabrosas.

1. La estudiante es deportista.
2. El helado es muy popular.
3. La bebida es horrible.
4. El pastel es malo para la salud.
5. La fruta es buena para la salud.
6. El refresco es sabroso.

Actividad 18 Gramática Hablar

En el club deportivo

In many parts of Latin America, young people exercise, practice sports, and get together for after-school activities at sports clubs. Work with a partner to describe the following kids who go to the Club Deportivo Águila.

Luis y Ricardo

Estudiante A

Flor y Carlos

Lisa y Pilar

Andrés y Carmen

Marco y Tomás

Paqui y Ramón

Micaela y Luisa

Estudiante B

perezoso	serio
artístico	atrevido
gracioso	talentoso
deportista	

● **Más práctica**

Practice Workbook 3B-5

Go Online
PHSchool.com
For: Practice with plural of adjectives
Visit: www.phschool.com
Web Code: jad-0313

Pronunciación

The letters *l* and *ll*

In Spanish, the letter *l* is pronounced much like the letter *l* in the English word *leaf*. Listen to and say these words:

lechuga	lunes	pasteles	helado
almuerzo	sol	abril	difícil

For most Spanish speakers, the letter combination *ll* is similar to the sound of the letter *y* in *yes*. Listen to and say these words:

llamo	silla	allí	llueve
cebolla	pollo	ella	mantequilla

Try it out!
Listen to this song and then sing it.

Canta el gallo, canta el gallo
con el kiri, kiri, kiri, kiri, kiri;
La gallina, la gallina
con el cara, cara, cara, cara, cara;
Los polluelos, los polluelos
con el pío, pío, pío, pío, pío, pío, pí.

Gramática

The verb *ser*

Ser, which means "to be," is an irregular verb. Use *ser* to describe what a person or thing is like. Here are the present-tense forms:

(yo)	**soy**	(nosotros) (nosotras)	**somos**
(tú)	**eres**	(vosotros) (vosotras)	**sois**
Ud. (él) (ella)	**es**	Uds. (ellos) (ellas)	**son**

¿Recuerdas?

In previous chapters, you learned how to talk about what a person is like.

—Tú **eres** muy deportista, ¿no?

—Sí, **soy** deportista.

—Mi amigo Pablo **es** deportista también.

GramActiva VIDEO

Want more help with the verb *ser*? Watch the **GramActiva** video.

19 Gramática **Escribir**

Amigos deportistas

Juan Pablo thinks that he and his friends are very athletic. Find out why by combining the appropriate phrases. Write the completed sentences on a sheet of paper.

1. Es muy deportista...
2. Somos muy deportistas...
3. Son muy deportistas...
4. Soy muy deportista...
5. Eres muy deportista...

a. porque ellos caminan todos los días.
b. porque yo corro cada tarde.
c. porque ella hace mucho ejercicio.
d. porque tú levantas pesas.
e. porque nosotros nadamos todas las noches.

20 Gramática **Leer/Escribir**

En el mercado de fruta

Rafe's mother is explaining to him how she likes to buy fruit at the local market. Complete her explanation by using the correct form of the verb *ser*. Write your answers on a separate sheet of paper.

Yo __1.__ muy práctica. Me gusta mucho comprar la fruta en el mercado Zarzalejos. La fruta nunca __2.__ mala. Los plátanos __3.__ sabrosos y las fresas __4.__ muy buenas también. La Sra. Zarzalejos y yo __5.__ buenas amigas. Ella trabaja en el mercado y __6.__ muy trabajadora. El Sr. y la Sra. Zarzalejos __7.__ muy simpáticos. Rafe, tú __8.__ muy trabajador, ¿por qué no trabajas en el mercado con ellos en el verano?

Fondo Cultural

Un mercado guatemalteco

Los mercados, or open-air markets, are common throughout Latin America. Many towns have a central market, held on a given day of the week, where people come from all around to buy and sell food, as well as flowers, crafts, and clothing.

- How does this market compare with the ways in which fruits and vegetables are bought in your community?

Actividad 21 Escuchar/Escribir

Escucha y escribe

You will hear comments from five customers about the food being sold in a market. On a sheet of paper, write the numbers 1–5. As you listen, write the comments next to the numbers.

Un mercado de fruta

Actividad 22 Gramática Escribir

En la cafetería

Write eight original sentences to describe the following people and things that you see while eating lunch in the cafeteria. Your sentences all need to make sense!

yo		inteligente	sabroso
el almuerzo		deportista	malo para la salud
las verduras		talentoso	horrible
mis amigos y yo	ser	simpático	perezoso
la leche		popular	bueno para la salud
los profesores			
tú		**¡Respuesta personal!**	
el helado			

Where did it come from?

The names of many foods in Spanish come from Latin as well as from other languages as diverse as Arabic, Italian, Greek, Turkish, and English. While it's clear that the word *espaguetis* comes from the Italian word *spaghetti,* it's not obvious that the word *zanahoria* comes from the Arabic word *safunariya.*

Try it out! Read the Spanish words on the left and match them up to their counterparts in their language of origin on the right.

agua	*piscatu* (Latin)
arroz	*aqua* (Latin)
pan	*beefsteak* (English)
bistec	*pane* (Latin)
salchichas	*pullu* (Latin)
pescado	*kahvé* (Turkish)
café	*salciccia* (Italian)
pollo	*óryza* (Greek)

Actividad 23 **Gramática** **Hablar**

¿Sabroso u horrible?

Work with a partner and express your opinions on various foods and beverages.

Modelo

A —¿Comes zanahorias en la cena?
B —No, no como zanahorias en la cena porque son horribles.
o: Sí, como zanahorias en la cena porque son buenas para la salud.

Estudiante A

Estudiante B

(muy) sabroso
bueno para la salud
malo para la salud
horrible

¡Respuesta personal!

1.  2. 3. 4.

5. 6. 7. 8.

9. 10. 11.

Fondo cultural

La Tomatina How would you like to attend a festival where a gigantic food fight with tomatoes is the highlight of the day? That's what happens at the annual *Fiesta de la Tomatina* in Buñol, Spain. After the town council distributes more than 130 tons of ripe tomatoes to participants, the two-hour-long tomato-throwing festival begins.

• Describe any festivals unique to your community or your state. How do they compare to *La Tomatina*?

La Tomatina en Buñol, España

Actividad 24

Leer/Escribir •

En el festival

Your friend Juanito has just attended the *Tomatina* festival and has written a postcard to tell you all about it. However, there were so many tomatoes flying around that some got on the postcard, and now you have to figure out what it says.

1 Number your paper 1–5 and write the forms of the verb *ser* that best complete the postcard.

2 Write your own postcard to a friend and describe people you know and things you are familiar with. Use Juanito's postcard as a model.

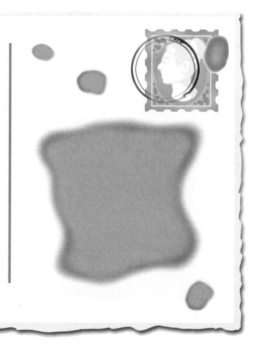

¡Hola!

Estoy en la Fiesta de la Tomatina en España. El festival __1.__ muy divertido. Yo __2.__ amigo de unos estudiantes en la escuela en Buñol. Nosotros __3.__ atrevidos y participamos[1] todos los años. Creo que los tomates __4.__ horribles. ¡No me gustan nada! Nunca como tomates, prefiero tirarlos.[2] Tú __5.__ atrevido, ¿verdad? Debes visitar Buñol.

Hasta pronto,

Juanito

[1]we participate   [2]to throw them

Actividad 25 **Leer/Escribir**

Una pizza para la buena salud

Read this ad for pizza and answer the
questions that follow.

Pizzería Lilia
¡Pizzas saludables!

A veces la pizza tiene muchas
calorías y grasas que no son
buenas para la salud.

La Pizzería Lilia tiene una variedad
de pizzas con ingredientes
que son buenos y saludables.

◆ Menos queso
◆ Usamos ingredientes nutritivos
  •Más verduras (tienen pocas calorías
   y son muy nutritivas)
◆ Evita[1] la combinación de carnes
  •Las carnes tienen mucho sodio y grasas
  •El pollo o el jamón es mejor[2] que
   las salchichas

¡Llámanos!
¡Estamos aquí para servirte!
372 42 89
Calle Independencia 28

[1]Avoid   [2]better

1. Find and list three cognates in this ad.
2. Write three recommendations for a healthier pizza.

Actividad 26 **Escribir/Hablar**

Y tú, ¿qué dices?

1. ¿Qué prefieres en tu pizza, cebolla o pollo?
2. Describe tu pizza favorita.
3. ¿Crees que la pizza es buena o mala
   para la salud? ¿Por qué?
4. ¿Qué verduras prefieres? ¿Qué verduras
   no te gustan?
5. ¿Qué comes cuando tienes hambre?

Rick Bayless's career as a world-class Mexican chef began at the age of 14, when he visited Mexico and decided to study Spanish. Since 1978, Rick has opened gourmet Mexican restaurants, created and starred in cooking shows, written cookbooks, and won many awards.

- How would Rick's Spanish skills be helpful in his career?

Para decir más...

doscientos	two hundred	**seiscientos**	six hundred
trescientos	three hundred	**setecientos**	seven hundred
cuatrocientos	four hundred	**ochocientos**	eight hundred
quinientos	five hundred	**novecientos**	nine hundred

Actividad 27

Leer/Escribir

Las calorías y la salud

Conexiones

La salud

You've probably noticed that the nutritional labels on the bottle of juice that you drink, the energy bar that you eat, or even the gum that you chew all have a listing for calories. Our bodies burn calories even when we are sleeping. We can burn more or fewer calories depending on how much we weigh and what kind of activities we do. Look at the chart at right and answer the questions that follow.

Promedio[1] de calorías quemadas[2] en una hora de ejercicio

Actividad	Peso[3] 55–59 kg	Peso 77–82 kg
Básquetbol	170–515	400–800
Bailar	115–400	160–560
Correr 10 km/h	575	800
Fútbol	290–690	400–960
Nadar	230–690	320–900
Tenis	230–515	320–720
Caminar 6 km/h	250	340

[1]Average [2]burned (*quemar* = to burn) [3]weight

1. ¿En qué actividad quemas más calorías si pesas (*you weigh*) 78 kilogramos?

2. Pablo nada por una hora y Paco corre por una hora. Ellos queman el máximo (*maximum*) número de calorías. ¿Quién quema más calorías?

3. Tú pesas 55 kg. Bailas por dos horas y quemas el máximo número de calorías. ¿Cuántas quemas?

4. Una barra de chocolate (*chocolate bar*) tiene 320 calorías. Pesas 59 kg. ¿Por cuántos minutos tienes que caminar para quemar las calorías? ¿Es mucho?

● **Más práctica**
Practice Workbook 3B-6, 3B-7

Go Online PHSchool.com
For: Practice with *ser*
Visit: www.phschool.com
Web Code: jad-0314

¡Adelante!

Objectives

- Read about a sports diet and learn some facts about an athlete
- Understand about cultural perspectives on healthcare
- Make a poster about good health habits
- Learn facts about the southern part of South America

Lectura

La comida de los atletas

Lee este artículo *(article)* de una revista deportiva. ¿Qué comen y qué beben los atletas profesionales para mantener la salud y estar en buena forma?

Strategy

Skimming
List three things that you would expect to find in an article about athletes' eating habits. Skim the article to find the information.

¿Qué come un jugador de fútbol?

Los jugadores[1] de fútbol comen comidas equilibradas con muchos carbohidratos, minerales y vitaminas. Ellos consumen cerca de 5.000 calorías en total todos los días.

17% Proteínas

13% Grasas

70% Carbohidratos

Para el desayuno el día de un partido,[2] un jugador típico come mucho pan con mantequilla y jalea,[3] yogur y té.

Para el almuerzo antes del[4] partido, come pan, pasta, pollo sin grasa, verduras, frutas y una ensalada.

Para la cena después del[5] partido, el atleta come papas, carne sin grasa y más verduras y frutas.

También es muy importante beber muchos líquidos. La noche antes del partido, el jugador bebe un litro de jugo de naranja y durante el partido bebe hasta[6] dos litros de agua y bebidas deportivas.

[1]players [2]game [3]jam [4]before the [5]after the [6]up to

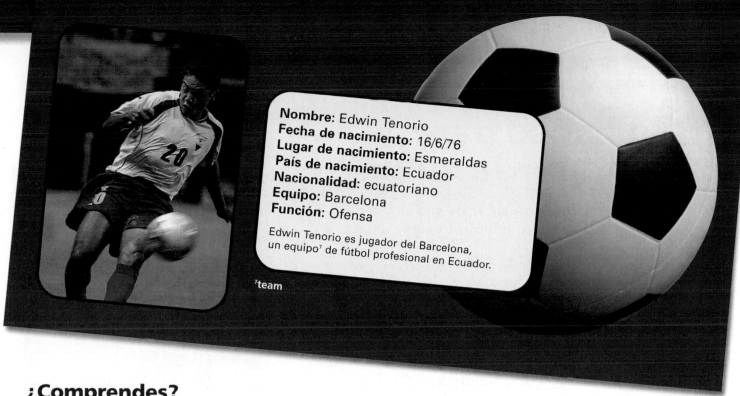

Nombre: Edwin Tenorio
Fecha de nacimiento: 16/6/76
Lugar de nacimiento: Esmeraldas
País de nacimiento: Ecuador
Nacionalidad: ecuatoriano
Equipo: Barcelona
Función: Ofensa

Edwin Tenorio es jugador del Barcelona, un equipo⁷ de fútbol profesional en Ecuador.

⁷team

¿Comprendes?

1. ¿Qué debe comer Edwin Tenorio antes de un partido de fútbol?

2. ¿Qué debe beber?

3. ¿Qué comida no debe comer Edwin?

4. ¿Es tu dieta diferente de la dieta de un jugador de fútbol profesional? ¿Cómo?

5. ¿Cuál es la fecha de nacimiento (birth date) de Edwin? Escribe tu fecha de nacimiento como lo hacen en los países hispanohablantes.

Go Online
PHSchool.com
For: Internet link activity
Visit: www.phschool.com
Web Code: jad-0315

Fondo cultural

¡Goooooooooooool! Scoring the winning *gol* is the most exciting moment of the game. *El fútbol* is the most popular sport in the world, and it has many *fanáticos* (fans) in every Spanish-speaking country. Every four years, teams throughout the world compete regionally in order to become one of the 32 teams to advance to the World Cup *(la Copa Mundial)* competition. Many Spanish-speaking countries compete in what has become the most widely watched sporting event in the world. Since the competition began in 1930, two Spanish-speaking countries have won the World Cup competition: Uruguay in 1930 and 1950 and Argentina in 1978 and 1986.

• How does the enthusiasm for soccer in the United States compare with the rest of the world's view of this sport? Why do you think this is so?

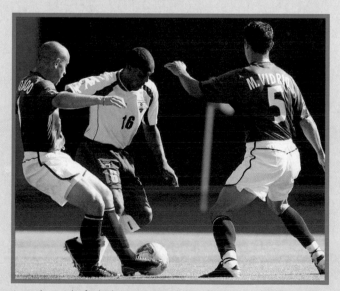

Jugadores de fútbol

¿Qué haces para mantener la salud?

Have you ever eaten chicken soup when you have a cold? How about putting aloe on a sunburn? In many countries, including those in the Spanish-speaking world, traditional remedies consisting of medicinal herbs have been used for centuries to treat common medical problems. In Mexico, a mint known as *yerbabuena* may be made into tea and given to someone with a stomachache. Remedies such as these may not be prescribed by licensed physicians, but people have confidence in them because they have been passed down through the generations. Many of those herbs are very safe, though some may have harmful side effects.

Researchers are studying traditional herbal remedies to find modern-day medical solutions. In the Amazon rainforest in South America, an amazing abundance of plant life may hold the key to treating a wide variety of common ailments and diseases. Drug companies are looking for cures found in these plants and herbs that could be reproduced in today's modern drugs.

En la selva de Amazonas, Perú

Increasingly, medicinal herbs are accepted not only as the basis for pharmaceutical drugs, but also for their own inherent healing qualities. In many countries, including the United States, herbal remedies are sometimes used in combination with conventional healthcare.

Check it out! What alternatives to conventional medical care are available in your community? Make a list of all the healthcare services you can think of that are not traditional physicians. Are there health stores that sell herbal medicines? What types of herbal medicines are being sold and what remedies are attributed to these medicines?

Think about it! In many Spanish-speaking cultures, herbal remedies have been accepted for centuries. Do you think that medicinal herbs can provide relief and cures? Why or why not?

En un mercado en la Ciudad de México

Para mantener la salud

Task
You are doing some research for your health class on good eating and exercise habits. Make a poster in Spanish with five suggestions for better health.

1 Prewrite Talk to classmates, teachers, the school nurse, your parents, and so on, about good eating and exercise habits, especially for teens. Then list their ideas under the following headings to help you organize your information:

- Debes comer…
- Debes beber…
- No debes comer mucho(a)…
- No debes beber mucho(a)…
- Debes _____ para mantener la salud.

> **Strategy**
>
> **Gathering information**
> Gathering information from a variety of sources helps you create a more complete presentation on a topic.

2 Draft Write the first draft. Decide how to present the information in a logical manner. Think about using visuals for clarity. Sketch them on your draft. Give the poster a title.

3 Revise Share your draft with a partner. Your partner should check the following:

- Have you communicated the five suggestions well?
- Do the visuals help convey meaning and make the poster attractive?
- Are the vocabulary and grammar correct?

Decide whether to use your partner's suggestions, and then rewrite your poster.

4 Publish Make a final copy, adding attractive illustrations or designs and making necessary changes. You might want to:

- post it in the nurse's office, at a local community center, or in your classroom
- include it in your portfolio

5 Evaluation Your teacher may give you a rubric for how the poster will be graded. You probably will be graded on:

- completion of task
- accuracy of vocabulary and grammar
- effective use of visuals

América del Sur

Parte sur

A large proportion of the people of Argentina, Uruguay, and Chile live in cities. As in the United States, these cities have been shaped by mass immigration from southern and eastern Europe during the nineteenth and twentieth centuries. Many more Paraguayans, in contrast, live in the countryside.

In the early 1900s, the area of *las cataratas de Iguazú* was made an Argentine national park. Three countries—Brazil, Argentina, and Paraguay—meet at these spectacular falls, which are four times the width of Niagara Falls and 50 percent higher. Hundreds of species of insects, birds, and mammals are found in the area, and at least 500 species of butterflies. As many as 15,000 tourists a day visit the falls, a worrisome number for environmental groups, who continue to lobby against nearby hotel construction projects.

¿Sabes que . . . ?

At 22,840 feet (7,021 meters), Argentina's Cerro Aconcagua is the highest point in the Western Hemisphere, but it is considered a relatively easy climb. Chile's Torres del Paine, three granite towers, are nearly 6,000 feet lower, but their sheer cliffs, high winds, and extreme cold make them some of the most challenging climbs in the world. Both mountains are part of the Andes, a range that extends from Colombia to the southern tip of South America.

Para pensar

Think about what it would be like to be an immigrant arriving in one of the countries of southern South America. Would you prefer the city life of Buenos Aires, Argentina, Montevideo, Uruguay, or Santiago, Chile? Or would the countryside of Paraguay be more appealing? Why?

Go Online PHSchool.com

For: Online Atlas
Visit: www.phschool.com
Web Code: jae-0002

The Spanish were able to topple large, centralized empires such as those of the Aztecs and Incas quickly, but they were never able to conquer the smaller indigenous groups in the more remote regions. Chile's Pehuenche suffered defeats in the nineteenth century, but they still struggle to maintain their lands and culture. ▶

Spain introduced horses, cows, sheep, and pigs to the Americas in the sixteenth century, transforming the ecology, culture, and economy of the region. In the nineteenth century, the growth of cities, the expansion of railways, and improvements in shipping created a worldwide market for South American meat and hides—and helped spur the development of the cowboy culture throughout the Americas. As on ranches in the western United States and northern Mexico, the main house of an Argentine or Uruguayan *estancia* served as a residence, office, and military stronghold.

With its wide boulevards, parks, museums, and diverse cultural life, Buenos Aires is considered one of the most cosmopolitan cities in the world. Argentina has produced world-class writers such as Jorge Luis Borges, Julio Cortázar, and José Hernández, who wrote a classic about the life of the *gauchos*. The tango, the first dance from Latin America to gain international popularity, is a favorite of the *porteños*—the residents of Buenos Aires.

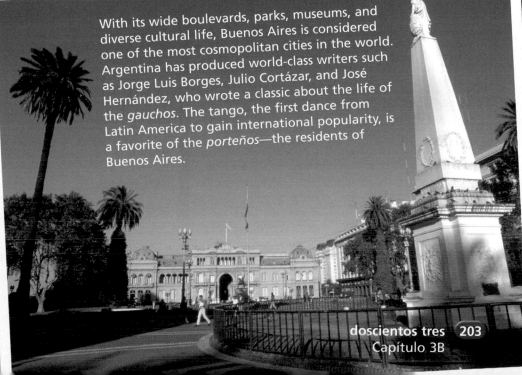

Repaso del capítulo

Vocabulario y gramática

Chapter Review

To prepare for the test, check to see if you . . .
- know the new vocabulary and grammar
- can perform the tasks on p. 205

to talk about food and beverages

la cena	dinner
el bistec	beefsteak
la carne	meat
el pescado	fish
el pollo	chicken
la cebolla	onion
los guisantes	peas
las judías verdes	green beans
la lechuga	lettuce
las papas	potatoes
los tomates	tomatoes
las uvas	grapes
las zanahorias	carrots
el arroz	rice
los cereales	grains
los espaguetis	spaghetti
las grasas	fats
la mantequilla	butter
el helado	ice cream
los pasteles	pastries
las bebidas	beverages

to talk about being hungry and thirsty

Tengo hambre.	I'm hungry.
Tengo sed.	I'm thirsty.

to discuss health

caminar	to walk
hacer ejercicio	to exercise
(yo) hago	I do
(tú) haces	you do
levantar pesas	to lift weights
para la salud	for one's health
para mantener la salud	to maintain one's health

For *Vocabulario adicional*, see pp. 268–269.

to indicate a preference

(yo) prefiero	I prefer
(tú) prefieres	you prefer
deber	should, must

to indicate agreement or disagreement

Creo que...	I think (that)...
Creo que sí / no.	I (don't) think so.
(No) estoy de acuerdo.	I (don't) agree.

to express a question or an answer

¿Por qué?	Why?
porque	because

to express quantity

algo	something
muchos, -as	many
todos, -as	all

to describe something

horrible	horrible
malo, -a	bad
sabroso, -a	tasty, flavorful

other useful words

cada día	every day

plurals of adjectives

Masculine	Feminine
Singular/Plural	Singular/Plural
sabroso/sabrosos	sabrosa/sabrosas
popular/populares	popular/populares

ser *to be*

soy	somos
eres	sois
es	son

● **Más práctica**

Practice Workbook Puzzle 3B-8
Practice Workbook Organizer 3B-9

Preparación para el examen

On the exam you will be asked to...	Here are practice tasks similar to those you will find on the exam...	If you need review...
1 Escuchar Listen and understand as people describe a healthy or unhealthy lifestyle	Listen as two people are interviewed about their habits. See if you can tell which one is an Olympic skier and which one is a drummer. Be prepared to explain your "educated guesses."	**pp. 178–183** *A primera vista* **p. 179** Actividad 2
2 Hablar Express your opinion about food preferences	During a telephone survey, you are asked some questions in Spanish about your food preferences. Say whether you think each food choice is good or bad for your health.	**p. 187** Actividad 11 **p. 188** Actividades 12, 14 **p. 194** Actividad 23 **p. 197** Actividad 27
3 Leer Read and compare what people do and eat in order to determine whether they lead a healthy or unhealthy lifestyle	Read the online conversation that you have just joined in a chat room. Decide whether each person has a healthy or unhealthy lifestyle, based on what they tell each other. Chato: *¿Qué hago yo? Cuando hace buen tiempo, corro por treinta minutos. Cuando llueve, levanto pesas.* Chispa: *No me gusta hacer ejercicio. Prefiero comer papas fritas. Son muy sabrosas.* Andrés: *¿Papas fritas? Son horribles para la salud. Para mantener la salud, nunca debes comer papas fritas.*	**pp. 178–183** *A primera vista* **p. 188** Actividad 13 **p. 189** Actividad 15 **p. 196** Actividad 25 **pp. 198–199** *Lectura*
4 Escribir Write a list of things a person should do to maintain a healthy lifestyle	Many people think that teens don't know anything about a healthy lifestyle. You and your friends are compiling a top-ten list of ways to improve teens' health. Write at least three suggestions for the list.	**p. 188** Actividad 13 **p. 189** Actividad 15 **p. 196** Actividad 25 **p. 201** *Presentación escrita*
5 Pensar Demonstrate an understanding of cultural perspectives regarding healthcare	Give an example of an herbal remedy that is accepted in a Spanish-speaking country as a remedy for a common ailment. Compare this with a similar herbal/natural remedy believed by many in the United States to be a cure for a common ailment.	**p. 200** *Perspectivas del mundo hispano*

Fondo cultural

El quitasol is a work by Spanish painter Francisco de Goya (1746–1828). He made this painting in 1777 as a design to be used in the manufacture of a royal tapestry. At that time Goya was already famous for the elegance of his artwork and his ability to capture ordinary events in realistic detail. The brilliant colors of this painting suggest a happy moment of relaxation for two young people.

• Why do people who live in the city go out to the country to relax?

El quitasol (1777), Francisco de Goya

Oil on canvas, 104 x 152 cm. Museo Nacional del Prado, Madrid, Spain.
Photo Credit: Scala / Art Resource, NY.

En la Gran Vía de Madrid, España

¿Adónde vas?

Chapter Objectives

- Talk about locations in your community
- Discuss leisure activities
- Talk about where you go and with whom
- Learn how to ask questions
- Understand cultural perspectives on leisure activities

Video Highlights

A primera vista: *Un chico reservado*

GramActiva Videos: the verb *ir;* asking questions

Country Connection

As you learn about leisure activities, you will make connections to these countries and places:

California   Texas   España
                  Illinois
Arizona   Luisiana
                      Florida
México   Puerto Rico
Nuevo México   Venezuela
Honduras   Colombia
Ecuador
Perú   Bolivia
Chile   Argentina

Go Online
PHSchool.com

For: Online Atlas
Visit: www.phschool.com
Web Code: jae-0002

A primera vista

Vocabulario y gramática en contexto

el gimnasio

el parque

el centro comercial

ir de compras

el trabajo

la lección de piano

el cine

ver una película

la biblioteca

la piscina

—En tu **tiempo libre después de** las clases, ¿qué haces?

   —**Voy al** gimnasio **para** levantar pesas y al parque para correr. ¿Y tú?

—Hoy voy **a** mi trabajo. No voy a mi lección de piano.

—**¿Con quién** vas al centro comercial?

   —Voy con Guillermo, y **después vamos** al cine. ¿Y tú?

—Voy a la biblioteca para estudiar. Después voy al **Café** del Mundo con Lucila.

la playa

el restaurante

el campo

las montañas

—¿Qué haces **los** domingos?

    —Voy **con mis amigos** a la playa. Allí comemos el almuerzo. Hay un restaurante muy bueno. ¿Y tú?

—**Generalmente** voy al campo o a las montañas.

> ### Más vocabulario
> **la iglesia** church
> **la mezquita** mosque
> **la sinagoga** synagogue
> **el templo** temple; Protestant church

 Actividad 1   Escuchar · · · · · · · · ·

¿Estás de acuerdo?

You will hear Elena describe where she does seven activities. If a statement is logical, give a "thumbs-up" sign. If it is not logical, give a "thumbs-down" sign.

 Actividad 2   Escuchar · · · · · · · · ·

¡Muchas actividades!

Listen to Antonio describe his weekly list of after-school activities. As he names his activities, touch the corresponding picture(s).

● **Más práctica** · · · · · · · · · · · · · ·
Practice Workbook 4A-1, 4A-2

Go Online
PHSchool.com
For: Vocabulary practice
Visit: www.phschool.com
Web Code: jad-0401

Un chico reservado

¿Qué pasa cuando Ignacio, Elena y Ana hablan con el estudiante nuevo *(new)?* Lee la historia.

España

Ignacio

Ana

Elena

Javier

Antes de leer

Strategy

Using visuals You can use visuals to predict what might happen in a story.

• Use the photos in the *Videohistoria* to predict what different activities Ana, Elena, Ignacio, and Javier are talking about. Then, look in the dialogues and find the corresponding word or phrase that describes each activity.

1. Does your school get many new students each year? If so, do you make a point to get to know them? Can you tell from the photos which person is the new student at this school?

2. What do you usually do after school? Do you have the same routine, or do your activities vary? Use the photos to compare the activities that these students participate in with your own pastimes.

1 Ignacio: Mira, el estudiante nuevo es un poco reservado, ¿verdad?

Elena: Ah sí... Está allí **solo.** ¿Por qué no hablamos con él?

Ignacio: Sí, ¡vamos!

2 Elena: Hola. Me llamo Elena. Él es Ignacio, y ella es Ana.

Javier: Mucho gusto. Me llamo Javier.

Elena: Encantada... **¿De dónde eres?**

Javier: Soy **de** Salamanca.

3 Ana: Pues, Javier, ¿vas después de las clases **con tus amigos?**

Javier: No, voy **a casa.**

4 Javier: **¿Adónde** vais* vosotros después de las clases?

Elena: Los lunes, miércoles y viernes voy a mi trabajo en el centro comercial.

Ignacio: Generalmente voy al gimnasio. Me gusta levantar pesas.

*Remember that in Spain, the *vosotros(as)* form of the verb is used when speaking to a group of people you would address individually with *tú.*

5 Ana: Los lunes voy a mi lección de piano y los martes, miércoles y jueves voy a la biblioteca para estudiar. Y Javier, ¿qué haces **los fines de semana?**

6 Javier: ¿Los fines de semana? **Me quedo en casa.** No tengo muchos amigos aquí.

Ignacio: ¿Qué te gusta hacer?

Javier: ¡Me gusta el fútbol!

7 Ana: ¡No me digas! Pues, nosotros vamos al parque para practicar fútbol.

Javier: ¿Cuándo?

Ana: El sábado.

Javier: Está bien.

8 Elena: Pero Ana, ¿fútbol?

Ana: ¿Por qué no? ¡No tiene muchos amigos y le gusta el fútbol!

Actividad 3 · **Leer/Escribir** ·

¿Comprendes?

Number your paper 1–6. Based on the *Videohistoria,* choose the response that best completes each statement below. Write the completed sentences on your paper.

1. Javier es de . . .
   a. Madrid.
   b. Barcelona.
   c. Salamanca.

2. Después de las clases Javier va . . .
   a. a la biblioteca para estudiar.
   b. a casa.
   c. al cine.

3. Después de las clases Ignacio va . . .
   a. al gimnasio.
   b. al centro comercial.
   c. al restaurante.

4. El jueves Ana va . . .
   a. a la lección de piano.
   b. a la biblioteca.
   c. a la iglesia.

5. A Javier le gusta practicar . . .
   a. el fútbol.
   b. el golf.
   c. el español.

6. Todos van al parque el . . .
   a. martes.
   b. jueves.
   c. sábado.

Actividad 4 · **Leer/Escribir** ·

La rutina de los estudiantes

You are trying to organize everybody's schedule. Copy the chart below onto a sheet of paper. Based on information in the *Videohistoria,* write what each person does on the various days of the week. Not all of the spaces on the chart will be filled.

	Ignacio	Elena	Ana	Javier
lunes				
martes				
miércoles				
jueves				
viernes				
sábado				
domingo				

● **Más práctica** · · · · · · · · · · · · · · · ·
Practice Workbook 4A-3, 4A-4

Go Online
PHSchool.com
For: Vocabulary practice
Visit: www.phschool.com
Web Code: jad-0402

Manos a la obra
Vocabulario y gramática en uso

Objectives
- Communicate about leisure activities
- Tell where you go and with whom
- Learn to use the verb *ir* and how to ask questions

Escribir

¿Qué haces en . . . ?

Using the pictures at right, complete the following sentences logically. Write the completed sentences on your paper.

1. Hago ejercicio en . . .
2. Nado en . . .
3. Veo películas en . . .
4. Leo libros y revistas en . . .
5. Esquío en . . .
6. Como el desayuno en . . .

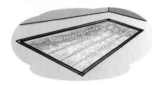

¡Respuesta personal!

Escribir

¿Vas mucho a . . . ?

On a sheet of paper, copy the diagram below and write the names of the places you go under the appropriate time expressions.

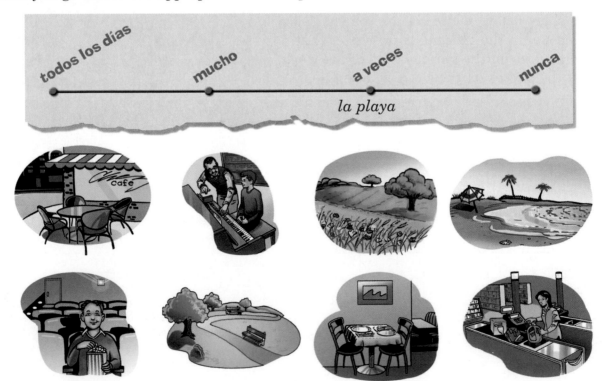

Hablar •

Actividad 7

¡No me digas!

Work with a partner. Using what you wrote for Actividad 6, take turns saying where you go and how often. React to your partner's statements. Follow the model.

Modelo

A —*Voy a la playa a veces.*
B —*¡No me digas! Yo voy a la playa a veces también.*
o: *¡No me digas! Yo nunca voy a la playa.*
o: *Pues, yo voy a la playa todos los días.*

 Nota

When *a* is used before *el,* the two words form the contraction *al (to the):*

$$a + el = al$$

• Voy **al** centro comercial a veces pero voy **a la** piscina mucho.

También se dice...

la piscina = la alberca *(México);* la pileta *(América del Sur)*

el restaurante = el restaurán *(América del Sur)*

  Escuchar/Escribir •

Actividad 8

Escucha y escribe

Look at this painting of Plaza Morazán in Tegucigalpa. You will hear six statements about the painting. Number your paper from 1–6 and write what you hear.

Fondo cultural

La Plaza Strolling through the main square, *la plaza,* of most towns and cities in Spanish-speaking countries is a popular activity for young and old alike. Plaza Morazán is the main square in Tegucigalpa, the capital city of Honduras. The square is named after Francisco Morazán (1792–1842), a Honduran general and head of state.

• What social gathering place in your community is similar to *la plaza?*

Plaza Morazán en Tegucigalpa (1969), José Antonio Velásquez

Origins of the Spanish days of the week

The word *sábado,* like many Spanish words, is based on Latin. The Spanish days of the week come from the Latin names for the gods, planets, sun, and moon, all of which were important in Roman daily life.

Try it out! Match the Spanish days of the week with their Latin origins.

1. lunes	**a.** *dies Mercurii:* named after Mercury, the god of commerce and travelers
2. martes	**b.** *dies Veneris:* named after Venus, the goddess of beauty and love
3. miércoles	**c.** *dies lunae:* the day dedicated to the moon *(luna)*
4. jueves	**d.** *dies solis:* named after the sun *(sol),* but later changed to *dies Dominicus,* which means "the Lord's day"
5. viernes	**e.** *dies Martis:* dedicated to Mars, the god of war
6. sábado	**f.** *dies Saturni:* named after Saturn; also called *dies Sabbati,* based on the Hebrew word *shabbath,* or "day of rest"
7. domingo	**g.** *dies Jovis:* named after Jove, or Jupiter, the ruler of the gods

- Since you know *día* means "day" in Spanish, what is the word for "day" in Latin?

Actividad 9

Hablar

¿Adónde vas?

With a partner, talk about the places you go at different times during the week.

Modelo

los lunes

A —¿Adónde vas <u>los lunes</u>?

B —Generalmente voy <u>a la lección de piano.</u>

o: Generalmente <u>me quedo en casa.</u>

 Nota

To say that something usually happens on a certain day every week, use *los* with the plural of the day of the week:

- Generalmente ellos van al campo **los viernes** o **los sábados.**

Estudiante A

1. los miércoles
2. los viernes
3. los sábados
4. los domingos
5. los fines de semana
6. después de las clases

Estudiante B

¡Respuesta personal!

Actividad 10
Pensar/Hablar •

Leer un mapa no es difícil

When you visit a new city or town in a Spanish-speaking country, you will often use a map to help you get to where you want to go. Although maps may vary from place to place, you will usually find some standard features that will help you find your way around. You should always look for the key (*la clave*). This will give you the symbols and other information that you need to read the map. Some maps are set up as a grid so that you can use an index to help you find streets or places of interest.

Conexiones
La geografía

You are visiting Madrid. With a partner, take turns asking and answering where you are going, based on the grid locations and the map.

1. F4   **2.** B7   **3.** E1   **4.** B8   **5.** E9   **6.** C10

Modelo

D9
A —*Estoy en D9. ¿Adónde voy?*
B —*Vas al restaurante.*

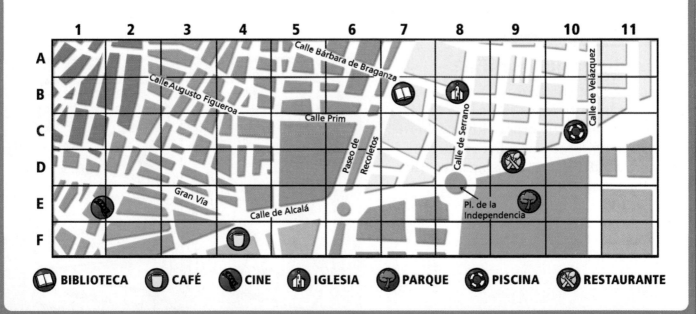

BIBLIOTECA   CAFÉ   CINE   IGLESIA   PARQUE   PISCINA   RESTAURANTE

Actividad 11
Escribir/Hablar •

Y tú, ¿qué dices?

1. ¿Dónde ves más películas, en casa o en el cine?

2. Cuando vas de compras, ¿adónde vas?

3. ¿Adónde vas los fines de semana? ¿Vas solo(a) o con tus amigos?

Gramática

The verb *ir*

To say where someone is going, use the verb *ir*. Here are its present-tense forms:

(yo)	**voy**	(nosotros) (nosotras)	**vamos**
(tú)	**vas**	(vosotros) (vosotras)	**vais**
Ud. (él) (ella)	**va**	Uds. (ellos) (ellas)	**van**

The verb *ir* is almost always followed by *a*. To ask where someone is going, use *¿Adónde?*

¿Adónde vas? *Where are you going?*

• You will often hear people say *¡Vamos!* This means, "Let's go!"

¿Recuerdas?

You have used the infinitive *ir* to talk about going to school.

• Me gusta **ir** a la escuela.

GramActiva VIDEO

Want more help with the verb *ir*? Watch the **GramActiva** video.

Voy al cine.

12 (Gramática) Escribir

¿Adónde va la familia?

The members of the Li family are always busy. They have to leave messages on the refrigerator to let the others know where they are going. Find out where everyone is going by putting the messages together. Write the complete sentences on a separate sheet of paper.

Actividad 13

Gramática **Leer/Escribir**

Chile

Un año en Chile

María, a student from Corpus Christi, Texas, is spending a year with a family in Santiago, Chile. Read the letter that she wrote to her friends back home and write the correct forms of the verb *ir* on a separate sheet of paper.

17 de julio

Querida Sonia,

¿Cómo estás? Yo, bien. Generalmente, paso tiempo en casa los fines de semana, pero a veces yo __1.__ a Portillo con mi familia para esquiar. Hace mucho frío allí y por eso la mamá no __2.__ siempre con nosotros. En Portillo hay una escuela para los esquiadores y muchos chicos simpáticos __3.__ a las lecciones. También hay un cibercafé con computadoras. Muchas personas __4.__ allí para pasar tiempo con los amigos. Nosotros __5.__ el domingo. Y tú, ¿ __6.__ a la playa todos los días con tus amigos?

Hasta luego,

María

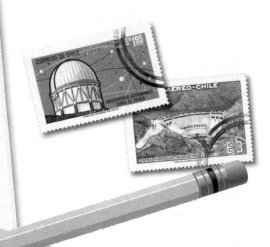

Actividad 14

Gramática **Leer/Hablar**

La carta

Read the letter in Actividad 13 again and answer the following questions about María's experience in Chile.

1. ¿Quién no va siempre con la familia a Portillo?
2. ¿Por qué a María le gusta ir a las lecciones de esquí?
3. ¿Adónde van para usar las computadoras?
4. ¿Cuándo van al cibercafé?
5. ¿Adónde van muchas personas para pasar tiempo con los amigos?

Esquiadores en Portillo, Chile

¿Adónde van todos?

Look at the pictures below. Number your paper 1–6 and, using the places in the word bank, write complete sentences telling where the following people are going.

Elena

Elena va a la biblioteca.

la piscina	el cine	la biblioteca
el restaurante	el centro comercial	el parque
el gimnasio		

1.

Luis

2.

yo

3.

Carlitos y Sandrina

4.

nosotros

5.

tú

6.

Uds.

¿Por qué van allí?

Where you go often depends on what you like to do. Using the sentences you wrote in Actividad 15, explain why the people go to those places.

Elena va a la biblioteca porque lee muchos libros.

Actividad 17 **Gramática** **Hablar** •

Voy allí porque me gusta...

Choose five of the following places. Working in pairs, ask your partner if he or she goes there and why.

Modelo

A —¿Vas al café?

B —Sí, por supuesto.

o: Claro que no.

A —¿Por qué (no) vas al café?

B —Voy porque me gusta pasar tiempo con mis amigos.

o: No voy porque no me gusta beber café.

Estudiante A

el café	la casa
la playa	el cine
la biblioteca	la escuela
las montañas	el centro comercial
el parque	el restaurante

Estudiante B

comer	ver
beber	hablar
pasar tiempo	comprar
con mis amigos	nadar
estudiar	esquiar
leer	

¡Respuesta personal!

Fondo cultural ■ ■ ◆ ◆ ◇ ◆ ◆ ◆

Estudiantes en el gimnasio

Sports clubs and gyms are very popular in Spanish-speaking countries. Since there are few school-based sports teams, many young people join private gyms for individual exercise, or play for privately sponsored teams, in order to compete in their favorite sports.

• What do you think students would do if your school did not offer opportunities for playing and competing in sports?

Actividad 18 · Gramática · Escribir/Hablar

Juego

1 With a partner, write five sentences telling what the two of you do in your free time and when. On a separate sheet of paper, write sentences telling where you go to do these activities.

> **Modelo**
> *Nosotros corremos después de las clases. Vamos al gimnasio.*

2 Get together with another pair of students and tell them what you and your partner do in your free time. Be sure not to tell them where you go! It's their job to guess where you go. If they guess correctly, their team gets a point. The team that earns the most points wins.

> **Modelo**
> **A** —*Nosotros corremos después de las clases.*
> **B** —*Uds. van al gimnasio, ¿verdad?*
> **A** —*Sí, vamos al gimnasio para correr.*
> **o:** *No, no vamos al gimnasio para correr. Vamos al parque.*

● Más práctica

Practice Workbook 4A-5

For: Practice with *ir*
Visit: www.phschool.com
Web Code: jad-0403

El español en la comunidad

In many businesses and neighborhoods in the United States, you can hear Spanish being spoken. For example, the Pilsen neighborhood in Chicago, Illinois, is home to one of the nation's largest Mexican communities. Colorful murals, thriving businesses, and popular restaurants give Pilsen its character.

● Are there areas near you where you can see expressions of community for Spanish speakers like those in Pilsen? What are they?

Un mural en la comunidad de Pilsen en Chicago

Stress and accents

How can you tell which syllable to stress, or emphasize, when you see words written in Spanish? Here are some general rules.

1. **When words end in a vowel, *n,* or *s* place the stress on the next-to-last syllable.** Copy each of these words and draw a line under the next-to-last syllable. Then listen to and say these words, making sure you stress the underlined syllable:

centro	pasteles	piscina
computadora	trabajo	parque
mantequilla	escriben	generalmente

2. **When words end in a consonant (except *n* or *s*) place the stress on the last syllable.** Listen to and say these words, making sure you stress the last syllable:

señor	nariz	escribir
profesor	reloj	arroz
español	trabajador	comer

3. **When a word has a written accent** place the stress on the **accented syllable.** One reason for written accents is to indicate exceptions to the first two rules. Listen to and say these words. Be sure to emphasize the accented syllable:

café	número	teléfono
difícil	película	lápiz
fácil	plátano	artístico

Try it out! Listen to the first verse of the song "La Bamba" and say each word with the stress on the correct syllable. Then listen to the recording again and see if you can sing along with the first verse.

Para bailar la bamba, para bailar la bamba

se necesita una poca de gracia,

una poca de gracia y otra cosita

y arriba y arriba,

y arriba y arriba y arriba iré,

yo no soy marinero, yo no soy marinero,

por ti seré, por ti seré, por ti seré.

Gramática

Asking questions

You use interrogative words (*who*, *what*, *where*, and so on) to ask questions.

¿Qué?	*What?*	**¿Adónde?**	*(To) Where?*
¿Cómo?	*How?, What?*	**¿De dónde?**	*From where?*
¿Quién?	*Who?*	**¿Cuál?**	*Which?, What?*
¿Con quién?	*With whom?*	**¿Por qué?**	*Why?*
¿Dónde?	*Where?*	**¿Cuándo?**	*When?*
¿Cuántos, -as?	*How many?*		

In Spanish, when you ask a question with an interrogative word, you put the verb before the subject.

¿Qué **come Elena** en el restaurante?   What *does Elena eat* at the restaurant?

¿Adónde **van Uds.** después de las clases?   Where *do you go* after classes?

¿Por qué **va Ignacio** a la playa todos los días?   Why *does Ignacio go* to the beach every day?

You have already used several interrogative words. Notice that all these words have a written accent mark.

For simple questions that can be answered by *sí* or *no*, you can indicate with your voice that you're asking a question:

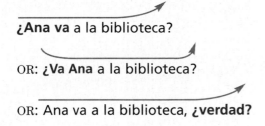

¿Ana va a la biblioteca?

OR: **¿Va Ana** a la biblioteca?

OR: Ana va a la biblioteca, **¿verdad?**

GramActiva VIDEO

Use the **GramActiva** video to help you learn more about asking questions.

¿Por qué?

---

19 Gramática **Leer/Escribir**

Un chico curioso

Joaquín is always asking you questions. Read his questions. Then, number your paper from 1–6 and write the appropriate responses.

1. ¿Qué haces tú después de las clases?

2. ¿Adónde van tú y tus amigos los fines de semana?

3. ¿Con quién comes tú en la cafetería?

4. ¿Por qué vas tú al gimnasio todos los días?

5. ¿Cuándo estudias tú?

6. ¿Quién es tu profesor favorito?

a. Yo estudio después de la cena.

b. Como el almuerzo con mis amigos.

c. Los sábados nosotros vamos a la biblioteca y los domingos estamos en casa.

d. Generalmente yo voy al centro comercial o al gimnasio.

e. Mi profesor favorito es el señor Rodríguez.

f. Voy porque me gusta mantener la salud.

Actividad 20 · Gramática · Pensar/Escribir

Preguntas revueltas

Your new pen pal from Bolivia has sent you an e-mail, but all of his questions are scrambled. Unscramble the words and write the questions in a logical order on a separate sheet of paper. Then answer your pen pal's questions.

1. ¿/ eres / de dónde / tú /?

2. ¿/ clases / tienes / cuántas /?

3. ¿/ Uds. / adónde / van / los fines de semana /?

4. ¿/ tú / qué / después de las clases / haces /?

5. ¿/ al centro comercial / cuándo / van / Uds. /?

6. ¿/ vas / tú / con quién / al centro comercial /?

Actividad 21 · Gramática · Leer/Pensar/Escribir

¿Cómo es el cine?

Read the advertisement for the *Cine Parque Arauco*. Then read the questions and answers below the advertisement. Number your paper from 1–5 and write the appropriate question words, based on what you read.

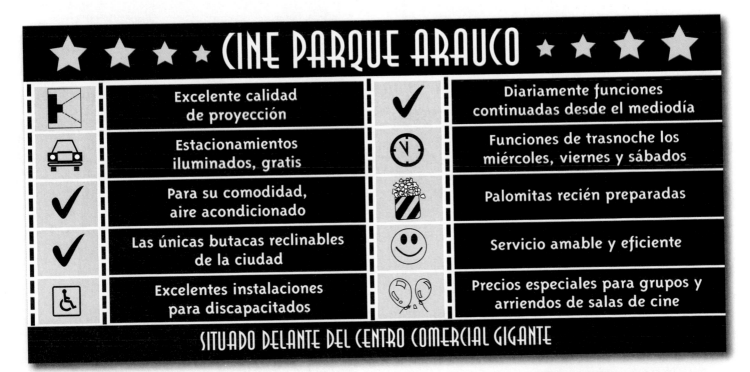

1. ¿____ es la calidad de la proyección en el cine? *Es excelente.*

2. ¿____ comen muchas personas allí? *Comen palomitas.*

3. ¿____ es el nombre del cine? *Es el Cine Parque Arauco.*

4. ¿____ van las personas a ver películas muy tarde (*late*) en la noche? *Van los miércoles, viernes y sábados.*

5. ¿____ está el cine? *Está delante del Centro Comercial Gigante.*

Cuándo	Cuál
Por qué	Dónde
Cómo	Qué

 **Gramática** **Escribir/Hablar** • • • • • • • • • • •

Los fines de semana

1 Copy a chart like this one on a separate sheet of paper. Write *yo* in the first column, and the name of a place that you go on the weekends in the second column. If there are people who go with you, write their names in the third column.

Nombre	¿Adónde vas?	¿Con quién?
yo	a la lección de guitarra	solo(a)
Laura	al centro comercial	con Selena

2 Follow the model to find out the same information about three of your classmates. Write the information on your chart.

> **Modelo**
> A —¿Adónde vas los fines de semana?
> B —Voy al centro comercial.
> A —¿Con quién vas?
> B —Voy con Selena.
> o: Voy solo(a).

3 Report the information you find to the class.

> **Modelo**
> Yo voy a mi lección de guitarra solo(a).
> Laura va al centro comercial con Selena.

Gramática 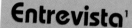 **Leer/Escribir/Hablar**

Una estrella de cine

1 *Estrella* magazine interviewed Luis Ramos, a famous movie star. Read the interview, then answer the questions below.

¿Comprendes?

1. What city is Luis Ramos from?
2. What is happening on September 15?
3. Who are María Rúa and Lorena Herrera?
4. What does Luis Ramos like to do in his free time?
5. Why is he an actor?

2 Write two additional questions that you might add to the interview with Luis Ramos.

3 Work with a partner to take turns playing the role of Luis or his co-star María. Ask him or her the additional questions that you wrote.

Entrevista¹ con **Luis Ramos**

▶ **¿De dónde eres?**
Soy de San Juan, Puerto Rico.

▶ **¿Cuándo vamos a ver tu nueva² película?**
El 15 de septiembre.

▶ **¿Con quién trabajas en la película y tú también?**
Trabajo con María Rúa y Lorena Herrera.

▶ **¿Cuándo tienes tiempo libre?**
No trabajo los fines de semana ni en diciembre.

▶ **¿Qué haces en tu tiempo libre?**
Generalmente yo voy al gimnasio todos los días. También me gusta ir a los restaurantes. Me quedo en casa cuando no trabajo en una nueva película.

▶ **¿Por qué eres actor?**
Soy actor porque me encantan las películas, y creo que soy talentoso.

▶ **¡Gracias!**
¡Gracias a usted! ¡Nos vemos!

¹Interview ²new

Actividad 24   Leer/Escribir

Estudiantes desordenados

At the Colegio de Ponce, a public school in Puerto Rico, the school newspaper staff is extremely disorganized today. They have the answers to the questions that they asked in an interview with a new student, but they lost the questions. Help them complete the article by reading the answers at right and then writing a logical question for each one.

| Modelo |

Me llamo Juliana Ramírez.
¿Cómo te llamas?

Me llamo Juliana Ramírez.

Yo soy de San Juan.

Yo estudio con mis amigos.

Mi clase favorita es matemáticas.

Después de las clases, voy al centro comercial.

Porque soy deportista y me gusta mucho
   practicar deportes.

Los sábados, voy a la playa o voy al cine para
   ver una película.

    Hablar/Escribir

Una entrevista con un amigo

Use the questions that you wrote for Actividad 24 to interview a partner. Present the information you find out to the class.

| Modelo |

Jaime es de Houston. Él va a la lección de piano después de las clases...

    Escribir/Hablar/GramActiva

Juego

1 With a partner, cut a sheet of blank paper into twelve squares, making sure that each square is the same size.

2 Write six questions, each on a different square. Use a different question word for each one. On the remaining six squares of paper, write a logical answer for each question.

3 Mix up the questions and answers, and spread them out facedown on the desk. Take turns turning two cards faceup, and read what they say aloud. If the cards are a logical question and answer match, pick them up and take another turn. If not, turn them facedown again and let your partner take a turn. The person with the most pairs wins. When you finish your game, switch cards with another pair of students.

| Modelo |

¿Cómo es Ana?

Ella es inteligente.

Escribir/Hablar •

Y tú, ¿qué preguntas?

1 Look at the photo and write four questions about the beach, the people, and the activities.

2 Ask your partner your questions and he or she will respond. Then switch roles.

Para decir más...

el hombre   man

la mujer   woman

la persona   person

tomar el sol   to sunbathe

Mucho jóvenes pasan el día en la playa en Perú.

Fondo cultural

■ ■ ◆ ◇ ◆ ◆ ◆

La música puertorriqueña In Puerto Rico, as in much of the Caribbean, music is an extremely important part of the identity of the people. Two of the musical styles that are often associated with Puerto Rico are *bomba* and *plena*. *Bomba* is a style of music with African roots where various people tend to call out and respond to the accompaniment of drums. *Plena* is a style of music where a singer tells a story or recounts an event to a musical accompaniment.

• What style of music do you listen to that is similar to *bomba* or *plena*?

Actividad 28 · Leer/Escribir

¡Vamos al Viejo San Juan!

Puerto Rico has been a commonwealth of the United States since 1952. It is an island with a fascinating past. Look at the pictures and read about a historic section of Puerto Rico's capital. Then answer the questions below.

Conexiones
La historia

El Viejo[1] San Juan es una zona histórica, pintoresca,[2] colonial y muy popular en la capital de Puerto Rico. Los jóvenes[3] pasan el tiempo con sus amigos en los parques, cafés y plazas. Allí cantan, bailan y comen en los restaurantes típicos.

El Morro fue construido[6] en el siglo[7] XVI para combatir los ataques de los piratas ingleses y franceses.[8]

Datos importantes:

- Cristóbal Colón llega[4] aquí durante su segunda visita a las Américas en 1493.
- El Viejo San Juan llega a ser[5] la capital de Puerto Rico en 1521.

La Catedral de San Juan tiene muchas obras de arte.[9] Allí descansan[10] los restos[11] de Juan Ponce de León, famoso explorador de la Florida.

[1]Old [2]picturesque [3]young people [4]arrives [5]becomes [6]was constructed [7]century [8]French [9]works of art [10]lie [11]remains

¿Comprendes?

1. For how many years has San Juan been the capital of Puerto Rico?
2. On which of his voyages did Christopher Columbus land on Puerto Rico?
3. Why did the Spaniards build *El Morro?*
4. What are two things you'll see when you visit the cathedral?

● **Más práctica**
Practice Workbook 4A-6, 4A-7

Go Online PHSchool.com
For: Practice with questions
Visit: www.phschool.com
Web Code: jad-0404

¡Adelante!

Al centro comercial

Lee las actividades diferentes que puedes hacer en la semana del 11 al 17 de enero durante tu tiempo libre.

Objectives

- Read about after-school and weekend activities offered at a mall
- Learn some nursery rhymes
- Role-play a new student's first day at school
- Learn facts about the history of the United States

Strategy

Using prior knowledge
Think about what you know about special-event weeks at shopping centers. List events from this calendar that you think might be offered at a mall.

¡Vamos a la Plaza del Sol!

Aquí en la Plaza del Sol, ¡siempre hay algo que hacer!

Actividades para el 11 al 17 de enero

11 lunes
8.00 P.M.   Música andina

12 martes
7.00 P.M.   Clase de yoga

13 miércoles
8.00 P.M.   Noche de jazz

14 jueves
7.00 P.M.   Clase de repostería[1]

15 viernes
8.00 P.M.   Música andina

16 sábado
1.30 P.M.   Exposición de fotografía
2.00 P.M.   Show infantil
4.00 P.M.   Exhibición de yoga
8.00 P.M.   Sábado flamenco

17 domingo
1.30 P.M.   Exposición de fotografía
2.00 P.M.   Show infantil
4.00 P.M.   Exhibición de yoga
8.00 P.M.   Noche de tango

Música andina

El grupo Sol Andino toca música andina fusionada con bossa nova y jazz los lunes y los viernes a las 8.00 P.M. Abierto[2] al público.

Clase de yoga

La práctica de yoga es todos los martes desde las 7.00 hasta las 9.00 P.M. La instructora Lucía Gómez Paloma enseña los secretos de esta disciplina. Inscríbase[3] al teléfono 224-24-16. Vacantes limitadas.

[1] pastry making   [2] Open   [3] Register

Sábado flamenco

El Sábado flamenco es el programa más popular de la semana. María del Carmen Ramachi baila acompañada por el guitarrista Ernesto Hermoza el sábado a las 8.00 P.M. Es una noche emocionante y sensacional de música y danza. Abierto al público.

Clase de repostería

Inscríbase gratis⁴ en la clase de repostería programada para el jueves a las 7.00 P.M. Preparamos unos pasteles deliciosos gracias a la Repostería Ideal y al maestro Rudolfo Torres. Inscríbase al teléfono 224-24-16. Vacantes limitadas.

⁴free

¿Comprendes?

1. You will be in town from January 9 through February 2. Will you be able to take part in these activities?

2. Which events require you to sign up in advance? Which don't?

3. You have to baby-sit your six-year-old sister. Which day(s) would be best to go?

4. According to the interests of these people, to what events mentioned in the *Lectura* are they going?

   Raquel: Me gusta mucho hacer ejercicio.

   Roberto: Me encantan los pasteles.

   Teresa: Estudio baile. Tomo lecciones todos los jueves.

   Alejandro: Me gusta escuchar música... toda clase de música.

5. What activities mentioned interest you the most?

For: Internet link activity
Visit: www.phschool.com
Web Code: jad-0405

Fondo cultural

Andean music Andean music has become popular worldwide. This style originated in the Andes mountains of Peru, Ecuador, Bolivia, and Chile. The music has a slightly haunting sound. Performers often wear typical Andean attire. Instruments commonly used in Andean music include the *quena* flute, *siku* panpipes, and a small guitar called a *charango*.

• The Andean sound is created using a particular set of instruments. What instruments define the music you enjoy?

Rimas infantiles

Can you remember the chants and songs you learned as a child? Or do you remember the rhymes you or your friends recited while jumping rope?

Here are some chants and songs that children in the Spanish-speaking world use when they play. The first one is a Spanish-language equivalent to "Eenie, meenie, minie, moe . . ." It is a nonsense rhyme used to select the person who will be "It" in various games.

Niños saltando a la cuerda

**Tin Marín de dopingüé
cucaramanga titirifuera.
Yo no fui,
fue Teté.
Pégale, pégale,
que ella fue.**

Niños jugando en San Sebastián, España

Here's a chant for jumping rope:

Salta, salta la perdiz	**The partridge jumps and jumps**
por los campos de maíz.	**Through the cornfields.**
Ten cuidado, por favor,	**Be careful, please!**
¡porque viene el cazador!	**Here comes the hunter!**
	(The jump rope then turns faster.)

Try it out! Here's a traditional game that combines Spanish, math, and hopping over a board. Place a long, narrow board on the floor. Take turns hopping with both feet from one side of the board to the other. Go forward as you hop. When you get to the end of the board, jump and turn in the air, facing the direction you came from. Continue hopping from side to side back to the other end. Be very careful! Try this in an area where you won't hurt yourself. As you are hopping, sing this song:

Brinca la tablita	**Jump over the board**
que yo la brinqué.	**That I already jumped.**
Bríncala tú ahora	**Now you jump**
que yo me cansé.	**Since I'm tired.**
Dos y dos son cuatro,	**Two and two are four,**
cuatro y dos son seis.	**Four and two are six.**
Seis y dos son ocho,	**Six and two are eight,**
y ocho dieciséis,	**And eight are sixteen,**
y ocho veinticuatro,	**And eight are twenty-four,**
y ocho treinta y dos.	**And eight are thirty-two.**
Y diez que le sumo	**And ten that I add**
son cuarenta y dos.	**Equals forty-two.**

Think about it! What rhymes and songs do you know? What purpose do they serve in play?

Un estudiante nuevo

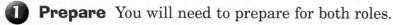

Task

This is a new student's first day at school. You and a partner will play the roles of a new student and a student who has been at the school for awhile. Find out information about the new student.

1 Prepare You will need to prepare for both roles.

Experienced student: Make a list of at least four questions. Find out where the new student is from, activities he or she likes to do and on what days of the week, and where he or she goes and with whom. Plan to greet the new student and introduce yourself.

New student: Look at the questions the experienced student will ask you and jot down answers.

Strategy

Using models
It helps to go back and review models that prepare you for a task like this role-play. Reread *A primera vista* (pp. 208–213). Pay attention to the different questions and answers that will help you with this task.

2 Practice Work in groups of four, with two experienced students and two new students. Practice different questions and responses. Be sure you are comfortable in both roles. Go through your presentation several times. You can use your notes in practice, but not during the role-play. Try to:

• obtain or provide information
• keep the conversation going
• speak clearly

3 Present Your teacher will tell you which role to play. The experienced student begins the conversation by greeting the new student. Listen to your partner's questions or responses and keep the conversation going.

4 Evaluation Your teacher may give you a rubric for how the presentation will be graded. You probably will be graded on:

• completion of task
• ability to keep the conversation going
• how well you were understood

Estados Unidos

Histórico

The oldest permanent European settlement in the United States, St. Augustine, Florida, was established by Spain in 1565—55 years before the Pilgrims landed at Plymouth Rock. For more than two centuries after that, the Spanish controlled a large territory in North America that included what is now Mexico, parts of the southern United States, the states of Texas, New Mexico, Arizona, California, and Nevada, and parts of Colorado and Utah.

Constructed as a mission in 1718, the Alamo (in San Antonio, Texas) today is best known as a key battleground in the secession of Texas from Mexico in 1836. The defeat of the Texans at the Alamo became a rallying cry for Texas independence, and Texas gained its freedom from Mexico two months later. ▶

¿Sabes que...?

The language of the Nahua peoples of central Mexico, which included the Aztecs, is related to the languages of the Shoshone, Comanche, and Hopi tribes in the United States. When Spaniards pushed north from the newly conquered central Mexico, they often followed ancient Native American trade routes and used Nahua people as guides.

Para pensar

You can find many Spanish names of cities, counties, and states in the United States. Work with a partner and write a list of at least ten places with Spanish names and then try to guess what they mean in English.

Go Online
PHSchool.com
For: Online Atlas
Visit: www.phschool.com
Web Code: jae-0002

◄ The French Quarter in New Orleans was named after the French who first settled here. In spite of its name, most of the buildings date to when Spain ruled Louisiana (1763–1803). Fires ravaged the area in 1788 and 1794, so when the rebuilding was done, the architectural style was Spanish. This can be seen in the landscaped patios and iron grillwork on balconies.

A network of Spanish Catholic missions once extended throughout the Americas. Many cities in the southwestern United States, including San Francisco, San Diego, and Santa Fe, were originally built around Catholic missions, which in turn were often located at Native American villages or religious sites. The Mission San Xavier del Bac, in Arizona, combines the name of a Catholic saint (San Xavier) with the name of the Papago village where it was built (Bac, which means "where the water emerges"). Constructed in the early 1700s, the mission is still used by the Papago people and is considered one of the world's architectural treasures. ▼

Spain built the Castillo de San Marcos to protect both St. Augustine (Florida) and the sea routes for ships returning to Spain from enemy attacks. This fort was started in 1672 and took 23 years to build. When Spain sold Florida to the United States in 1821, the fort was renamed Fort Marion. The Castillo has been a National Monument since 1924.

Repaso del capítulo

Vocabulario y gramática

To prepare for the test, check to see if you . . .
- know the new vocabulary and grammar
- can perform the tasks on p. 237

to talk about leisure activities

ir de compras	to go shopping
ver una película	to see a movie
la lección de piano	piano lesson (class)
Me quedo en casa.	I stay at home.

to talk about places

la biblioteca	library
el café	café
el campo	countryside
la casa	home, house
en casa	at home
el centro comercial	mall
el cine	movie theater
el gimnasio	gym
la iglesia	church
la mezquita	mosque
las montañas	mountains
el parque	park
la piscina	swimming pool
la playa	beach
el restaurante	restaurant
la sinagoga	synagogue
el templo	temple, Protestant church
el trabajo	work, job

to ask and tell where you go

a	to (prep.)
a la, al (a + el)	to the
¿Adónde?	(To) Where?
a casa	(to) home

to ask and tell with whom you go

con mis/tus amigos	with my/your friends
¿Con quién?	With whom?
solo, -a	alone

to talk about when things are done

¿Cuándo?	When?
después	afterwards
después (de)	after
los fines de semana	on weekends
los lunes, los martes . . .	on Mondays, on Tuesdays . . .
tiempo libre	free time

to talk about where someone is from

¿De dónde eres?	Where are you from?
de	from, of

to indicate how often

generalmente	generally

other useful words and expressions

¡No me digas!	You don't say!
para + infinitive	in order to + infinitive

ir *to go*

voy	vamos
vas	vais
va	van

For *Vocabulario adicional*, see pp. 268–269.

● **Más práctica**
Practice Workbook Puzzle 4A-8
Practice Workbook Organizer 4A-9

Preparación para el examen

On the exam you will be asked to...	Here are practice tasks similar to those you will find on the exam...	If you need review...
1 Escuchar Listen and understand as people ask questions about weekend events	Two friends are trying to make plans for the weekend. Based on their dialogue, what do they finally agree on? a) who is going b) where they are going c) when they are going	**pp. 208–213** *A primera vista* **p. 226** Actividad 22
2 Hablar Talk about places to go and things to do on the weekend	Your parents want to know what you're doing this weekend. Mention at least three places you plan to go or things you plan to do. For example, you might say *Voy de compras con mis amigos.*	**pp. 208–213** *A primera vista* **p. 215** Actividad 7 **p. 216** Actividad 9 **p. 221** Actividad 17 **p. 222** Actividad 18 **p. 226** Actividad 22

3 Leer Read about what a person does on particular days of the week	Someone has left his or her planner at your house. Read the schedule for two days to try to figure out what type of person owns it. Indicate whether you agree or disagree with the statements about the person.
	
	MARTES: 6:00 Desayuno 4:00 Lección de piano
	          5:00 Trabajo 8:30 Clase aeróbica
	
	JUEVES: 3:30 Gimnasio 4:30 Piscina
	         6:00 Trabajo 8:00 Biblioteca
	
	¿Estás de acuerdo o no?
	a) *Es muy perezoso(a).*
	b) *Es atlético(a).*
	c) *Le gusta ir de compras.*
		pp. 208–213 *A primera vista*
		p. 214 Actividad 5
		p. 219 Actividad 13
		pp. 230–231 *Lectura*

4 Escribir Write a short note to a friend to let him or her know where you are going after school	Your friend is taking a make-up test after school, so you need to write her a short note to tell her what you are doing after school today. In the note, tell her where you are going and then at what time you are going home.	**p. 214** Actividad 5 **p. 217** Actividad 11 **p. 220** Actividad 15 **p. 222** Actividad 18 **p. 228** Actividad 27
5 Pensar Demonstrate an understanding of rhymes, songs, and games from Spanish-speaking cultures	Think about your favorite childhood game. How does it compare to the children's games you learned about in this chapter? Describe a traditional game from a Spanish-speaking country.	**p. 232** *La cultura en vivo*

Fondo cultural

Los juegos Paralímpicos Starting with the first Paralympics Games in Rome in 1960, the International Paralympics Committee has organized summer and winter games that follow the Olympic Games and are hosted by the same city. Athletes with all types of disabilities compete in the Paralympics. More than 160 nations participate in this nonprofit organization, with over 6,000 participants worldwide.

• How do you think athletes benefit from competing in the Paralympics or in similar local events?

¿Quieres ir conmigo?

Chapter Objectives

- **Talk about activities outside of school**
- **Extend, accept, and decline invitations**
- **Tell when an event happens**
- **Understand cultural perspectives on after-school activities**

Video Highlights

A primera vista: *¡A jugar!*
GramActiva Videos: *ir + a + infinitive;*
the verb *jugar*

Country Connection

As you learn about after-school activities, you will make connections to these countries and places:

España
Estados Unidos
México
Chile

Go Online
PHSchool.com
For: Online Atlas
Visit: www.phschool.com
Web Code: jae-0002

En los juegos paralímpicos de 1996, Atlanta, Georgia

A primera vista

Vocabulario y gramática en contexto

Club Deportivo León
Parque de la Independencia

¿Te gustan los deportes? ¡Puedes practicar con uno de nuestros expertos!
¿Juegas bien o juegas mal? ¡No importa! Hay un deporte para ti.

8.00		el fútbol
8.00		el vóleibol
10.00		el golf
10.00		el tenis
13.00		el béisbol
13.00		el básquetbol
16.00		el fútbol americano

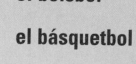

—¿Qué **quieres** hacer **a las ocho de la mañana, jugar al** fútbol o al vóleibol?

—A ver . . . No **quiero** jugar al fútbol. **Juego muy mal.** Prefiero jugar al vóleibol. Necesito practicar más. ¿Y qué **te gustaría** hacer a las cuatro **esta tarde?**

—**Me gustaría** jugar al fútbol americano.

el concierto

la fiesta

el baile

el partido

—¡Hola! Soy Rosa. ¿Quieres hacer algo **conmigo este fin de semana?** Hay un concierto en el parque.

—**Lo siento,** pero no **puedo.** Estoy **demasiado ocupado** y tengo mucha tarea.

—No puedo porque **tengo que** trabajar. Trabajo **esta noche** a las siete y mañana trabajo **a la una de la tarde. Voy a estar** un poco **cansada. ¡Ay! ¡Qué pena!**

—¡Qué **triste!** No, no puedo ir **contigo.** Estoy **un poco enferma.**

ir de cámping

ir de pesca

—**¡Qué buena idea!** Pero no me gustan los conciertos. Prefiero ir de cámping. Siempre estoy muy **contenta** cuando voy de cámping. **¿A qué hora?** ¿Mañana a las cinco de la tarde? **Entonces,** nos vemos.

Actividad 1
Escuchar •

¡Deportemanía!

Marcela is a sports fanatic! As she lists the days on which she will play the various sports, touch the picture of each sport.

Actividad 2
Escuchar •

¿Cómo estás?

You will hear how five people are feeling. Act out the adjectives that you hear.

● **Más práctica** • • • • • •
Practice Workbook 4B-1, 4B-2

Go Online
PHSchool.com
For: Vocabulary practice
Visit: www.phschool.com
Web Code: jad-0411

¡A jugar!

Ignacio, Javier, Ana y Elena están en el Parque del Retiro en Madrid.
¿Qué van a jugar y hacer? ¿De qué hablan? Lee la historia.

España

Javier

Ana

Elena

Ignacio

Antes de leer

 **Strategy**

Look to find key questions Before you read the story, skim to find where the characters are asking questions. The answers may point to important information in the story.

- Look at the questions. Which characters are offering invitations? What do you think they will do?

1. Look through the text for words that you already know. What clues do they give you about how the students are spending their weekend?

2. Think about how you spend your weekends. How does your weekend compare with what you see the students doing in the pictures?

3. Using the pictures, try to determine what each person is like. What can you tell about each student's interests based on what you see?

1 *Hoy es sábado y hace buen tiempo. Ignacio, Javier, Ana y Elena están en el parque para jugar al fútbol.*

2 **Ignacio:** ¡Oye, Javier! ¡Sabes jugar muy bien al fútbol!

Javier: Y tú también... pero necesito practicar más. Ana, ¿quieres jugar?

Ana: ¡Por supuesto! Vamos a jugar.

3 **Elena:** Estoy demasiado cansada y tengo sed. ¿Por qué no tomamos un refresco?

Ignacio: ¡Genial! Yo también estoy un poco cansado.

4 **Ana:** ¿Juegas al vóleibol esta tarde?

Elena: Sí, a las seis.

5 Ignacio: Oye, hay una fiesta esta noche. Ana, tú y Elena vais, ¿verdad?

Ana: ¡Claro!

Elena: Javier, ¿quieres ir con nosotros a la fiesta?

Ana: ¡Qué buena idea!

6 Javier: ¿A qué hora es la fiesta?

Ana: A las nueve **de la noche,** en la escuela.

7 Javier: ¿Tengo que bailar?

Ana: Pues, sí. Puedes bailar conmigo y con Elena.

Javier: No **sé** bailar muy bien.

Ana: ¡Vamos, Javier!

Javier: Bien, voy.

8 Javier: Hasta las nueve entonces.

Ignacio: ¡Genial! Hasta más tarde.

Leer/Escribir •

Una postal de Javier

Before going to the party, Javier decides to write a postcard to his friend in Salamanca, telling him about his new friends in Madrid. Number your paper from 1–6. Use the words in the box to complete his postcard. Base your answers on the *Videohistoria*.

fiesta	bailar
Elena	fútbol
sábado	nueve

Querido José,

¿Cómo estás? Estoy bien en mi nueva¹ escuela. Tengo tres amigos: Ignacio, Ana y __1.__. Ellos son muy divertidos. Hoy es __2.__, y fuimos² al parque para jugar al __3.__. Esta noche, vamos a una __4.__. Vamos a las __5.__ de la noche. Según mi amiga, yo tengo que __6.__. ¡Pero no sé bailar muy bien! Bueno, son las ocho y media y debo ir.

¡Hasta pronto!
Javier

José Romero-Manterola
15-D, c/Luchana
37008 Salamanca

¹new   ²we went

Escribir/Hablar •

¿Quién habla?

Who is speaking: Ana, Ignacio, Elena, or Javier?

Ana	**Ignacio**	**Elena**	**Javier**

1. No sé bailar bien.
2. Juego al vóleibol a las seis.
3. Necesito beber algo después de jugar al fútbol.
4. Necesito practicar más el fútbol.
5. Voy a la fiesta a las nueve.
6. Sé jugar al fútbol muy bien.

● **Más práctica** • • • • • • • • • • • • • •
Practice Workbook 4B-3, 4B-4

For: Vocabulary practice
Visit: www.phschool.com
Web Code: jad-0412

Manos a la obra

Vocabulario y gramática en uso

Objectives

- Talk about activities outside of school
- Extend, accept, and decline invitations
- Tell when an event happens
- Say what you are going to do
- Learn to use *ir + a +* infinitive and the verb *jugar*

Actividad 5 Hablar

Me gustaría ir . . .

Say whether or not you would like to do these things this weekend.

Modelo

Me gustaría ir a una fiesta este fin de semana.

o: *No me gustaría ir a una fiesta este fin de semana.*

1.
2.
3.
4.
5.

Actividad 6 Escribir/Hablar

No sé jugar . . .

Number your paper from 1–6. Indicate whether or not you know how to play the sports pictured below.

Modelo

Sé jugar al béisbol muy bien.

o: *No sé jugar al béisbol.*

1.
2.
3.

4.
5.
6.

Actividad 7 Hablar

¿Qué deportes practicas?

Using the information from Actividad 6, ask and tell about which sports you know, or don't know, how to play.

Modelo

A —¿Sabes jugar al béisbol?

B —¡Por supuesto! Sé jugar al béisbol muy bien.

o: No, no sé jugar al béisbol.

Actividad 8 · Escribir

La fiesta de Marta

Marta is having a party, and many of her classmates in her class are there. While some people are having a great time, others are not. Number your paper from 1–6. Use the adjectives in the word box to write six sentences describing the people in the picture below.

triste
ocupado, -a
cansado, -a
contento, -a
enfermo, -a
mal

Modelo

Felipe y María están contentos.

Fondo cultural

La noche de los rábanos is just one of the many kinds of *fiestas* in the Spanish-speaking world. On the evening of December 23, people set up booths around the *zócalo* (town square) of Oaxaca, Mexico, to display and sell radishes (*los rábanos*) sculpted into a fantastic array of shapes. *Oaxaqueños* and visitors alike crowd the square to view the amazing creations.

• Do you know communities or regions in the United States that are known for particular crafts or products?

Rábanos esculpidos (*sculpted*), Oaxaca, México

Actividad 9

  Hablar

Lo siento

Ask your partner if he or she wants to do these activities with you. Your partner can't go and will offer excuses to explain why.

Modelo

A —¡Oye! ¿Quieres *patinar conmigo esta tarde?*

B —*Lo siento. Hoy no puedo. Estoy demasiado enfermo(a).*

Estudiante A

1.
2.
3.
4.
5.

Estudiante B

muy	ocupado, -a
demasiado	enfermo, -a
un poco	cansado, -a
	triste
	mal

¡Respuesta personal!

Actividad 10

Escuchar/Escribir

Escucha y escribe

You will hear three invitations to events and the responses given. On a sheet of paper, write the numbers 1–3. As you listen, write what each invitation is for and whether the person accepted it (write *sí*) or turned it down (write *no*).

Actividad 11

 Escribir

Un estudiante muy popular

You have a busy Saturday and your friends are asking you to do things. Respond by telling them why you cannot accept.

Modelo

¿Quieres ir al cine a la una y media de la tarde?
No puedo. Tengo que ir a la biblioteca con Ramón.

1. ¿Te gustaría ir al café a las diez de la mañana?
2. ¿Puedes jugar al vóleibol a las tres de la tarde?
3. ¿Quieres ir al concierto esta noche a las siete?
4. ¿Puedes ir al restaurante con la clase esta tarde?
5. ¿Quieres ir a la fiesta de Beto esta noche?
6. ¿Te gustaría ir de pesca a las doce del mediodía?

sábado: el 26 de abril

10:00	ir a la lección de piano
12:00	jugar al fútbol americano con mis amigos
1:30	ir a la biblioteca con Ramón
3:00	jugar al básquetbol con Silvia y Jaime
5:30	comer en casa
7:00	ir al baile
9:30	ir a la fiesta de Julia

¿A qué hora?

Take turns asking and telling what time the following activities take place.

 8:00

1.  9:00

2.  2:30

3.  1:30

4.  8:30

5. 7:30

6. 7:00

Nota

To ask and tell what time something happens, you say:

- **¿A qué hora** vas?
- Voy **a la** una.
- Voy **a las** tres y media.

To specify what part of the day, add:

de la mañana*   in the morning (A.M.)
de la tarde   in the afternoon (P.M.)
de la noche   in the evening, at night (P.M.)

Mañana means "tomorrow"; *la mañana* means "morning."

Exploración del lenguaje

Spanish words borrowed from English

Languages often borrow words from one another. For example, *rodeo* and *patio* are Spanish words that have found their way into English. There are also many examples of English words that have entered Spanish. By recognizing these familiar words, you can increase your vocabulary in Spanish.

Try it out! Read the sentences and identify the "borrowed words." Don't forget to pronounce the words correctly in Spanish.

Quiero hacer videos.
¿Quieres jugar al básquetbol conmigo?
Practico el rugby y el ráquetbol.
Juego al fútbol cuando voy de cámping.
¡Me encantan los sándwiches!

Actividad 13 · Hablar

Una invitación para el sábado

Invite your partner to these places, and tell at what time you will go. Your partner will accept or decline. Follow the model.

 1:30

Modelo
A —¿Te gustaría *ir al concierto el sábado?*
B —¿A qué hora?
A —*A la una y media de la tarde.*
B —*¡Genial! Nos vemos el sábado.*

Estudiante A

1.  7:30

2.  1:00

3.  8:30

4.  4:15

5.   5:30

6.  11:00

Estudiante B

¡Por supuesto! Me gustaría mucho.
Lo siento, pero no puedo.
¡Ay! ¡Qué pena! Tengo que trabajar.
¡Genial! Nos vemos el sábado.
¡Qué buena idea! ¡Gracias!

¡Respuesta personal!

Actividad 14

Escribir/Hablar •

Una invitación para mi amigo

viernes, el _____ de _____

la mañana _____

la tarde _____

la noche _____

sábado, el _____ de _____

la mañana _____

la tarde _____

la noche _____

domingo, el _____ de _____

la mañana _____

la tarde _____

la noche _____

1 Copy this page of an agenda book onto a sheet of paper. Then, fill in each space with what you will be doing this weekend. Try to include specific times whenever possible.

2 After you have completed your schedule, work with a partner to invite him or her to various activities. Your partner will accept or decline, based on the information in his or her agenda book.

Actividad 15

Escribir/Hablar •

Y tú, ¿qué dices?

1. ¿Qué haces los fines de semana?
2. ¿Qué prefieres, practicar un deporte o ver la televisión? ¿Por qué?
3. ¿Cómo estás después de practicar tu deporte favorito? ¿Cómo estás cuando pasas tiempo con tus amigos?
4. ¿Qué te gustaría hacer esta noche? ¿Y mañana?
5. ¿Qué tienes que hacer este fin de semana?

Gramática

Ir + a + infinitive

Just as you use "going" + infinitive in English to say what you are going to do, in Spanish you use a form of the verb *ir + a +* an infinitive to express the same thing:

Voy a jugar al tenis hoy.
I'm going to play tennis today.

¿Tú **vas a jugar** al golf esta tarde?
Are you going to play golf this afternoon?

Mis amigas **van a ir de cámping** mañana.
My friends are going camping tomorrow.

Javier: ¿**Van a jugar** conmigo, o no?
Ana: Sí, **vamos a jugar** contigo.

GramActiva VIDEO

Want more help with *ir + a* + infinitive? Watch the **GramActiva** video.

Voy a comer.

16 Gramática · Escribir

¿Qué van a hacer todos?

You and the people you know have a lot to do this weekend. Tell what everyone is going to do by matching the people in the first column with any of the activities in the third column. Use the appropriate form of the verb *ir*. Write the sentences you create on a sheet of paper.

1. yo 2. mis amigos 3. mi mamá 4. mi papá y yo 5. mi profesor(a) y director(a) 6. tú	ir a	ver una película ir de pesca jugar al golf estudiar trabajar pasar tiempo con amigos **¡Respuesta personal!**

17 Gramática · Escuchar/Escribir

Escucha y escribe

Rosario and Pablo have left messages on your answering machine telling you what they are going to do and inviting you to join them. Copy this chart on your paper. As you listen to each message, complete the chart with information given in the message.

	Rosario	Pablo
1. ¿Adónde quiere ir?		
2. ¿Qué va a hacer?		
3. ¿A qué hora va a ir?		

Actividad 18 Gramática  Escribir ·

Este fin de semana vamos a...

On your paper, write sentences telling what the Ríos family is going to do this weekend.

Esteban /  / 8:00

Modelo

Esteban va a estudiar a las ocho de la noche.

1. Angélica /  / 3:30

4. Los señores Ríos /  / 7:30

2. Angélica y el Sr. Ríos / / 7:00

5. Esteban y un amigo / / 10:00

3. yo / / 4:00

6. Angélica, Esteban y yo /  / 8:00

Actividad 19 Gramática  Hablar ·

En mi tiempo libre voy a...

Work with a partner and talk about what you are going to do in your free time and when.

Modelo

A —¿*Cuándo vas a correr?*
B —*Voy a correr esta tarde.*
o: *Nunca voy a correr.*

Estudiante A

correr en el parque
estudiar español
hacer ejercicio
trabajar
comer en un restaurante
ver una película

¡Respuesta personal!

Estudiante B

a la(s)...
esta tarde
esta noche
este fin de semana
nunca

¡Respuesta personal!

The letter *d*

In Spanish, the pronunciation of the letter *d* is determined by its location in a word. When *d* is at the beginning of a word, or when it comes after *l* or *n*, it sounds similar to the *d* in "dog." Listen to and say these words:

diccionario	doce	donde
domingo	desayuno	día
deportes	calendario	bandera

When *d* comes between vowels and after any consonant except *l* or *n*, it sounds similar to the *th* of "the." Listen to and say these words:

cansado	ocupado	puedes
idea	sábado	partido
tarde	ensalada	atrevido

Try it out! Here is a tongue twister to give you practice in pronouncing the letter *d*, and also to give you something to think about!

> **Porque puedo, puedes,**
> **porque puedes, puedo;**
> **Pero si no puedes,**
> **yo tampoco puedo.**

   Escribir/Hablar

Actividad 20

¿Qué vas a hacer?

1 Make a chart like this one to describe five things you're going to do, when you're going to do them, and with whom. Use the following words to say when you're going to do these things: *esta tarde, esta noche, mañana, el (jueves), este fin de semana.*

¿Qué?	¿Cuándo?	¿Con quién?
tocar la guitarra	esta tarde	mis amigos

2 Ask your partner what his or her plans are.

Modelo

A —*¿Qué vas a hacer esta tarde?*
B —*Esta tarde mis amigos y yo vamos a tocar la guitarra.*

Actividad 21 — Leer/Escribir

El teléfono celular

Answer the following questions about this ad for a cellular phone. Then create your own ad by writing at least five things that you want to do.

1. ¿Por qué es bueno tener un teléfono celular?

2. ¿Te gusta hablar por teléfono celular? ¿Con quién?

3. ¿Crees que es bueno o malo usar un teléfono celular en un restaurante? ¿Por qué?

¿Te gustaría . . .

pasar más tiempo con tus amigos?

ir de compras?

ir al cine?

ir a conciertos?

escuchar música?

hablar por teléfono?

¡Por supuesto!
¡Con un teléfono celular puedes hacer planes para hacerlo todo!

Actividad 22 — Hablar

Una conversación por teléfono celular

You're calling a friend to invite him or her to do something. Your friend turns down the invitation and explains why. Make at least three invitations each.

Modelo

A —*Hola, Sara. Soy Rosa. ¿Puedes jugar al tenis conmigo esta tarde?*

B —*Lo siento, hoy no puedo. Voy a estudiar para mi clase de inglés.*

A —*¡Ay! ¡Qué pena!*

Actividad 23 — Escribir/Hablar

Y tú, ¿qué dices?

1. ¿Con quién te gustaría ir a una fiesta? ¿Por qué?

2. ¿Qué prefieres: ir de pesca o ir a un baile?

3. ¿Qué vas a hacer mañana a las ocho de la noche?

4. ¿Qué vas a hacer este fin de semana?

5. ¿Te gustaría ver un partido de fútbol o ir a un concierto?

Más práctica

Practice Workbook 4B-5, 4B-6

Go Online
PHSchool.com

For: Practice with *ir* + *a* + infinitive
Visit: www.phschool.com
Web Code: jad-0413

Gramática

The verb *jugar*

Use the verb *jugar* to talk about playing a sport or a game. Even though *jugar* uses the same endings as the other *-ar* verbs, it has a different stem in some forms. For those forms, the *u* becomes *ue*. This kind of verb is called a "stem-changing verb." Here are the present-tense forms:

(yo)	**juego**	(nosotros) (nosotras)	**jugamos**
(tú)	**juegas**	(vosotros) (vosotras)	**jugáis**
Ud. (él) (ella)	**juega**	Uds. (ellos) (ellas)	**juegan**

Nota

Many Spanish speakers always use *jugar a* and the name of the sport or game:

• ¿Juegas **al** vóleibol?

Others do not use the *a:*

• ¿Juegas vóleibol?

GramActiva VIDEO

Use the **GramActiva** video to help you learn more about the verb *jugar.*

---

24 **Gramática** Escribir

¿A qué juegan?

Write sentences telling what sports the following people play.

Alejandro

Modelo

Alejandro juega al béisbol.

También se dice...

el básquetbol = el baloncesto *(muchos países)*

el fútbol = el balompié *(muchos países)*

el vóleibol = el balonvolea *(España)*

1.

Natalia

2.

los estudiantes en mi clase

3.

nosotros

4.

Sara

5.

Uds.

6.

tú

Juego

1 On each of two index cards, draw a picture that represents a sport or game and write *muy bien, bien,* or *mal* to show how well you play that sport or game. Don't let your classmates see your cards.

2 Get together with five other students. Put all the cards face down in the center of your group. Choose a card and try to identify who drew it by asking the others how well they play what is pictured. Keep track of what you learn about your classmates.

Modelo

A —*Enrique, ¿juegas bien al tenis?*
B —*No, juego muy mal al tenis.*

3 Write six sentences describing the sports and games the students in your group play.

Modelo

Óscar y Nacho juegan muy bien al fútbol.
Teresa y yo jugamos bien al béisbol.

Estos jugadores de Managua, Nicaragua juegan muy bien al béisbol.

Actividad 26

Leer/Escribir/Hablar • • • • • • • • •

La ciudad deportiva

Read about Iván Zamorano's dream and
answer the questions.

1. ¿Qué es el sueño de Iván Zamorano?
2. ¿Qué deportes juegan en la Ciudad
   Deportiva de Iván?
3. ¿Qué día empieza *(begins)* la
   inscripción para las escuelas?
   ¿A qué hora?
4. ¿A qué hora empiezan las actividades?
5. ¿Te gustaría ir a la Ciudad Deportiva
   de Iván Zamorano? ¿Por qué?

Mi sueño[1]

Quiero una ciudad[2] dedicada al deporte, a la familia y a
los niños.[3] Quiero servicios de calidad internacional, con
profesores de excelencia. En mi sueño, los niños y jóvenes
juegan y practican deportes para ser mejores.[4] Este sueño
ya es realidad y quiero compartirlo contigo.

El lugar[5] para hacer deporte en familia.
Escuelas de Fútbol, Tenis, Hockey

Inicio de Inscripción[6]: 23 de marzo, a las 8
Inicio de Actividades: 1 de abril, a las 14 horas

Avenida Pedro Hurtado 2650, Las Condes, Santiago, Chile
Teléfono: 212 2711

[1]dream [2]city [3]children [4]better [5]place [6]Registration

El español en el mundo del trabajo

Una voluntaria en un hospital

There are many opportunities to use
Spanish in the health care field—in
hospitals, emergency rooms, and
neighborhood clinics. This young
woman volunteers in a California
hospital. Since many of the patients
come from Spanish-speaking homes,
she is able to speak with them and
their families in Spanish. *"Para mí,
trabajar como voluntaria es una de
mis actividades favoritas. Creo que
mi trabajo es importante."*

• What opportunities are there in your
  community to do volunteer work
  where speaking Spanish is helpful?

Actividad 27

Leer/Pensar/Escribir •

¡Vamos de cámping!

Tourism is an important industry in Spain. Many tourists prefer to go camping rather than stay in hotels. Read the following brochure about a campground and then answer the questions.

Conexiones
Las matemáticas

Cámping Playa Tropicana

Alcossebre (Castellón)
Teléfono: 462 41 42 73   Fax: 964 01 55 05

240 kilómetros al sur de Barcelona
52 kilómetros al norte de Castellón

- Un cámping verdaderamente recomendable
- Siempre algo nuevo
- La mejor opción para su dinero

Con abundante vegetación y mucha sombra,[1] directamente sobre una fabulosa playa. Ideal para niños. La mejor zona de pesca de la Costa de Azahar.

[1]shade

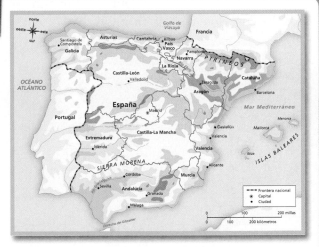

1. ¿Qué distancia en millas[2] hay entre[3] Barcelona y el Cámping Playa Tropicana?

2. ¿Qué distancia hay entre Castellón y el Cámping Playa Tropicana?

(Para convertir kilómetros en millas, es necesario dividir el número de kilómetros por 1.6.)

[2]miles [3]between

> **Para decir más...**
>
> **200**   doscientos

Actividad 28

Escribir/Hablar •

Y tú, ¿qué dices?

1. ¿Qué deporte juegas bien? ¿Qué deporte juegas mal?

2. ¿Quién juega al básquetbol muy bien? ¿Al golf?

3. ¿Dónde juegan tú y tus amigos al vóleibol?

4. ¿Qué deportes juegan tú y tus amigos para la escuela?

5. ¿Qué deportes juegan tú y tus amigos en invierno?

● **Más práctica** • • • • • • • • • • •
Practice Workbook 4B-7

Go Online
PHSchool.com
For: Practice with *jugar*
Visit: www.phschool.com
Web Code: jad-0414

¡Adelante!

Objectives

- Read about and compare the lives of two famous golfers
- Recognize specialized sports vocabulary
- Understand cultural perspectives regarding extracurricular activities
- Write an invitation to an event
- Learn facts about the contemporary United States

Lectura

Sergio y Lorena: El futuro del golf

Lee este artículo de una revista deportiva.
Vas a conocer a[1] Sergio García y a Lorena
Ochoa Reyes, dos atletas famosos.

Strategy

Cognates
Use the cognates in the following articles to help you understand what is being said about the golfers.

Sergio García

Nombre: Sergio García

Fecha de nacimiento: 9/1/80

Lugar de nacimiento:
Borriol, Castellón (España)

Club: Club de Campo
del Mediterráneo

Su objetivo: Ser el mejor
del mundo

Profesional: Desde abril
del 99

Aficiones[2]: Real Madrid,
tenis, fútbol, videojuegos

Sergio García es uno de los golfistas más populares en el mundo del golf profesional.

Sergio juega para el Club de Campo del Mediterráneo en Borriol, Castellón, donde su padre Víctor es golfista profesional. Juega al golf desde la edad[3] de tres años y a los 12 años es campeón[4] del Club de Campo. Es el golfista más joven en competir en el campeonato PGA desde Gene Sarazen en 1921 y gana[5] segundo lugar.[6] Tiene el nombre "El niño". A los 15 años, juega en un torneo del circuito europeo de profesionales. Y a la edad de 17 años gana su primer torneo de profesionales.

Es evidente que este español tiene el talento para realizar su objetivo.

---

[1]You will meet [2]Interests [3]age [4]champion [5]he wins [6]second place

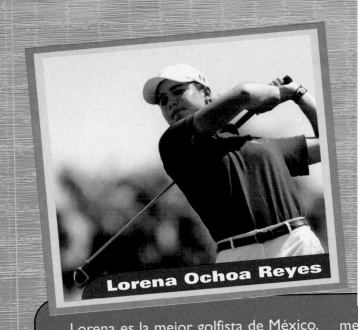

Nombre:
Lorena Ochoa Reyes

Fecha de nacimiento:
15/11/81

Lugar de nacimiento:
Guadalajara, México

Su objetivo: Ser la golfista número uno del mundo

Universidad: Universidad de Arizona

Aficiones: básquetbol, tenis, bicicleta de montaña, correr, nadar, comida italiana

Lorena es la mejor golfista de México. Juega al golf desde los seis años de edad. A los 21 años, gana su primer torneo de profesionales. Es la única[7] mexicana en calificar al torneo U.S. Women's Open. Ella dice que está muy emocionada porque quiere jugar mejor[8] y competir en los Estados Unidos. Ella dice que es importante practicar y entrenar[9] todos los días. Un día ella quiere ser la golfista número uno del mundo.

[7]only [8]better [9]to train

¿Comprendes?

Copy this Venn diagram on a sheet of paper. Make a list in English of at least eight facts that you learned about Sergio and Lorena. Write the facts on your Venn diagram. Include information about Sergio in the left oval, information about Lorena in the right oval, and any fact that applies to both of them in the overlapping oval.

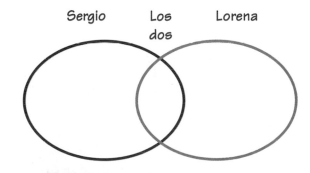

Sergio   Los dos   Lorena

Go Online
PHSchool.com

For: Internet link activity
Visit: www.phschool.com
Web Code: jad-0415

Fondo cultural

Una jugadora profesional Rebecca Lobo is a professional basketball player. After winning a gold medal in the 1996 Olympics, she became one of the WNBA's original players. Rebecca wrote a book called The Home Team, which tells about her life and her mother's struggle against breast cancer. In 2001, she established a college scholarship fund to assist minority students who plan to pursue careers in the healthcare field.

• Rebecca Lobo is a popular motivational speaker. What message do you think she gives to her audiences?

¿Qué haces en tu tiempo libre?

In many Spanish-speaking countries, extracurricular activities traditionally play a much smaller role in school life than in the United States. Students usually participate in activities such as music and athletics at clubs and institutions outside of school.

Although some schools have teams, many students who are interested in sports attend clubs such as el Club Deportivo General San Martín. At these clubs teens practice and compete on teams. They also participate in individual sports such as tennis. The competition between clubs is sometimes more intense than the competition between schools.

Students with artistic talents often go to a private institute to take music, dance, or art lessons. They might attend el Instituto de Música Clásica or el Instituto de Danza Julio Bocca.

Many students spend their time outside of classes studying a foreign language. They might learn English at la Cultura Inglesa or French at la Alianza Francesa.

In general, students do not hold jobs. They spend their time studying, being with family and friends, and participating in different activities.

Check it out! Take a survey of your friends to find out what they do after school. Do they work a part-time job? Do they participate in a sport with a school team or in extracurricular activities at school? Do they belong to a club or organization outside of school?

Think about it! How do the practices in your community compare with what you have learned about young people's after-school activities in Spanish-speaking countries?

Jugando al hockey en Buenos Aires, Argentina

¿Te gusta jugar al ajedrez?

Trabajando después de las clases

Presentación escrita

Una invitación

Task
A special event is coming up on the calendar and you want to invite a friend to go with you.

1 **Prewrite** Think about an event that you would invite a friend to attend, such as a concert, sporting event, or party. Write an invitation that includes:

- the name of the event
- when, where, and at what time the event is taking place
- who is going

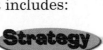

Strategy

Organizing information
Thinking about the correct format and necessary information beforehand will help you create a better invitation.

2 **Draft** Use the information from Step 1 to write a first draft of your invitation. Begin your invitation with *¡Hola...!* and close with *Tu amigo(a)* and your name.

3 **Revise** Read your note and check for correct spelling and verb forms. Share your invitation with a partner. Your partner should check the following:

- Did you give all the necessary information?
- Is there anything you should add or change?
- Are there any errors?

4 **Publish** Write a final copy of your invitation, making any necessary changes. You may want to give it to your friend or include it in your portfolio.

5 **Evaluation** Your teacher may give you a rubric for how the invitation will be graded. You probably will be graded on:

- how complete the information is
- use of vocabulary expressions
- accuracy of sentence structures

Estados Unidos

Contemporáneo

According to the 2000 census, 32,800,000 people (about 12 percent of the total population of the United States) classified themselves as being of Spanish or Hispanic descent. Out of that number, 30,700,800 indicated that they were of either Mexican, Puerto Rican, or Cuban descent. The remaining 2,099,200 people checked "Other Spanish/Hispanic" on their census questionnaires. This broad category included people who came from or who had ancestral ties to other Spanish-speaking countries in the Caribbean, Central and South America, or Spain.

Born in Costa Rica, Dr. Franklin Chang-Díaz (left) was the first Hispanic astronaut to fly in space. He was selected by NASA in 1980 and is a veteran of seven space flights. In 1990, Californian Dr. Ellen Ochoa (right) became the first Hispanic female astronaut. Since then she has logged more than 480 hours in space. Her dream is to help build a space station, which she considers "critical . . . to human exploration in space." Both Dr. Ochoa and Dr. Chang-Díaz are the recipients of many honors for their technical contributions and their scholarship. ▶

¿Sabes que...?

The influence of Spanish-speaking cultures is evident throughout the United States. Musical artists such as Enrique Iglesias, Shakira, and Marc Anthony sell millions of CDs. Actors such as Salma Hayek, Jennifer Lopez, Benjamin Bratt, and Edward James Olmos earn great acclaim for their work. And in politics, Spanish-speaking Americans serve in Congress and top-level Cabinet posts.

Para pensar

Work with a partner and interview a classmate, friend, or acquaintance who is Spanish-speaking or who has ties to a Spanish-speaking country. What is the person's name? Where did the family come from, and when? Why did the family move to your community? If this person had one thing to say to you and your classmates about the immigrant experience and cultural differences, what might that be? Write a short account of the interview and present it to your class or to a small group.

Go Online
PHSchool.com

For: Online Atlas
Visit: www.phschool.com
Web Code: jae-0002

The music and poetry of New York City's Puerto Rican community are a creative blend of English and Spanish. *Nuyoricans* of the *Loisaida* (Lower East Side) rub shoulders with people of diverse ethnic backgrounds creating sounds and rhythms unlike any other in the world. The Nuyorican Poets Café has become an institution on the *Loisaida,* where poets, writers, performance artists, musicians, and visual artists of all nationalities can find an outlet for their work.

More than half of Miami's population is of Spanish-speaking descent. Calle Ocho is the heart of Little Havana, the largest Cuban American community in the United States. The Calle Ocho Festival, which takes place at the end of Carnaval Miami, is a great time to sample Cuban food and dance to some of the world's greatest salsa artists.

More Mexicans visit the border town of Laredo, Texas, than any other city in the United States; and more United States citizens visit the Mexican border town of Tijuana than any other foreign city. Most of the visitors come from nearby areas and stay for only a few hours to visit or shop.

Repaso del capítulo

Vocabulario y gramática

to talk about leisure activities

el baile	dance
el concierto	concert
la fiesta	party
ir + a + *infinitive*	to be going + infinitive
ir de cámping	to go camping
ir de pesca	to go fishing
jugar al básquetbol	to play basketball
jugar al béisbol	to play baseball
jugar al fútbol	to play soccer
jugar al fútbol americano	to play football
jugar al golf	to play golf
jugar al tenis	to play tennis
jugar al vóleibol	to play volleyball
el partido	game, match
(yo) sé	I know (how)
(tú) sabes	you know (how)

to describe how someone feels

cansado, -a	tired
contento, -a	happy
enfermo, -a	sick
mal	bad, badly
ocupado, -a	busy
triste	sad

to extend, accept, or decline invitations

conmigo	with me
contigo	with you
(yo) puedo	I can
(tú) puedes	you can
¡Ay! ¡Qué pena!	Oh! What a shame!
¡Genial!	Great!
lo siento	I'm sorry
¡Oye!	Hey!
¡Qué buena idea!	What a good/nice idea!
(yo) quiero	I want
(tú) quieres	you want
¿Te gustaría?	Would you like?
Me gustaría	I would like
Tengo que ___.	I have to ___.

to tell what time something happens

¿A qué hora?	(At) what time?
a la una	at one (o'clock)
a las ocho	at eight (o'clock)
de la mañana	in the morning
de la noche	in the evening, at night
de la tarde	in the afternoon
esta noche	this evening
esta tarde	this afternoon
este fin de semana	this weekend

other useful words and expressions

demasiado	too
entonces	then
un poco (de)	a little

jugar (a) *to play (games, sports)*

juego	jugamos
juegas	jugáis
juega	juegan

For *Vocabulario adicional,* see pp. 268–269.

● **Más práctica**

Practice Workbook Puzzle 4B-8
Practice Workbook Organizer 4B-9

Preparación para el examen

On the exam you will be asked to...	Here are practice tasks similar to those you will find on the exam...	If you need review...
1 Escuchar Listen to and understand messages that give information about when and where to meet someone	On your answering machine, you hear your friend asking if you can go somewhere with her this weekend. Based on her message, try to tell: a) where she is going; b) what she is going to do; and c) what time she wants to go.	**pp. 240–245** *A primera vista* **p. 248** Actividad 10 **p. 252** Actividad 17
2 Hablar Make excuses for not accepting an invitation	You and a friend have planned a camping trip this weekend, but another friend now wants you to do something with him. With a partner, take turns rehearsing excuses for declining his invitation.	**p. 246** Actividad 5 **p. 248** Actividad 9 **p. 250** Actividad 13 **p. 255** Actividad 22
3 Leer Read and understand short messages about accepting or declining invitations	You find notes under your desk that were written to the person who was sitting there before you. Read them to see why people declined an invitation to a party: (a) Me gustaría, pero no puedo. Tengo que estudiar para un examen. (b) ¡Genial! ¡Una fiesta! Ay, pero no puedo— voy de cámping. (c) ¿A las siete? No puedo. Juego un partido de vóleibol a las siete y media. Lo siento.	**pp. 240–245** *A primera vista* **pp. 260–261** *Lectura*
4 Escribir Write a short note telling what you are going to do during the week	As a counselor for an after-school program for children, you must write a note to the parents telling them at least three things their children are going to do during the week. (Hint: Start your note with *¡Hola! Esta semana . . .*)	**pp. 240–245** *A primera vista* **p. 253** Actividad 18 **p. 254** Actividad 20 **p. 263** *Presentación escrita*
5 Pensar Demonstrate an understanding of cultural differences regarding extracurricular activities	Think about what you and your friends typically do after school. Are your activities usually school-related? How would you compare what you do to what some Spanish-speaking teens do in their after-school time?	**p. 262** *Perspectivas del mundo hispano*

Vocabulario adicional

Tema 1

Las actividades

coleccionar sellos / monedas to collect stamps / coins

jugar al ajedrez to play chess

patinar sobre hielo to ice-skate

practicar artes marciales (f.) to practice martial arts

tocar to play (an instrument)

  el bajo bass

  la batería drums

  el clarinete clarinet

  el oboe oboe

  el saxofón, pl. **los saxofones** saxophone

  el sintetizador synthesizer

  el trombón, pl. **los trombones** trombone

  la trompeta trumpet

  la tuba tuba

  el violín, pl. **los violines** violin

Tema 2

Las clases

el alemán German

el álgebra (f.) algebra

el anuario yearbook

la banda band

la biología biology

el cálculo calculus

el drama drama

la fotografía photography

el francés French

la geografía geography

la geometría geometry

el latín Latin

la química chemistry

la trigonometría trigonometry

Las cosas para la clase

la grapadora stapler

las grapas staples

el sujetapapeles, pl. **los sujetapapeles** paper clip

las tijeras scissors

Tema 3

Las comidas

Las frutas

el aguacate avocado

la cereza cherry

la ciruela plum

el coco coconut

el durazno peach

la frambuesa raspberry

el limón, *pl.* **los limones** lemon

el melón, *pl.* **los melones** melon

la pera pear

la sandía watermelon

la toronja grapefruit

Las verduras

el apio celery

el brócoli broccoli

la calabaza pumpkin

el champiñón, *pl.* **los champiñones** mushroom

la col cabbage

la coliflor cauliflower

los espárragos asparagus

las espinacas spinach

el pepino cucumber

La carne

la chuleta de cerdo pork chop

el cordero lamb

la ternera veal

Los condimentos

la mayonesa mayonnaise

la mostaza mustard

la salsa de tomate ketchup

Otro tipo de comidas

los fideos noodles

Los lugares y actividades

el banco bank

el club club

el equipo de . . . ___ team

la farmacia pharmacy

la oficina office

la práctica de . . . ___ practice

la reunión, *pl.* **las reuniones de . . .** ___ meeting

el supermercado supermarket

Resumen de gramática

Grammar Terms

Adjectives describe nouns: *a **red** car.*

Adverbs usually describe verbs; they tell when, where, or how an action happens: *He read it **quickly**.* Adverbs can also describe adjectives or other adverbs: ***very** tall, **quite** well.*

Articles are words in Spanish that can tell you whether a noun is masculine, feminine, singular, or plural. In English, the articles are *the, a,* and *an.*

Commands are verb forms that tell people to do something: ***Study!, Work!***

Comparatives compare people or things.

Conjugations are verb forms that add endings to the stem in order to tell who the subject is and what tense is being used: *escrib**o**, escrib**iste**.*

Conjunctions join words or groups of words. The most common ones are ***and, but,*** and ***or.***

Direct objects are nouns or pronouns that receive the action of a verb: *I read the **book**. I read **it**.*

Gender in Spanish tells you whether a noun, pronoun, or article is masculine or feminine.

Indirect objects are nouns or pronouns that tell you to whom / what or for whom / what something is done: *I gave **him** the book.*

Infinitives are the basic forms of verbs. In English, infinitives have the word "to" in front of them: ***to walk.***

Interrogatives are words that ask questions: ***What** is that? **Who** are you?*

Nouns name people, places, or things: ***students, Mexico City, books.***

Number tells you if a noun, pronoun, article, or verb is singular or plural.

Prepositions show relationship between their objects and another word in the sentence: *He is **in** the classroom.*

Present tense is used to talk about actions that always take place, or that are happening now: *I always **take** the bus; I **study** Spanish.*

Present progressive tense is used to emphasize that an action is happening *right now: I **am doing** my homework; he **is finishing** dinner.*

Preterite tense is used to talk about actions that were completed in the past: *I **took** the train yesterday; I **studied** for the test.*

Pronouns are words that take the place of nouns: ***She** is my friend.*

Subjects are the nouns or pronouns that perform the action in a sentence: ***John** sings.*

Superlatives describe which things have the most or least of a given quality: *She is the **best** student.*

Verbs show action or link the subject with a word or words in the predicate (what the subject does or is): *Ana **writes**; Ana **is** my sister.*

Nouns, Number, and Gender

Nouns refer to people, animals, places, things, and ideas. Nouns are singular or plural. In Spanish, nouns have gender, which means that they are either masculine or feminine.

Singular Nouns		Plural Nouns	
Masculine	**Feminine**	**Masculine**	**Feminine**
libro	carpeta	libros	carpetas
pupitre	casa	pupitres	casas
profesor	noche	profesores	noches
lápiz	ciudad	lápices	ciudades

Definite Articles

El, la, los, and *las* are definite articles and are the equivalent of "the" in English. *El* is used with masculine singular nouns; *los* with masculine plural nouns. *La* is used with feminine singular nouns; *las* with feminine plural nouns. When you use the words *a* or *de* before *el,* you form the contractions *al* and *del: Voy* **al** *centro; Es el libro* **del** *profesor.*

Masculine		Feminine	
Singular	**Plural**	**Singular**	**Plural**
el libro	los libros	la carpeta	las carpetas
el pupitre	los pupitres	la casa	las casas
el profesor	los profesores	la noche	las noches
el lápiz	los lápices	la ciudad	las ciudades

Indefinite Articles

Un and *una* are indefinite articles and are the equivalent of "a" and "an" in English. *Un* is used with singular masculine nouns; *una* is used with singular feminine nouns. The plural indefinite articles are *unos* and *unas.*

Masculine		Feminine	
Singular	**Plural**	**Singular**	**Plural**
un libro	unos libros	una revista	unas revistas
un escritorio	unos escritorios	una mochila	unas mochilas
un baile	unos bailes	una bandera	unas banderas

Pronouns

Subject pronouns tell who is doing the action. They replace nouns or names in a sentence. Subject pronouns are often used for emphasis or clarification: *Gregorio escucha música.* **Él** *escucha música.*

After most prepositions, you use *mí* and *ti* for "me" and "you." The forms change with the preposition *con: conmigo, contigo.* For all other persons, you use subject pronouns after prepositions.

Subject Pronouns		Objects of Prepositions	
Singular	**Plural**	**Singular**	**Plural**
yo	nosotros, nosotras	(para) mí, conmigo	nosotros, nosotras
tú	vosotros, vosotras	(para) ti, contigo	vosotros, vosotras
usted (Ud.)	ustedes (Uds.)	Ud.	Uds.
él, ella	ellos, ellas	él, ella	ellos, ellas

Interrogative Words

You use interrogative words to ask questions. When you ask a question with an interrogative word, you put the verb before the subject. All interrogative words have a written accent mark.

¿Adónde?	¿Cuándo?	¿Dónde?
¿Cómo?	¿Cuánto, -a?	¿Por qué?
¿Con quién?	¿Cuántos, -as?	¿Qué?
¿Cuál?	¿De dónde?	¿Quién?

Adjectives

Words that describe people and things are called adjectives. In Spanish, most adjectives have both masculine and feminine forms, as well as singular and plural forms. Adjectives must agree with the noun they describe in both gender and number. When an adjective describes a group including both masculine and feminine nouns, use the masculine plural form.

Masculine	
Singular	Plural
alto	altos
inteligente	inteligentes
trabajador	trabajadores
fácil	fáciles

Feminine	
Singular	Plural
alta	altas
inteligente	inteligentes
trabajadora	trabajadoras
fácil	fáciles

Shortened Forms of Adjectives

When placed before masculine singular nouns, some adjectives change into a shortened form.

bueno	buen chico
malo	mal día
primero	primer trabajo
tercero	tercer plato
grande	gran señor

One adjective, **grande,** changes to a shortened form before any singular noun: *una gran señora, un gran libro.*

Possessive Adjectives

Possessive adjectives are used to tell what belongs to someone or to show relationships. Like other adjectives, possessive adjectives agree in number with the nouns that follow them.

Only *nuestro* and *vuestro* have different masculine and feminine endings. *Su* and *sus* can have many different meanings: *his, her, its, your,* or *their.*

Singular	Plural
mi	mis
tu	tus
su	sus
nuestro, -a	nuestros, -as
vuestro, -a	vuestros, -as
su	sus

Demonstrative Adjectives

Like other adjectives, demonstrative adjectives agree in gender and number with the nouns that follow them. Use *este, esta, estos, estas* ("this" / "these") before nouns that name people or things that are close to you. Use *ese, esa, esos, esas* ("that" / "those") before nouns that name people or things that are at some distance from you.

Singular	Plural
este libro	estos libros
esta casa	estas casas

Singular	Plural
ese niño	esos niños
esa manzana	esas manzanas

Verbos

Regular Present Tense

Here are the conjugations for regular *-ar*, *-er*, and *-ir* verbs in the present tense.

Infinitive	Present	
estudiar	estudio estudias estudia	estudiamos estudiáis estudian
correr	corro corres corre	corremos corréis corren
escribir	escribo escribes escribe	escribimos escribís escriben

Stem-changing Verbs

Here is an alphabetical list of the stem-changing verbs.

Infinitive	Present	
doler (o → ue)	duele	duelen
dormir (o → ue)	duermo duermes duerme	dormimos dormís duermen
empezar (e → ie)	empiezo empiezas empieza	empezamos empezáis empiezan
jugar (u → ue)	juego juegas juega	jugamos jugáis juegan
llover (o → ue)	llueve	
nevar (e → ie)	nieva	
pensar (e → ie)	pienso piensas piensa	pensamos pensáis piensan
preferir (e → ie)	preflero prefieres prefiere	preferimos preferís prefieren

Irregular Verbs

These verbs have irregular patterns.

Infinitive	Present	
estar	estoy estás está	estamos estáis están
hacer	hago haces hace	hacemos hacéis hacen
ir	voy vas va	vamos vais van
poder	puedo puedes puede	podemos podéis pueden
querer	quiero quieres quiere	queremos queréis quieren
saber	sé sabes sabe	sabemos sabéis saben
ser	soy eres es	somos sois son
tener	tengo tienes tiene	tenemos tenéis tienen
ver	veo ves ve	vemos veis ven

Expresiones útiles para conversar

The following are expressions that you can use when you find yourself in a specific situation and need help to begin, continue, or end a conversation.

Greeting someone

Buenos días. Good morning.

Buenas tardes. Good afternoon.

Buenas noches. Good evening. Good night.

Making introductions

Me llamo . . . My name is . . .

Soy . . . I'm . . .

¿Cómo te llamas? What's your name?

Éste es mi amigo *m.* **. . .** This is my friend . . .

Ésta es mi amiga *f.* **. . .** This is my friend . . .

Se llama . . . His / Her name is . . .

¡Mucho gusto! It's a pleasure!

Encantado, -a. Delighted.

Igualmente. Likewise.

Asking how someone is

¿Cómo estás? How are you?

¿Cómo andas? How's it going?

¿Cómo te sientes? How do you feel?

¿Qué tal? How's it going?

Estoy bien, gracias. I'm fine, thank you.

Muy bien. ¿Y tú? Very well. And you?

Regular. Okay. Alright.

Más o menos. More or less.

(Muy) mal. (Very) bad.

¡Horrible! Awful!

¡Excelente! Great!

Talking on the phone

Aló. Hello.

Diga. Hello.

Bueno. Hello.

¿Quién habla? Who's calling?

Habla . . . It's [name of person calling].

¿Está . . . , por favor? Is . . . there, please?

¿De parte de quién? Who is calling?

¿Puedo dejar un recado? May I leave a message?

Un momento. Just a moment.

Llamo más tarde. I'll call later.

¿Cómo? No le oigo. What? I can't hear you.

Making plans

¿Adónde vas? Where are you going?

Voy a . . . I'm going to . . .

¿Estás listo, -a? Are you ready?

Tengo prisa. I'm in a hurry.

¡Date prisa! Hurry up!

Sí, ahora voy. OK, I'm coming.

Todavía necesito . . . I still need . . .

¿Te gustaría . . . ? Would you like to . . . ?

Sí, me gustaría . . . Yes, I'd like to . . .

¡Claro que sí (no)! Of course (not)!

¿Quieres . . . ? Do you want to . . . ?

Quiero . . . I want to . . .

¿Qué quieres hacer hoy? What do you want to do today?

¿Qué haces después de las clases? What do you do after school (class)?

¿Qué estás haciendo? What are you doing?

Te invito. It's my treat.

¿Qué tal si . . . ? What about . . . ?

Primero . . . First . . .

Después . . . Later . . .

Luego . . . Then . . .

Making an excuse

Estoy ocupado, -a. I'm busy.

Lo siento, pero no puedo. I'm sorry, but I can't.

¡Qué lástima! What a shame!

Ya tengo planes. I already have plans.

Tal vez otro día. Maybe another day.

Being polite

Con mucho gusto. With great pleasure.

De nada. You're welcome.

Disculpe. Excuse me.

Lo siento. I'm sorry.

Muchísimas gracias. Thank you very much.

Te (Se) lo agradezco mucho. I appreciate it a lot.

Muy amable. That's very kind of you.

Perdón. Pardon me.

¿Puede Ud. repetirlo? Can you repeat that?

¿Puede Ud. hablar más despacio? Can you speak more slowly?

Keeping a conversation going

¿De veras? Really?

¿Verdad? Isn't that so? Right?

¿En serio? Seriously?

¡No lo puedo creer! I don't believe it!

¡No me digas! You don't say!

Y entonces, ¿qué? And then what?

¿Qué hiciste? What did you do?

¿Qué dijiste? What did you say?

¿Crees que . . . ? Do you think that . . . ?

Me parece bien. It seems alright.

Perfecto. Perfect.

¡Qué buena idea! What a good idea!

¡Cómo no! Of course!

De acuerdo. Agreed.

Está bien. It's all right.

Giving a description when you don't know the name of someone or something

Se usa para . . . It's used to / for . . .

Es la palabra que significa . . . It's the word that means . . .

Es la persona que . . . It's the person who . . .

Ending a conversation

Bueno, tengo que irme. Well, I have to go.

Chao. (Chau.) Bye.

Hasta pronto. See you soon.

Hasta mañana. See you tomorrow.

Vocabulario español-inglés

The *Vocabulario español-inglés* contains all active vocabulary from the text, including vocabulary presented in the grammar sections.

A dash (—) represents the main entry word. For example, **pasar la —** after **la aspiradora** means **pasar la aspiradora.**

The number following each entry indicates the chapter in which the word or expression is presented. The letter *P* following an entry refers to the *Para empezar* section.

The following abbreviations are used in this list: *adj.* (adjective), *dir. obj.* (direct object), *f.* (feminine), *fam.* (familiar), *ind. obj.* (indirect object), *inf.* (infinitive), *m.* (masculine), *pl.* (plural), *prep.* (preposition), *pron.* (pronoun), *sing.* (singular).

A

a to *(prep.)* (4A)

   — **casa** (to) home (4A)

   — **la una de la tarde** at one (o'clock) in the afternoon (4B)

   — **las ocho de la mañana** at eight (o'clock) in the morning (4B)

   — **las ocho de la noche** at eight (o'clock) in the evening / at night (4B)

   — **mí también** I do (like to) too (1A)

   — **mí tampoco** I don't (like to) either (1A)

   ¿— **qué hora?** (At) what time? (4B)

   — **veces** sometimes (1B)

   — **ver** Let's see (2A)

al *(a + el)*, **a la,** to the (4A)

al lado de next to (2B)

abril April (P)

aburrido, -a boring (2A)

acuerdo:

   Estoy de —. I agree. (3B)

   No estoy de —. I don't agree. (3B)

¡Adiós! Good-bye! (P)

¿Adónde? (To) where? (4A)

agosto August (P)

el **agua** *f.* water (3A)

al *(a + el)*, **a la,** to the (4A)

   — **lado de** next to (2B)

algo something (3B)

allí there (2B)

el **almuerzo** lunch (2A)

   en el — for lunch (3A)

el **año** year (P)

aquí here (2B)

el **arroz** rice (3B)

el **arte:**

   la clase de — art class (2A)

artístico, -a artistic (1B)

asco:

   ¡Qué —! How awful! (3A)

atrevido, -a daring (1B)

¡Ay! ¡Qué pena! Oh! What a shame / pity! (4B)

B

bailar to dance (1A)

el **baile** dance (4B)

la **bandera** flag (2B)

el **básquetbol: jugar al —** to play basketball (4B)

beber to drink (3A)

las **bebidas** beverages (3B)

béisbol: jugar al — to play baseball (4B)

la **biblioteca** library (4A)

bien well (P)

el **bistec** beefsteak (3B)

la **boca** mouth (P)

el **bolígrafo** pen (P)

el **brazo** arm (P)

bueno (buen), -a good (1B)

   Buenas noches. Good evening. (P)

   Buenas tardes. Good afternoon. (P)

   Buenos días. Good morning. (P)

C

la **cabeza** head (P)

cada día every day (3B)

el **café** coffee (3A); café (4A)

la **calculadora** calculator (2A)

calor: Hace —. It's hot. (P)

caminar to walk (3B)

el **campo** countryside (4A)

cansado, -a tired (4B)

cantar to sing (1A)

la **carne** meat (3B)

la **carpeta** folder (P)

   la — de argollas three-ring binder (2A)

el **cartel** poster (2B)

la **casa** home, house (4A)

   a — (to) home (4A)

   en — at home (4A)

catorce fourteen (P)

la **cebolla** onion (3B)

la **cena** dinner (3B)

el **centro: el — comercial** mall (4A)

el **cereal** cereal (3A)

cero zero (P)

la **chica** girl (1B)

el **chico** boy (1B)

cien one hundred (P)

las **ciencias:**

   la clase de — naturales science class (2A)

   la clase de — sociales social studies class (2A)

cinco five (P)

cincuenta fifty (P)

el **cine** movie theater (4A)

la **clase** class (2A)

   la sala de clases classroom (P)

comer to eat (3A)

la **comida** food, meal (3A)

¿Cómo?:

¿— eres? What are you like? (1B)

¿— es? What is he / she like? (1B)

¿— está Ud.? How are you? *formal* (P)

¿— estás? How are you? *fam.* (P)

¿— se dice . . . ? How do you say . . . ? (P)

¿— se escribe . . . ? How is . . . spelled? (P)

¿— se llama? What's his / her name? (1B)

¿— te llamas? What is your name? (P)

compartir to share (3A)

comprender to understand (3A)

la **computadora** computer (2B)

usar la — to use the computer (1A)

con with (3A)

— mis / tus amigos with my / your friends (4A)

¿— quién? With whom? (4A)

el **concierto** concert (4B)

conmigo with me (4B)

contento, -a happy (4B)

contigo with you (4B)

correr to run (1A)

creer:

Creo que . . . I think . . . (3B)

Creo que no. I don't think so. (3B)

Creo que sí. I think so. (3B)

el **cuaderno** notebook (P)

¿Cuál? Which?, What? (3A)

¿— es la fecha? What is the date? (P)

¿Cuándo? When? (4A)

¿Cuántos, -as? How many? (P)

cuarenta forty (P)

cuarto, -a fourth (2A)

y — quarter past *(in telling time)* (P)

menos — *(time)* quarter to (P)

cuatro four (P)

D ••••••••••••••••••

de of (2B); from (4A)

¿— dónde eres? Where are you from? (4A)

— la mañana / la tarde / la noche in the morning / afternoon / evening (4B)

debajo de underneath (2B)

deber should, must (3B)

décimo, -a tenth (2A)

decir to say, to tell

¿Cómo se dice . . . ? How do you say . . . ? (P)

¡No me digas! You don't say! (4A)

¿Qué quiere — . . . ? What does . . . mean? (P)

Quiere — . . . It means . . . (P)

Se dice . . . You say . . . (P)

el **dedo** finger (P)

delante de in front of (2B)

demasiado too (4B)

deportista athletic, sports-minded (1B)

el **desayuno** breakfast (3A)

en el — for breakfast (3A)

desordenado, -a messy (1B)

después (de) after, afterwards (4A)

detrás de behind (2B)

el **día** day (P)

Buenos —s. Good morning. (P)

cada — every day (3B)

¿Qué — es hoy? What day is today? (P)

todos los —s every day (3A)

dibujar to draw (1A)

el **diccionario** dictionary (2A)

diciembre December (P)

diecinueve nineteen (P)

dieciocho eighteen (P)

dieciséis sixteen (P)

diecisiete seventeen (P)

diez ten (P)

difícil difficult (2A)

el **disquete** diskette (2B)

divertido, -a amusing, fun (2A)

doce twelve (P)

domingo Sunday (P)

dónde:

¿—? Where? (2B)

¿De — eres? Where are you from? (4A)

dos two (P)

E ••••••••••••••••••

educación física: la clase de — physical education class (2A)

el **ejercicio: hacer —** to exercise (3B)

el **el** the *m. sing.* (1B)

él he (1B)

ella she (1B)

ellas they *f. pl.* (2A)

ellos they *m. pl.* (2A)

en in, on (2B)

— casa at home (4A)

— la . . . hora in the . . . hour (class period) (2A)

encantado, -a delighted (P)

encantar to please very much, to love

me / te encanta(n) . . . I / you love . . . (3A)

encima de on top of (2B)

enero January (P)

enfermo, -a sick (4B)

la **ensalada** salad (3A)

la — de frutas fruit salad (3A)

enseñar to teach (2A)

entonces then (4B)

¿Eres . . . ? Are you . . . ? (1B)

es is (P); (he / she / it) is (1B)

— el *(number)* **de** *(month)* it is the . . . of . . . *(in telling the date)* (P)

— el primero de *(month).* It is the first of . . . (P)

— la una. It is one o'clock. (P)

— un(a) . . . it's a . . . (2B)

escribir:

  ¿Cómo se escribe . . . ? How is . . . spelled? (P)

  — cuentos to write stories (1A)

  Se escribe . . . It's spelled . . . (P)

el **escritorio** desk (2B)

escuchar música to listen to music (1A)

los **espaguetis** spaghetti (3B)

el **español: la clase de —** Spanish class (2A)

esquiar (i → í) to ski (1A)

la **estación,** *pl.* **las estaciones** season (P)

estar to be (2B)

  ¿Cómo está Ud.? How are you? *formal* (P)

  ¿Cómo estás? How are you? *fam.* (P)

  Estoy de acuerdo. I agree. (3B)

  No estoy de acuerdo. I don't agree. (3B)

este, esta this

  esta noche this evening (4B)

  esta tarde this afternoon (4B)

  este fin de semana this weekend (4B)

el **estómago** stomach (P)

estos, estas these

  ¿Qué es esto? What is this? (2B)

  Estoy de acuerdo. I agree. (3B)

el/la **estudiante** student (P)

estudiar to study (2A)

estudioso, -a studious (1B)

F

fácil easy (2A)

favorito, -a favorite (2A)

febrero February (P)

la **fecha: ¿Cuál es la —?** What is the date? (P)

la **fiesta** party (4B)

el **fin de semana:**

  este — this weekend (4B)

  los fines de semana on weekends (4A)

las **fresas** strawberries (3A)

frío: Hace —. It's cold. (P)

el **fútbol: jugar al —** to play soccer (4B)

el **fútbol americano: jugar al —** to play football (4B)

G

la **galleta** cookie (3A)

generalmente generally (4A)

¡Genial! Great! (4B)

el **gimnasio** gym (4A)

el **golf: jugar al —** to play golf (4B)

gracias thank you (P)

gracioso, -a funny (1B)

los **guisantes** peas (3B)

gustar:

  (A mí) me gusta . . . I like to . . . (1A)

  (A mí) me gusta más . . . I like to . . . better (I prefer to . . .) (1A)

  (A mí) me gusta mucho . . . I like to . . . a lot (1A)

  (A mí) no me gusta . . . I don't like to . . . (1A)

  (A mí) no me gusta nada . . . I don't like to . . . at all. (1A)

  Le gusta . . . He / She likes . . . (1B)

  Me gusta . . . I like . . . (3A)

  Me gustaría . . . I would like . . . (4B)

  No le gusta . . . He / She doesn't like . . . (1B)

  ¿Qué te gusta hacer? What do you like to do? (1A)

  ¿Qué te gusta hacer más? What do you like better (prefer) to do? (1A)

  Te gusta . . . You like . . . (3A)

  ¿Te gusta . . . ? Do you like to . . . ? (1A)

  ¿Te gustaría . . . ? Would you like . . . ? (4B)

H

hablar to talk (2A)

  — por teléfono to talk on the phone (1A)

hacer to do (3B)

  Hace calor. It's hot. (P)

  Hace frío. It's cold. (P)

  Hace sol. It's sunny. (P)

  — ejercicio to exercise (3B)

  ¿Qué tiempo hace? What's the weather like? (P)

  (yo) hago I do (3B)

  (tú) haces you do (3B)

hambre: Tengo —. I'm hungry. (3B)

la **hamburguesa** hamburger (3A)

hasta:

  — luego. See you later. (P)

  — mañana. See you tomorrow. (P)

Hay There is, There are (2B)

el **helado** ice cream (3B)

la **hoja de papel** sheet of paper (P)

¡Hola! Hello! (P)

la **hora:**

  en la . . . — in the . . . hour (class period) (2A)

  ¿A qué hora? (At) what time? (4B)

el **horario** schedule (2A)

horrible horrible (3B)

hoy today (P)

los **huevos** eggs (3A)

I

la **iglesia** church (4A)

igualmente likewise (P)

impaciente impatient (1B)

el **inglés: la clase de —** English class (2A)

inteligente intelligent (1B)

intercsante interesting (2A)

el invierno winter (P)

ir to go (4A)

— a + *inf.* to be going to + *verb* (4B)

— a la escuela to go to school (1A)

— de cámping to go camping (4B)

— de compras to go shopping (4A)

— de pesca to go fishing (4B)

J

las judías verdes green beans (3B)

jueves Thursday (P)

jugar (a) (u → ue) to play (*games, sports*) (4B)

— al básquetbol to play basketball (4B)

— al béisbol to play baseball (4B)

— al fútbol to play soccer (4B)

— al fútbol americano to play football (4B)

— al golf to play golf (4B)

— al tenis to play tennis (4B)

— al vóleibol to play volleyball (4B)

— videojuegos to play video games (1A)

el jugo:

— de manzana apple juice (3A)

— de naranja orange juice (3A)

julio July (P)

junio June (P)

L

la the *f. sing.* (1B)

lado: al — de next to, beside (2B)

el lápiz, *pl.* los lápices pencil (P)

las the *f. pl.* (2B)

le (to / for) him, her

— gusta . . . He / She likes . . . (1B)

No — gusta . . . He / She doesn't like . . . (1B)

la lección, *pl.* las lecciones de piano piano lesson (class) (4A)

la leche milk (3A)

la lechuga lettuce (3B)

leer revistas to read magazines (1A)

levantar pesas to lift weights (3B)

el libro book (P)

la limonada lemonade (3A)

llamar:

¿Cómo se llama? What's his / her name? (1B)

¿Cómo te llamas? What is your name? (P)

Me llamo . . . My name is . . . (P)

llover (o → ue): Llueve. It's raining. (P)

lo it, him

— siento. I'm sorry. (4B)

los the *m. pl.* (2B)

— fines de semana on weekends (4A)

— lunes, los martes . . . on Mondays, on Tuesdays . . . (4A)

lunes Monday (P)

los lunes on Mondays (4A)

M

mal bad, badly (4B)

malo, -a bad (3B)

la mano hand (P)

mantener: para — la salud to maintain one's health (3B)

la mantequilla butter (3B)

la manzana apple (3A)

el jugo de — apple juice (3A)

mañana tomorrow (P)

la mañana:

a las ocho de la — at eight (o'clock) in the morning (4B)

de la — in the morning (4B)

martes Tuesday (P)

los martes on Tuesdays (4A)

marzo March (P)

más:

— . . . que more . . . than (2A)

— o menos more or less (3A)

las matemáticas: la clase de — mathematics class (2A)

mayo May (P)

me (to / for) me

— gustaría I would like (4B)

— llamo . . . My name is . . . (P)

— quedo en casa. I stay at home. (4A)

media, -o half (P)

y — thirty, half past (*in telling time*) (P)

menos: más o — more or less (3A)

el mes month (P)

la mcsa table (2B)

la mezquita mosque (4A)

mi my (2B)

mí:

a — también I do (like to) too (1A)

a — tampoco I don't (like to) either (1A)

miércoles Wednesday (P)

la mochila bookbag, backpack (2B)

las montañas mountains (4A)

montar:

— en bicicleta to ride a bicycle (1A)

— en monopatín to skateboard (1A)

mucho, -a a lot (2A)

— gusto pleased to meet you (P)

muchos, -as many (3B)

muy very (1B)

— bien very well (P)

N ....

nada nothing (P)

  (A mí) no me gusta — . . .
  I don't like to . . . at all. (1A)

nadar to swim (1A)

la **naranja: el jugo de —** orange
  juice (3A)

la **nariz,** *pl.* **las narices** nose (P)

necesitar:

  (yo) necesito I need (2A)

  (tú) necesitas you need (2A)

nevar (e → ie) Nieva. It's
  snowing. (P)

ni . . . ni neither . . . nor, not . . .
  or (1A)

No estoy de acuerdo. I don't
  agree. (3B)

¡No me digas! You don't say! (4A)

noche:

  a las ocho de la — at eight
    (o'clock) in the evening, at
    night (4B)

  Buenas —s. Good evening. (P)

  de la — in the evening, at
    night (4B)

  esta — this evening (4B)

nos (to / for) us

  ¡— vemos! See you later! (P)

nosotros, -as we (2A)

noveno, -a ninth (2A)

noventa ninety (P)

noviembre November (P)

nueve nine (P)

nunca never (3A)

O ....

o or (1A)

ochenta eighty (P)

ocho eight (P)

octavo, -a eighth (2A)

octubre October (P)

ocupado, -a busy (4B)

el **ojo** eye (P)

once eleven (P)

ordenado, -a neat (1B)

el **otoño** fall, autumn (P)

¡Oye! Hey! (4B)

P ....

paciente patient (1B)

el **pan** bread (3A)

  el — tostado toast (3A)

la **pantalla** (computer) screen (2B)

las **papas** potatoes (3B)

  las — fritas French fries (3A)

la **papelera** wastepaper basket (2B)

para for (2A)

  — + *inf.* in order to (4A)

  — la salud for one's health (3B)

  — mantener la salud to
    maintain one's health (3B)

el **parque** park (4A)

el **partido** game, match (4B)

pasar:

  — tiempo con amigos to
    spend time with friends (1A)

  ¿Qué pasa? What's
    happening? (P)

los **pasteles** pastries (3B)

patinar to skate (1A)

la **película:** film, movie

  ver una — to see a movie (4A)

perezoso, -a lazy (1B)

pero but (1B)

el **perrito caliente** hot dog (3A)

pesas: levantar — to lift
  weights (3B)

el **pescado** fish (3B)

el **pie** foot (P)

la **pierna** leg (P)

la **piscina** pool (4A)

la **pizza** pizza (3A)

el **plátano** banana (3A)

la **playa** beach (4A)

  poco: un — (de) a little (4B)

poder (o → ue) to be able

  (yo) puedo I can (4B)

  (tú) puedes you can (4B)

el **pollo** chicken (3B)

por:

  ¿— qué? Why? (3B)

  — supuesto of course (3A)

porque because (3B)

practicar deportes to play
  sports (1A)

práctico, -a practical (2A)

preferir (e → ie) to prefer

  (yo) prefiero I prefer (3B)

  (tú) prefieres you prefer (3B)

la **primavera** spring (P)

primer (primero), -a first (2A)

el **profesor, la profesora** teacher
  (P)

puedes: (tú) — you can (4B)

puedo: (yo) — I can (4B)

la **puerta** door (2B)

pues well *(to indicate pause)* (1A)

el **pupitre** student desk (P)

Q ....

Qué:

  ¡— asco! How awful! (3A)

  ¡— buena idea! What a
    good / nice idea! (4B)

  ¿— día es hoy? What day is
    today? (P)

  ¿— es esto? What is this? (2B)

  ¿— hora es? What time is it?
    (P)

  ¿— pasa? What's happening?
    (P)

  ¡— pena! What a shame /
    pity! (4B)

  ¿— quiere decir . . . ? What
    does . . . mean? (P)

  ¿— tal? How are you? (P)

  ¿— te gusta hacer? What do
    you like to do? (1A)

¿**— te gusta hacer más?**
What do you like better
(prefer) to do? (1A)

¿**— tiempo hace?** What's the
weather like? (P)

querer (e → ie) to want

¿**Qué quiere decir . . . ?**
What does . . . mean? (P)

Quiere decir . . .
It means . . . (P)

(yo) quiero I want (4B)

(tú) quieres you want (4B)

¿**Quién?** Who? (2A)

quince fifteen (P)

quinto, -a fifth (2A)

R

el **ratón**, *pl.* **los ratones**
(computer) mouse (2B)

el **refresco** soft drink (3A)

regular okay, so-so (P)

el **reloj** clock (2B)

reservado, -a reserved, shy (1B)

el **restaurante** restaurant (4A)

S

sábado Saturday (P)

saber to know (how)

(yo) sé I know (how to) (4B)

(tú) sabes you know (how to)
(4B)

sabroso, -a tasty, flavorful (3B)

el **sacapuntas**, *pl.* **los sacapuntas**
pencil sharpener (2B)

la **sala de clases** classroom (P)

la **salchicha** sausage (3A)

la **salud:**

para la — for one's health (3B)

para mantener la — to
maintain one's health (3B)

el **sándwich de jamón y queso**
ham and cheese sandwich (3A)

sé: (yo) — I know (how to) (1B)

sed: Tengo —. I'm thirsty. (3B)

según according to (1B)

— mi familia according to
my family (1B)

segundo, -a second (2A)

seis six (P)

la **semana** week (P)

este fin de — this weekend
(4B)

los fines de — on weekends
(4A)

señor (Sr.) sir, Mr. (P)

señora (Sra.) madam, Mrs. (P)

señorita (Srta.) miss, Miss (P)

septiembre September (P)

séptimo, -a seventh (2A)

ser to be (3B)

¿**Eres . . . ?** Are you . . . ? (1B)

es he / she is (1B)

no soy I am not (1B)

soy I am (1B)

serio, -a serious (1B)

scscnta sixty (P)

setenta seventy (P)

sexto, -a sixth (2A)

sí yes (1A)

siempre always (3A)

siento: lo — I'm sorry (4B)

siete seven (P)

la **silla** chair (2B)

simpático, -a nice, friendly (1B)

sin without (3A)

la **sinagoga** synagogue (4A)

sociable sociable (1B)

el **sol: Hace —.** It's sunny. (P)

solo, -a alone (4A)

Son las . . . It is . . . *(in telling
time)* (P)

la **sopa de verduras** vegetable
soup (3A)

soy I am (1B)

supuesto: por — of course (3A)

T

tal: ¿Qué —? How are you? (P)

talentoso, -a talented (1B)

también also, too (1A)

a mí — I do (like to) too (1A)

tampoco: a mí — I don't (like
to) either (1A)

tarde afternoon (4B)

a la una de la — at one
(o'clock) in the afternoon (4B)

Buenas —s. Good afternoon.
(P)

de la tarde in the afternoon
(4B)

esta — this afternoon (4B)

la **tarea** homework (2A)

te (to / for) you

¿**— gusta . . . ?** Do you like
to . . . ? (1A)

¿**— gustaría . . . ?** Would you
like . . . ? (4B)

el **té** tea (3A)

el — helado iced tea (3A)

el **teclado** (computer) keyboard (2B)

la **tecnología** technology /
computers (2A)

la clase de — technology /
computer class (2A)

el **templo** temple; Protestant
church (4A)

tener to have

(yo) tengo I have
(2A)

(tú) tienes you have
(2A)

Tengo hambre. I'm hungry.
(3B)

Tengo que . . .
I have to . . . (4B)

Tengo sed. I'm thirsty. (3B)

el **tenis: jugar al —** to play tennis
(4B)

tercer (tcrccro), -a third (2A)

ti you *fam. after prep.*

¿**Y a —?** And you? (1A)

el **tiempo:**

el — **libre** free time (4A)

pasar — con amigos to spend time with friends (1A)

¿Qué — hace? What's the weather like? (P)

tocar la guitarra to play the guitar (1A)

el **tocino** bacon (3A)

todos, -as all (3B)

— **los días** every day (3A)

los **tomates** tomatoes (3B)

trabajador, -ora hardworking (1B)

trabajar to work (1A)

el **trabajo** work, job (4A)

trece thirteen (P)

treinta thirty (P)

treinta y uno thirty-one (P)

tres three (P)

triste sad (4B)

tu your (2B)

tú you *fam.* (2A)

U ● ● ● ● ● ● ● ● ● ● ● ● ● ● ● ● ●

Ud. (usted) you *formal sing.* (2A)

Uds. (ustedes) you *formal pl.* (2A)

un, una a, an (1B)

un poco (de) a little (4B)

la **una: a la —** at one o'clock (4B)

uno one (P)

unos, -as some (2B)

usar la computadora to use the computer (1A)

usted (Ud.) you *formal sing.* (2A)

ustedes (Uds.) you *formal pl.* (2A)

las **uvas** grapes (3B)

V ● ● ● ● ● ● ● ● ● ● ● ● ● ● ● ● ●

veinte twenty (P)

veintiuno (veintiún) twenty-one (P)

la **ventana** window (2B)

ver:

a — Let's see (2A)

¡Nos vemos! See you later! (P)

— **la tele** to watch television (1A)

— **una película** to see a movie (4A)

el **verano** summer (P)

¿Verdad? Really?, Right? (3A)

la **vez,** *pl.* **las veces:**

a veces sometimes (1B)

los **videojuegos: jugar —** to play video games (1A)

viernes Friday (P)

el **vóleibol: jugar al —** to play volleyball (4B)

vosotros, -as you *pl.* (2A)

Y ● ● ● ● ● ● ● ● ● ● ● ● ● ● ● ● ●

y and (1A)

¿— a ti? And you? (1A)

— **cuarto** quarter past *(in telling time)* (P)

— **media** thirty, half past *(in telling time)* (P)

¿— tú? And you? *fam.* (P)

¿— usted (Ud.)? And you? *formal* (P)

yo I (1B)

el **yogur** yogurt (3A)

Z ● ● ● ● ● ● ● ● ● ● ● ● ● ● ● ● ●

las **zanahorias** carrots (3B)

English-Spanish Vocabulary

The *English-Spanish Vocabulary* contains all active vocabulary from the text, including vocabulary presented in the grammar sections.

A dash (—) represents the main entry word. For example, **to play —** after **baseball** means **to play baseball.**

The number following each entry indicates the chapter in which the word or expression is presented. The letter *P* following an entry refers to the *Para empezar* section.

The following abbreviations are used in this list: *adj.* (adjective), *dir. obj.* (direct object), *f.* (feminine), *fam.* (familiar), *ind. obj.* (indirect object), *inf.* (infinitive), *m.* (masculine), *pl.* (plural), *prep.* (preposition), *pron.* (pronoun), *sing.* (singular).

A

a, an un, una (1B)

  a little un poco (de) (4B)

  a lot mucho, -a (2A)

according to según (1B)

  — my family según mi familia (1B)

after después (de) (4A)

afternoon:

  at one (o'clock) in the afternoon a la una de la tarde (4B)

  Good —. Buenas tardes. (P)

  in the — de la tarde (4B)

  this — esta tarde (4B)

afterwards después (4A)

agree:

  I —. Estoy de acuerdo. (3B)

  I don't —. No estoy de acuerdo. (3B)

all todos, -as (3B)

alone solo, -a (4A)

also también (1A)

always siempre (3A)

am:

  I — (yo) soy (1B)

  I — not (yo) no soy (1B)

amusing divertido, -a (2A)

and y (1A)

  ¿— you? ¿Y a ti? *fam.* (1A); ¿Y tú? *fam.* (P); ¿Y usted (Ud.)? *formal* (P)

apple la manzana (3A)

  — juice el jugo de manzana (3A)

April abril (P)

Are you . . . ? ¿Eres . . . ? (1B)

arm el brazo (P)

art class la clase de arte (2A)

artistic artístico, -a (1B)

at:

  — eight (o'clock) a las ocho (4B)

  — eight (o'clock) at night a las ocho de la noche (4B)

  — eight (o'clock) in the evening a las ocho de la noche (4B)

  — eight (o'clock) in the morning a las ocho de la mañana (4B)

  — home en casa (4A)

  — one (o'clock) a la una (4B)

  — one (o'clock) in the afternoon a la una de la tarde (4B)

  — what time? ¿A qué hora? (4B)

athletic deportista (1B)

August agosto (P)

autumn el otoño (P)

B

backpack la mochila (2B)

bacon el tocino (3A)

bad malo, -a (3B); mal (4B)

badly mal (4B)

banana el plátano (3A)

baseball: to play — jugar al béisbol (4B)

basketball: to play — jugar al básquetbol (4B)

to be ser (3B); estar (2B)

  to — going to + *verb* ir a + *inf.* (4B)

beach la playa (4A)

because porque (3B)

beefsteak el bistec (3B)

behind detrás de (2B)

beverages las bebidas (3B)

bicycle: to ride a — montar en bicicleta (1A)

binder: three-ring — la carpeta de argollas (2A)

book el libro (P)

bookbag la mochila (2B)

boring aburrido, -a (2A)

boy el chico (1B)

bread el pan (3A)

breakfast el desayuno (3A)

  for — en el desayuno (3A)

busy ocupado, -a (4B)

but pero (1B)

butter la mantequilla (3B)

C

café el café (4A)

calculator la calculadora (2A)

can:

  I — (yo) puedo (4B)

  you — (tú) puedes (4B)

carrots las zanahorias (3B)

cereal el cereal (3A)

chair la silla (2B)

chicken el pollo (3B)

church la iglesia (4A)

  Protestant — el templo (4A)

class la clase (2A)

classroom la sala de clases (P)

clock el reloj (2B)

coffee el café (3A)

cold: It's —. Hace frío. (P)

computer la computadora (2B)

  — keyboard el teclado (2B)

  — mouse el ratón (2B)

  — screen la pantalla (2B)

  —s / technology la tecnología (2B)

  to use the — usar la computadora (1A)

concert el concierto (4B)

cookie la galleta (3A)

countryside el campo (4A)

D •••••••••••••••••••

dance el baile (4B)

to **dance** bailar (1A)

daring atrevido, -a (1B)

date: What is the —? ¿Cuál es la fecha? (P)

day el día (P)

    every — todos los días (3A); cada día (3B)

    What — is today? ¿Qué día es hoy? (P)

December diciembre (P)

delighted encantado, -a (P)

desk el pupitre (P); el escritorio (2B)

dictionary el diccionario (2A)

difficult difícil (2A)

dinner la cena (3B)

diskette el disquete (2B)

to **do** hacer (3B)

    — you like to … ? ¿Te gusta . . . ? (1A)

    I — (yo) hago (3B)

    you — (tú) haces (3B)

door la puerta (2B)

to **draw** dibujar (1A)

to **drink** beber (3A)

E •••••••••••••••••••

easy fácil (2A)

to **eat** comer (3A)

eggs los huevos (3A)

eight ocho (P)

eighteen dieciocho (P)

eighth octavo, -a (2A)

eighty ochenta (P)

either tampoco (1A)

    I don't (like to) — a mí tampoco (1A)

eleven once (P)

English class la clase de inglés (2A)

evening:

    Good —. Buenas noches. (P)

    in the — de la noche (4B)

    this — esta noche (4B)

every day cada día (3B); todos los días (3A)

to **exercise** hacer ejercicio (3B)

eye el ojo (P)

F •••••••••••••••••••

fall el otoño (P)

favorite favorito, -a (2A)

February febrero (P)

fifteen quince (P)

fifth quinto, -a (2A)

fifty cincuenta (P)

finger el dedo (P)

first primer (primero), -a (2A)

fish el pescado (3B)

    to go —ing ir de pesca (4B)

five cinco (P)

flag la bandera (2B)

flavorful sabroso, -a (3B)

folder la carpeta (P)

food la comida (3A)

foot el pie (P)

football: to play — jugar al fútbol americano (4B)

for para (2A)

    — breakfast en el desayuno (3A)

    — lunch en el almuerzo (3A)

forty cuarenta (P)

four cuatro (P)

fourteen catorce (P)

fourth cuarto, -a (2A)

free time el tiempo libre (4A)

French fries las papas fritas (3A)

Friday viernes (P)

friendly simpático, -a (1B)

from de (4A)

    Where are you —? ¿De dónde eres? (4A)

fruit salad la ensalada de frutas (3A)

fun divertido, -a (2A)

funny gracioso, -a (1B)

G •••••••••••••••••••

game el partido (4B)

generally generalmente (4A)

girl la chica (1B)

to **go** ir (4A)

    to be —ing to +*verb* ir a + *inf.* (4B)

    to — camping ir de cámping (4B)

    to — fishing ir de pesca (4B)

    to — shopping ir de compras (4A)

    to — to school ir a la escuela (1A)

golf: to play — jugar al golf (4B)

good bueno (buen), -a (1B)

    — afternoon. Buenas tardes. (P)

    — evening. Buenas noches. (P)

    — morning. Buenos días. (P)

Good-bye! ¡Adiós! (P)

grapes las uvas (3B)

Great! ¡Genial! (4B)

green verde

    — beans las judías verdes (3B)

guitar: to play the — tocar la guitarra (1A)

gym el gimnasio (4A)

H •••••••••••••••••••

half media, -o (P)

    — past y media *(in telling time)* (P)

ham and cheese sandwich el sándwich de jamón y queso (3A)

hamburger la hamburguesa (3A)

hand la mano (P)

happy contento, -a (4B)

hardworking trabajador, -ora (1B)

to have: I — to . . . tengo que + *inf.* (4B)

he él (1B)

he / she is es (1B)

head la cabeza (P)

health:

    for one's — para la salud (3B)

    to maintain one's — para mantener la salud (3B)

Hello! ¡Hola! (P)

here aquí (2B)

Hey! ¡Oye! (4B)

home la casa (4A)

    at — en casa (4A)

    (to) — a casa (4A)

homework la tarea (2A)

horrible horrible (3B)

hot:

    — dog el perrito caliente (3A)

    It's —. Hace calor. (P)

hour: in the . . . — en la . . . hora (class period) (2A)

house la casa (4A)

how: — awful! ¡Qué asco! (3A)

How? ¿Cómo? (P)

    — are you? ¿Cómo está Ud.? *formal* (P); ¿Cómo estás? *fam.* (P); ¿Qué tal? *fam.* (P)

    — do you say . . . ? ¿Cómo se dice . . . ? (P)

    — is . . . spelled? ¿Cómo se escribe . . . ? (P)

    — many? ¿Cuántos, -as? (P)

hundred: one — cien (P)

hungry: I'm —. Tengo hambre. (3B)

I

I yo (1B)

    — am soy (1B)

    — am not no soy (1B)

    — do too a mí también (1A)

    — don't either a mí tampoco (1A)

— don't think so. Creo que no. (3B)

— stay at home. Me quedo en casa. (4A)

— think . . . Creo que . . . (3B)

— think so. Creo que sí. (3B)

— would like Me gustaría (4B)

—'m hungry. Tengo hambre. (3B)

—'m sorry. Lo siento. (4B)

—'m thirsty. Tengo sed. (3B)

ice cream el helado (3B)

iced tea el té helado (3A)

impatient impaciente (1B)

in en (P, 2B)

    — front of delante de (2B)

    — order to para + *inf.* (4A)

    — the . . . hour en la . . . hora (class period) (2A)

intelligent inteligente (1B)

interesting interesante (2A)

is es (P)

    he / she — es (1B)

it la, lo

    — is . . . Son las (in telling time) (P)

    — is one o'clock. Es la una. (P)

    — is the . . . of . . . Es el (number) de (month) (in telling the date) (P)

    — is the first of . . . Es el primero de (month). (P)

    —'s a . . . es un / una . . . (2B)

    —'s cold. Hace frío. (P)

    —'s hot. Hace calor. (P)

    —'s raining. Llueve. (P)

    —'s snowing. Nieva. (P)

    —'s sunny. Hace sol. (P)

J

January enero (P)

job el trabajo (4A)

juice:

    apple — el jugo de manzana (3A)

orange — el jugo de naranja (3A)

July julio (P)

June junio (P)

K

keyboard (computer) el teclado (2B)

to know saber (4B)

    I — (how to) (yo) sé (4B)

    you — (how to) (tú) sabes (4B)

L

later: See you — ¡Hasta luego!, ¡Nos vemos! (P)

lazy perezoso, -a (1B)

leg la pierna (P)

lemonade la limonada (3A)

Let's see A ver . . . (2A)

lettuce la lechuga (3B)

library la biblioteca (4A)

to lift weights levantar pesas (3B)

to like:

    Do you — to . . . ? ¿Te gusta . . . ? (1A)

    He / She doesn't — . . . No le gusta . . . (1B)

    He / She —s . . . Le gusta . . . (1B)

    I don't — to . . . (A mí) no me gusta . . . (1A)

    I don't — to . . . at all. (A mí) no me gusta nada . . . (1A)

    I — . . . Me gusta . . . (3A)

    I — to . . . (A mí) me gusta . . . (1A)

    I — to . . . a lot (A mí) me gusta mucho . . . (1A)

    I — to . . . better (A mí) me gusta más . . . (1A)

    I would — Me gustaría (4B)

    What do you — better (prefer) to do? ¿Qué te gusta hacer más? (1A)

    What do you — to do? ¿Qué te gusta hacer? (1A)

Would you —? ¿Te gustaría?
(4B)

You — . . . Te gusta . . . (3A)

likewise igualmente (P)

to **listen to music** escuchar música
(1A)

little: a — un poco (de) (4B)

lot: a — mucho, -a (2A)

to **love** encantar

I / You — . . . Me / Te
encanta(n) . . . (3A)

lunch el almuerzo (2A)

for — en el almuerzo (3A)

M • • • • • • • • • • • • • • • •

madam (la) señora (Sra.) (P)

to **maintain one's health** para
mantener la salud (3B)

mall el centro comercial (4A)

many muchos, -as (3B)

How —? ¿Cuántos, -as? (P)

March marzo (P)

match el partido (4B)

mathematics class la clase de
matemáticas (2A)

May mayo (P)

me me

— too a mí también (1A)

with — conmigo (4B)

meal la comida (3A)

to **mean:**

It —s . . . Quiere decir . . . (P)

What does . . . —? ¿Qué quiere
decir . . . ? (P)

meat la carne (3B)

messy desordenado, -a (1B)

milk la leche (3A)

miss, Miss (la) señorita (Srta.) (P)

Monday lunes (P)

on Mondays los lunes (4A)

month el mes (P)

more:

— . . . than más . . . que (2A)

— or less más o menos (3A)

morning:

Good —. Buenos días. (P)

in the — de la mañana (4B)

mosque la mezquita (4A)

mountains las montañas (4A)

mouse (computer) el ratón (2B)

mouth la boca (P)

movie la película

to see a — ver una película (4A)

— theater el cine (4A)

Mr. (el) señor (Sr.) (P)

Mrs. (la) señora (Sra.) (P)

music: to listen to — escuchar
música (1A)

must deber (3B)

my mi (2B)

— name is . . . Me llamo . . . (P)

N • • • • • • • • • • • • • • • •

name:

My — is . . . Me llamo . . . (P)

What is your —? ¿Cómo te
llamas? (P)

What's his / her —? ¿Cómo se
llama? (1B)

neat ordenado, -a (1B)

to **need**

I — necesito (2A)

you — necesitas (2A)

neither . . . nor ni . . . ni (1A)

never nunca (3A)

next to al lado de (2B)

nice simpático, -a (1B)

night: at — de la noche (4B)

nine nueve (P)

nineteen diecinueve (P)

ninety noventa (P)

ninth noveno, -a (2A)

nose la nariz, *pl.* las narices (P)

not . . . or ni . . . ni (1A)

notebook el cuaderno (P)

nothing nada (P)

November noviembre (P)

O • • • • • • • • • • • • • • • •

o'clock:

at eight — a las ocho (4B)

at one — a la una (4B)

October octubre (P)

of de (2B)

— course por supuesto (3A)

Oh! What a shame / pity! ¡Ay!
¡Qué pena! (4B)

okay regular (P)

on en (2B)

— Mondays, on Tuesdays . . .
los lunes, los martes . . . (4A)

— top of encima de (2B)

— weekends los fines de
semana (4A)

one uno (un), -a (P)

at — (o'clock) a la una (4B)

one hundred cien (P)

onion la cebolla (3B)

or o (1A)

orange: — juice el jugo de
naranja (3A)

P • • • • • • • • • • • • • • • •

paper: sheet of — la hoja de papel
(P)

park el parque (4A)

party la fiesta (4B)

pastries los pasteles (3B)

patient paciente (1B)

peas los guisantes (3B)

pen el bolígrafo (P)

pencil el lápiz, *pl.* los lápices (P)

— sharpener el sacapuntas,
pl. los sacapuntas (2B)

phone: to talk on the — hablar
por teléfono (1A)

physical education class la clase
de educación física (2A)

piano lesson (class) la lección,
pl. las lecciones de piano (4A)

pizza la pizza (3A)

to **play** jugar (a) (u → ue) *(games,
sports)* (4B); tocar *(an instrument)*
(1A)

to — **baseball** jugar al béisbol (4B)

to — **basketball** jugar al básquetbol (4B)

to — **football** jugar al fútbol americano (4B)

to — **golf** jugar al golf (4B)

to — **soccer** jugar al fútbol (4B)

to — **sports** practicar deportes (1A)

to — **tennis** jugar al tenis (4B)

to — **the guitar** tocar la guitarra (1A)

to — **video games** jugar videojuegos (1A)

to — **volleyball** jugar al vóleibol (4B)

pleased to meet you mucho gusto (P)

pool la piscina (4A)

poster el cartel (2B)

potatoes las papas (3B)

practical práctico, -a (2A)

to **prefer** preferir (e → ie)

I — (yo) prefiero (3B)

I — to . . . (a mí) me gusta más . . . (1A)

you — (tú) prefieres (3B)

Q ● ● ● ● ● ● ● ● ● ● ● ● ● ● ● ●

quarter past y cuarto *(in telling time)* (P)

R ● ● ● ● ● ● ● ● ● ● ● ● ● ● ● ●

rain: It's —ing. Llueve. (P)

to **read magazines** leer revistas (1A)

Really? ¿Verdad? (3A)

reserved reservado, -a (1B)

restaurant el restaurante (4A)

rice el arroz (3B)

to **ride: to — a bicycle** montar en bicicleta (1A)

Right? ¿Verdad? (3A)

to **run** correr (1A)

S ● ● ● ● ● ● ● ● ● ● ● ● ● ● ● ● ● ● ●

sad triste (4B)

salad la cnsalada (3A)

fruit — la ensalada de frutas (3A)

sandwich: ham and cheese — el sándwich de jamón y queso (3A)

Saturday sábado (P)

sausage la salchicha (3A)

to **say** decir

How do you —? ¿Cómo se dice? (P)

You — . . . Se dice . . . (P)

You don't —! ¡No me digas! (4A)

schedule el horario (2A)

science: — class la clase de ciencias naturales (2A)

screen: computer — la pantalla (2B)

season la estación, *pl.* las estaciones (P)

second segundo, -a (2A)

to **see** ver

Let's — A ver . . . (2A)

— you later! ¡Nos vemos!, Hasta luego. (P)

— you tomorrow. Hasta mañana. (P)

to — a movie ver una película (4A)

September septiembre (P)

serious serio, -a (1B)

seven siete (P)

seventeen diecisiete (P)

seventh séptimo, -a (2A)

seventy setenta (P)

to **share** compartir (3A)

she ella (1B)

sheet of paper la hoja de papel (P)

should deber (3B)

shy reservado, -a (1B)

sick enfermo, -a (4B)

to **sing** cantar (1A)

sir (el) señor (Sr.) (P)

six seis (P)

sixteen dieciséis (P)

sixth sexto, -a (2A)

sixty sesenta (P)

to **skate** patinar (1A)

to **skateboard** montar en monopatín (1A)

to **ski** esquiar (i → í) (1A)

snow: It's —ing. Nieva. (P)

so-so regular (P)

soccer: to play — jugar al fútbol (4B)

sociable sociable (1B)

social studies class la clase de ciencias sociales (2A)

soft drink el refresco (3A)

some unos, -as (2B)

something algo (3B)

sometimes a veces (1B)

sorry: I'm —. Lo siento. (4B)

soup: vegetable — la sopa de verduras (3A)

spaghetti los espaguetis (3B)

Spanish class la clase de español (2A)

to **spell:**

How is . . . spelled? ¿Cómo se escribe . . . ? (P)

It's spelled . . . Se escribe . . . (P)

to **spend time with friends** pasar tiempo con amigos (1A)

sports:

to play — practicar deportes (1A)

—-minded deportista (1B)

spring la primavera (P)

to **stay: I — at home.** Me quedo en casa. (4A)

stomach el estómago (P)

stories: to write — escribir cuentos (1A)

strawberries las fresas (3A)

student el / la estudiante (P)

studious estudioso, -a (1B)

to **study** estudiar (2A)

summer el verano (P)

Sunday domingo (P)

sunny: It's —. Hace sol. (P)

to **swim** nadar (1A)

synagogue la sinagoga (4A)

T • • • • • • • • • • • • • • • •

table la mesa (2B)

talented talentoso, -a (1B)

to **talk** hablar (2A)

    to — on the phone hablar por teléfono (1A)

tasty sabroso, -a (3B)

tea el té (3A)

    iced — el té helado (3A)

to **teach** enseñar (2A)

teacher el profesor, la profesora (P)

technology / computers la tecnología (2A)

technology / computer class la clase de tecnología (2A)

television: to watch — ver la tele (1A)

temple el templo (4A)

ten diez (P)

tennis: to play — jugar al tenis (4B)

tenth décimo, -a (2A)

thank you gracias (P)

the el, la (1B); los, las (2B)

theater: movie — el cine (4A)

then entonces (4B)

there allí (2B)

    — is / are hay (2B)

they ellos, ellas (2A)

to **think** pensar (e → ie)

    I don't — so. Creo que no. (3B)

    I — . . . Creo que . . . (3B)

    I — so. Creo que sí. (3B)

third tercer (tercero), -a (2A)

thirsty: I'm —. Tengo sed. (3B)

thirteen trece (P)

thirty treinta (P); y media *(in telling time)* (P)

thirty-one treinta y uno (P)

this este, esta

    — afternoon esta tarde (4B)

    — evening esta noche (4B)

    — weekend este fin de semana (4B)

    What is —? ¿Qué es esto? (2B)

three tres (P)

three-ring binder la carpeta de argollas (2A)

Thursday jueves (P)

time:

    At what —? ¿A qué hora? (4B)

    free — el tiempo libre (4A)

    to spend — with friends pasar tiempo con amigos (1A)

    What — is it? ¿Qué hora es? (P)

tired cansado, -a (4B)

to **a** *(prep.)* (4A)

    in order — para + *inf.* (4A)

    — the a la, al (4A)

toast el pan tostado (3A)

today hoy (P)

tomatoes los tomates (3B)

tomorrow mañana (P)

    See you —. Hasta mañana. (P)

too también (1A); demasiado (4B)

    I do (like to) — a mí también (1A)

    me — a mí también (1A)

top: on — of encima de (2B)

Tuesday martes (P)

    on —s los martes (4A)

twelve doce (P)

twenty veinte (P)

twenty-one veintiuno (veintiún) (P)

two dos (P)

U • • • • • • • • • • • • • • • •

underneath debajo de (2B)

to **understand** comprender (3A)

to **use: to — the computer** usar la computadora (1A)

V • • • • • • • • • • • • • • • •

vegetable soup la sopa de verduras (3A)

very muy (1B)

    — well muy bien (P)

video games: to play — jugar videojuegos (1A)

volleyball: to play — jugar al vóleibol (4B)

W • • • • • • • • • • • • • • • •

to **walk** caminar (3B)

to **want** querer (e → ie)

    I — (yo) quiero (4B)

    you — (tú) quieres (4B)

wastepaper basket la papelera (2B)

to **watch television** ver la tele (1A)

water el agua *f.* (3A)

we nosotros, -as (2A)

weather: What's the — like? ¿Qué tiempo hace? (P)

Wednesday miércoles (P)

week la semana (P)

weekend:

    on —s los fines de semana (4A)

    this — este fin de semana (4B)

well bien (P); pues *(to indicate pause)* (1A)

    very — muy bien (P)

What? ¿Cuál? ¿Qué? (3A)

    — are you like? ¿Cómo eres? (1B)

    (At) — time? ¿A qué hora? (4B)

    — day is today? ¿Qué día es hoy? (P)

    — do you like better (prefer) to do? ¿Qué te gusta hacer más? (1A)

— do you like to do? ¿Qué te gusta hacer? (1A)

— does . . . mean? ¿Qué quiere decir . . . ? (P)

— is she / he like? ¿Cómo es? (1B)

— is the date? ¿Cuál es la fecha? (P)

— is this? ¿Qué es esto? (2B)

— is your name? ¿Cómo te llamas? (P)

— time is it? ¿Qué hora es? (P)

—'s happening? ¿Qué pasa? (P)

—'s his / her name? ¿Cómo se llama? (1B)

—'s the weather like? ¿Qué tiempo hace? (P)

What!:

— a good / nice idea! ¡Qué buena idea! (4B)

— a shame / pity! ¡Qué pena! (4B)

When? ¿Cuándo? (4A)

Where? ¿Dónde? (2B)

— are you from? ¿De dónde eres? (4A)

(To) —? ¿Adónde? (4A)

Which? ¿Cuál? (3A)

Who? ¿Quién? (2A)

Why? ¿Por qué? (3B)

window la ventana (2B)

winter el invierno (P)

with con (3A)

— me conmigo (4B)

— my / your friends con mis / tus amigos (4A)

— whom? ¿Con quién? (4A)

— you contigo (4B)

without sin (3A)

work el trabajo (4A)

to work trabajar (1A)

Would you like . . . ? ¿Te gustaría . . . ? (4B)

to write: to — stories escribir cuentos (1A)

Y ·

year el año (P)

yes sí (1A)

yogurt el yogur (3A)

you *fam. sing.* tú (2A); *formal sing.* usted (Ud.) (2A); *fam. pl.* vosotros, -as (2A); *formal pl.* ustedes (Uds.) (2A); *fam. after prep.* ti (1A)

And —? ¿Y a ti? (1A)

with — contigo (4B)

— don't say! ¡No me digas! (4A)

— say . . . Se dice . . . (P)

your *fam.* tu (2B)

Z ·

zero cero (P)

Grammar Index

Structures are most often presented first in *A primera vista*, where they are practiced lexically. They are then explained later in a *Gramática* section or a *Nota*. Light face numbers refer to the pages where structures are initially presented or, after explanation where student reminders occur. **Bold face numbers** refer to pages where structures are explained or are otherwise highlighted.

a 26–30, 218
> + definite article 208–209, **215**
> after **jugar** 240, **256**
> in time telling 240–241, **250**
> with **ir** + infinitive 241, **252**

accent marks **13**, 38, **223**
> in interrogative words **224**

adjectives:
> agreement and formation 56–57, **64, 82, 190,** 204
> comparative 87
> demonstrative 240–241
> plural. *See* adjectives: agreement and formation
> position of **72**
> possessive 29, 118, 144

alphabet 12

-ar verbs 36
> present 87, 89–90, **100,** 114, 160

articles:
> definite **11, 70, 82, 132,** 144
> definite, with **a** 208–209, **215**
> definite, with days of the week 216
> definite, with **de 125**
> definite, with titles of respect 94
> indefinite **70, 82, 132,** 144

cognates 40, 68

comparison 87

compound subject **98**

dates 14–15

de:
> + definite article 125
> in compound nouns **156**
> in prepositional phrases 119, 125
> possessive 119, **135**

derivation of words 94, 194, 216, 249

encantar 149, **164**

-er verbs 36
> present 148–149, **160,** 174

estar 118–119, **128,** 144

Exploración del lenguaje:
> Cognates **40**
> Cognates that begin with **es** + consonant **68**
> Connections between Latin, English, and Spanish **94**
> Language through gestures **127**
> Origins of the Spanish days of the week **216**
> Punctuation and accent marks **13**
> Señor, señora, señorita **2**
> Spanish words borrowed from English **249**
> **Tú** vs. **usted 5**
> Using a noun to modify another noun **156**
> Where did it come from? **194**

gender **11**
> of adjectives agreeing with nouns **64,** 82, **190,** 204
> of articles **70,** 82
> of pronouns **98**

gustar 26, 52, **164**

hacer 26, 179
> use of in weather expressions 18

hay 14

infinitive **36**
> after **ir a** 241, **252**
> after **para** 208
> after **tener que** 241

interrogative words **224**

ir 30, 208, **218,** 236
> + **a** + infinitive 241, **252**
> with future meaning 241, **252**

-ir verbs 36
> present 152, **160,** 174

jugar 27, 240, **256, 266**

negative 27, **42, 44,** 72, 105
> **nada** used for emphasis 27, **42**
> **ni . . . ni** 27, **42**
> **tampoco** 27, **44**

nouns **11,** 64
> compound **156**
> plural **132,** 190
> used with **gustar / encantar 164**

numbers 7
> in dates 15
> in telling time **8**
> ordinal 86

plurals:
> of adjectives **190,** 204
> of nouns **132,** 190

poder 241

possession:
> adjectives 29, 118
> with **de** 119, 135

preferir 181

prepositions 119

present. *See individual verb listings*

pronouns:
> **conmigo / contigo** 241
> prepositional, used for agreement, clarity, or emphasis 26–27, **44**

subject 56, 60, **98,** 114

subject, omission of **100,** 163

subject, use of for clarification or emphasis 100

Pronunciation:

a, e, i 35

accent marks 223

c 107

d 254

g 137

h / j 167

l / ll 191

o / u 71

stress 223

punctuation marks **13**

querer 240

question formation **224**

accent marks 224

with **¿no?** 90

with **¿verdad?** 149

saber 243–244

ser 28, 57, **192,** 204

in telling time 8

stem-changing verbs. *See* verbs, stem-changing

subject, of a sentence **98.** *See also* pronouns, subject

tener 86, 89

expressions with 179, 181

with **que** + infinitive 241

time telling **8,** 240–241, **250**

tú vs. **usted** 4, **5, 98**

ver 27, **160**

verbs 36

-ar 87, **100,** 114, 160

-er 148, **160,** 174

-ir 152, **160,** 174

irregular. *See individual listings*

stem-changing **u → ue** 240, **256,** 266

weather expressions 18

word order with adjectives **72,** 82

Acknowledgments

Cover Design Tamada Brown & Associates

Program Graphic Development Herman Adler Design

Maps Mapping Specialists
Technical Illustration/Additional Graphics Herman Adler Design; New England Typographic Services; Publicom; John Reece; Joseph Taylor

Ilustrations Wilkinson Studios Artists; Bob Brugger: **pp. 167, 254**; Dennis Dzielak: **pp. 8, 79, 94, 118, 119**; Seitu Hayden: **pp. 6, 12, 16, 27, 32, 34, 36, 208, 209, 214, 246, 248, 249**; Reggie Holladay: **pp. 43, 67, 103, 230, 231**; Tim Jones: **pp. 16, 26, 62, 65, 74, 86, 91, 95, 134, 136, 191, 220, 241, 247, 253**, Victor Kennedy: **p. 35**; Gary Krejca: **pp. 32, 36**; Miguel Luna: **pp. 7, 191**; Jonathan Massie: **p. 179**; Tom Mc Kee: **pp. 2, 15, 188, 232, 257**; Donna Perrone: **pp.103, 154, 156, 159, 178, 185, 186, 187, 194**; Judy Stead: **pp. 3, 18, 70, 125, 240, 250**; Nicole Wong: **pp. 8, 209, 214**

Photography Front and back covers: Parque del Buen Retiro, Madrid, Spain, Lonely Planet Images; (front cover inset) Café on the waterfront, Barcelona, Spain, Robert Frerck/Odyssey/Chicago;
Photographers who contributed to the studio/location photography: Bill Burlingham, Burlingham Photography and John Morrison, Morrison Photography.

x–xi, José Fuste Raga/CORBIS; **x inset**, Danny Lehman/CORBIS; **xi inset**, www.corbis.com/Phil Schermeister; **xiii–xiii**, Danny Lehman/CORBIS; **xiv–xv**, David Zimmerman/CORBIS; **xiv inset**, Stuart Westmorland/CORBIS; **xvi–xvii**, Jim Erickson/CORBIS; **xviii–xix**, ©Galen Rowell/CORBIS; **xx–xxi**, Paul Hardy/CORBIS; **xx inset**, Mark L. Stephenson; **xxi inset**, José Fuste Raga/CORBIS; **xxii–xxiii**, ©Craig Turtle/CORBIS; **xxii inset**, Strauss/Curtis/CORBIS; **xxiii br inset**, Ron Watts/CORBIS; **xxiii bl inset**, Corbis Royalty Free; **xxiv tl**, Pablo Picasso (1881-1973) ©ARS, NY ©Erich Lessing/Art Resource, NY; **xxiv tr**, Paul Barton/CORBIS; **xxiv bm**, ©S. P. Gillette/CORBIS; **xxvi**, LatinFocus.com; **1 t**, Robert Frerck/Odyssey Productions, Inc.; **1 br**, Bill Bachmann/PhotoEdit; **3 (1)**, Bob Daemmrich/Stock Boston; **3 (2)**, Spencer Grant/Stock Boston; **3 (3)**, David Young-Wolff/PhotoEdit; **3 (4)**, M. Ferguson/PhotoEdit; **3 (5)**, Bachmann/Stock Boston; **3 (6)**, Mary Kate Denny/PhotoEdit; **5**, Spencer Grant/Stock Boston; Mary Kate Denny/PhotoEdit; **8**, A.K.G., Berlin/SuperStock; **13**, Museo Nacional de Antropología, Mexico City, Mexico/Bridgeman Art Library International, Ltd.; **15**, David Young-Wolff/PhotoEdit; **16**, A. Ramey/PhotoEdit; **17**, Peter Wilson/Dorling Kindersley Media Library © CONACULTA-INAH-MEX. Authorized reproduction by the *Instituto Nacional de Antropología e Historia*; **18 all**, George Gold/SuperStock, Inc.; **19 (1)**, © Gordon R. Gainer/CORBIS; **19 (2)**, Rocio Escobar; **19 (3)**, Joseph Nettis/Photo Researchers, Inc.; **19 (4)**, *Causes and Effects*, Philip Steele; **20 tl**, Spencer Swanger/Tom Stack & Associates, Inc.; **20 tr**, Ann Duncan/Tom Stack & Associates, Inc.; **20 bl**, J. Schulte/D. Donne Bryant Stock Photography; **20 br**, Ricardo Carrasco/D. Donne Bryant Stock Photography; **20 m**, © ESA/ELI/CORBIS; **24–25**, David Young-Wolff/Photo Edit ; **24 inset**, Picasso, Pablo (1881-1973). (c) ARS, NY. *Three Musicians*. 1921. Oil on canvas, 6' 7" x 7' 3 3/4". Mrs. Simon Guggenheim Fund. (55.1949). Museum of Modern Art, New York, N.Y., U.S.A./The Bridgeman Art Library International, Ltd.; **28 m**, Roberto M. Arakaki/ImageState/International Stock Photography Ltd.; **29 tm**, Spencer Grant/PhotoEdit; **29 bm**, SuperStock, Inc.; **30 r**, Buddy Mays/ImageState/International Stock Photography, Ltd.; **33**, Peter Menzel/Stock Boston; **35 tl**, Ernest Manewal/SuperStock, Inc.; **35 tr**, M. Paganelli/Woodfin Camp & Associates; **38**, David Simson/Stock Boston; **40 m**, Museo Bellapart; **41 ml**, Bonnie Kamin/PhotoEdit; **41 bl**, PictureQuest; **41 t**, Blaine Harrington; **41 mr**, David Young-Wolff/PhotoEdit; **41 br**, HIRB/Index Stock Imagery; **45**, Getty Images, Inc.; **45 b**, Wolfgang Kaehler/CORBIS; **45 tl**, Larry Prosor/SuperStock, Inc.; **46 t**, David Young-Wolff/PhotoEdit; **46 b**, Marisol Diaz/Latin Focus Photo Agency; **47 t**, © Robert Frerck/Odyssey/Chicago; **47 ml**, Myrleen Ferguson Cate/PhotoEdit Inc. 48, Danilo Boschung/eStock Photography LLC; **49 t**, Bob Daemmrich Photography, Inc.; **49 b**, Kathy Ferguson-Johnson/PhotoEdit; **50–51, background image** Reinhard Eisele/CORBIS, **inset tr**, Richard Bickel, **inset mr**, Roger Resmeyer/CORBIS, **inset br**, Jan Burchofsky-Houser/CORBIS; **51 t**, Robert Frerck/Woodfin Camp & Associates; **51**, Dave Bartruff/Stock Boston; **51 m**, Patrick Ward/CORBIS; **51 b**, Robert Frerck/Odyssey Productions, Inc.; **52**, Robert Frerck/Odyssey Productions, Inc.; **54–55**, David Simson/Stock Boston; **54 inset**, Albright-Knox Art Gallery; **57 b**, Paul Mark Smith/Panos Pictures; **63 (1, 2, 3, 7, 8)** Ulrike Welsch Photography; **63 (4)**, Robert Frerck/Odyssey Productions, Inc.; **63 (5)**, PhotoDisc/GettyImages; **63 (6)**, Robert Frerck/Odyssey Productions, Inc.; **66**, Copyright © Mary Kate Denny/PhotoEdit All rights reserved; **68 t**, The Bridgeman Art Library International, Ltd.; **68 b**, David Simson/Stock Boston; **69 b**, David Sanger Photography; **73 t**, Robert Fried Photography/Stock Boston; **73 b**, H. Huntly Hersch/D. Donne Bryant Stock Photography; **75**, Robert Fried Photography; **77**, Robert Frerck/Odyssey/Chicago; **78 tr**, Rhoda Sidney/Stock Boston; **78 br**, David Simson/Stock Boston; **78 tl**, Tony Arruza/CORBIS; **78 bl**, Robert Fried Photography; **78**, H. Huntly Hersch/D.Donne Bryant Stock Photography; **79 t**, David Young-Wolff/PhotoEdit; **79 b**, David Young-Wolff/PhotoEdit; **80–81**, Reinhard Eisele/CORBIS; **81 t inset**, Richard Bickel/COR-